UKRAINIAN SCORPIONS

UKRAINIAN SCORPIONS

A TALE OF LARCENY AND GREED

GRAND CHIEF RONALD M DERRICKSON

Published by ECW Press
665 Gerrard Street East
Toronto, Ontario, Canada M4M 1Y2
416-694-3348 / info@ecwpress.com

To the best of his abilities, the author has related
experiences, places, people, and organizations from his
memories of them. In order to protect the privacy of others,
he has, in some instances, changed the names of certain
people and details of events and places.

LIBRARY AND ARCHIVES CANADA CATALOGUING
IN PUBLICATION

Title: Ukrainian scorpions : a tale of larceny and greed /
Grand Chief Ronald M. Derrickson.

Names: Derrickson, Ronald M., author.

Identifiers: Canadiana (print) 20230147941 | Canadiana
(ebook) 20230147968

ISBN 978-1-77041-567-6 (softcover)
ISBN 978-1-77852-161-4 (Kindle)
ISBN 978-1-77852-159-1 (ePub)
ISBN 978-1-77852-160-7 (PDF)

Subjects: LCSH: Derrickson, Ronald M. | LCSH:
Corruption—Ukraine. | LCSH: Political corruption—
Ukraine. | LCSH: Ukraine—Politics and government—1991- |
LCSH: Ukraine—Economic conditions—1991-

Classification: LCC HV6771.U38 D47 2023 | DDC
364.1/32309477—dc23

This book is funded in part by the Government of Canada. *Ce livre est financé en partie par le gouvernement du Canada.*
We also acknowledge the support of the Government of Ontario through the Ontario Book Publishing Tax Credit, and
through Ontario Creates.

PRINTED AND BOUND IN CANADA   PRINTING: FRIESENS   5   4   3   2   1

We are punished by our sins, not for them.

— ELBERT HUBBARD

CONTENTS

FOREWORD

When Ron Derrickson asked me to write the foreword to a book he was working on about his adventures and misadventures in Ukraine, I wondered why he would want to share this unpleasant episode in his otherwise incredibly successful business career, and what good it might do *him*. As the deadline for the foreword approached, I slowly began to understand Ron's commitment to this book. He instinctively knew at the outset of his fourth book what it would take me many months to work out.

Before I discuss Ron's legendary foresight in such things, I would like to tell you more about the man himself. Despite his outwardly tough, sometimes unnervingly blunt exterior, Ron has a level of wisdom, intelligence, experience and ability in both his personal and business dealings that never ceases to astonish me. His willingness to help those who have fallen into hard times is legendary. Ron shows loyalty — when he is your friend he will stand in your corner come hell or high water — and he values honesty above all other qualities.

You will see these qualities again and again in this book. You will also see his uncanny ability to predict the future. I cannot count the times I've watched him make major decisions on the spot, which made no sense to me at the time, that weeks or often many months later proved to be the right call. And that is very much the case with this book. In our future relations with the heroic people of Ukraine, we had better heed the warnings he is giving.

You see, that is Ron's superpower: his ability to know instinctively, ahead of everyone else, how things will turn out. In *Ukrainian Scorpions*, Ron is forewarning and forearming potential donors and future investors who are already planning for the aftermath of the shameful illegal war being waged by Russia against the people of Ukraine.

As the international community discusses how it will invest billions of much-needed dollars in reconstruction funding once the war is won by the courageous Ukrainian men and women on the front lines, governments and potential donors must know that there are powerful forces in Ukraine that are plotting against them from inside the country. The criminal elements described in this book are still there and they will be applying significant energy, not to protecting the innocent or helpless or rebuilding the country, but to stealing, misappropriating or diverting every dollar that is paid into Ukraine, and they will have put mechanisms in place to cover up their theft.

This has always been the case at the highest levels in Ukraine, and it will be the case again. Winning the war is the free world's top priority today, and rightly so. But they must know that the forces of corruption in Ukraine are even today using the fog of war to obscure their treacherous activities. While their compatriots fight and die, the crooks and scammers, corrupt police and judges, and gangster politicians remain at the heart of Ukraine business and even today are planning how they will funnel the post-war funds into their personal offshore bank accounts.

Along with Ron, I have witnessed first-hand the astonishing criminal behaviour that has made Ukraine the most corrupt country in Europe. In fact, I first met Ron due to having built a similar business in Ukraine in the 2000s. I faced similar challenges with criminal classes, bureaucrats, tax offices and local thugs who spend all of their time and energy not in creating wealth but in scheming, with the help of corrupt politicians, judges and police, about ways to steal it.

In Ron's case, the corrupt Ukrainian directors of his company rushed to steal and defraud him of the company with a mafia organization supported by senior Ukrainian public officials, police, secret service and criminals; ironically for far less financial gain to themselves than they would have received had they sold the business legally to me after I offered to purchase it. This process exposed theft on a grand scale, premeditated misappropriation of assets and a disgusting level of stupidity, amateurism and criminality that in any other country in the world would have seen them all in prison within months and the company and its assets returned to Ron. But this was in the most lawless region of one of the most corrupt countries in the world.

Those who are ready to help rebuild Ukraine must heed Ron's warnings and go into Ukraine with their eyes wide open. Donors and investors cannot allow themselves to fall for the scams of the past or pretend that the scorpions have disappeared in post-war Ukraine. They have not. They are waiting for us. We must be aware of this and make sure we do not allow them a free ride, because they will sink Ukraine before it gets to the other shore. And Ukraine, especially after all it has endured, deserves to enjoy the rewards of peace and prosperity. But only by confronting corruption head-on in the aftermath of the war will Ukraine at last reach its place in the sun.

— RICHARD SPINKS
September 2022

AUTHOR'S PREFACE

I watched the Russian invasion of Ukraine, the country where I had spent much of the past 20 years, with a kind of anguish. While their neighbours were secure within the European Union and protected by membership in the NATO alliance, Ukrainians were standing against Russia. And certainly not by choice. Ukraine had been systematically shut out of the European club for 30 years because of the rampant political and economic corruption that has crippled the country.

This book tells the story of my personal battles in Ukraine and of the country's much wider struggle to shake off the gangsterism that has plagued it since the 1990s and shaped, or rather misshaped, so much of its history. In my 20 years of doing business there, I became a reluctant expert on the country as I fought in its courts, in the halls of power and briefly with an armed force to get back millions of dollars in property that was stolen from me. The process took me down the rabbit hole of Ukrainian political and economic life into a land where gangsters control not only the heights of the economy but also the police, the courts and even the national parliament.

It was no accident that virtually all of the people directly or. indirectly involved in the theft were at the time, or had recently been, People's Deputies in the national parliament or regional governors. To understand Ukraine it's essential to understand that for 30 years after independence, it was largely a criminal enterprise. In 2019, when the *Kyiv Post* looked at the 450 deputies elected to the current parliament, journalists identified more than 350 with corrupt pasts. When they looked a bit further, they could see that only two of the dozen or so oligarchs controlled 170 deputies between them, giving them effective control of parliament. This deeply embedded corruption is what made Ukraine such a pariah in the world.

On a financial level, my decades-long foray into Ukraine came at a high cost. But I am fortunate to be in the rare position that my life is largely unaffected by the loss of US$28 million in property. Instead, the terrible weight of the corruption in Ukraine is borne by its people, who face lives of crushing poverty while the political and financial criminal class feast on the spoils. Despite the fabulous wealth of the gangster class, Ukraine vied with Moldova for the position of the poorest country in Europe even before the war. Ukraine had an average income less than one-quarter of that of their Polish and Hungarian neighbours and even — and this is a surprise to many — one-third that of Russians. According to a 2020 study, there were more hungry people in Ukraine than any other country in Europe, and it was the only country where that number was growing.[1]

Denys Shmyhal, the prime minister of Ukraine, calculated that corruption cost Ukraine a trillion dollars in GDP over the previous decade.

Despite the West's endless finger-wagging and tut-tutting about corruption in Ukraine over the past 30 years, it has refused to put serious conditions on its aid to the country. In this choice, they ignore the true anti-corruption

---

1   Yuriy Lifanse, "Faces of Poverty in Ukraine": A study conducted by the Dmitry F. Chebotarev Institute of Gerontology of the National Academy of Medical Sciences of Ukraine, *Mission Crossroads*, Fall 2021, http://onlinedigitalpublishing.com/publication/?m=60707&i=720014&view=articleBrowser&article _id=4108427&ver=html5.

fighters in Ukraine, who have been pleading with the West to stop funding the state without enforcing stringent safeguards against corruption.

Canada is perhaps the biggest disappointment in this regard. The country has close ties to Ukraine and, before the war, had the largest Ukrainian population outside of Ukraine and Russia. Canada was in fact the first country in the world to recognize Ukraine independence in 1991, and it provided financial and military aid and complete diplomatic cover for a country that was crumbling from corruption.

In these pages, you will hear the truth about Ukraine, which you will not read in the papers or see on newscasts or hear about in political speeches. This book will reveal Ukraine as it was behind the scenes in the weeks before the outbreak of the war with Russia. Among the shadowy characters you will meet is a joint Canadian-Ukrainian citizen with a house in Westmount, Quebec — down the street from former prime minister Brian Mulroney's — whose extraparliamentary activities include bank robbery and murder. You will also meet a former governor who was accused of attempted murder and bank fraud, and a parliamentarian who was a hero of the Maidan revolution but now operates a private militia he hires out to criminal enterprises for violent business takeovers. Every one of these characters was a People's Deputy in the national parliament and, in one case, a provincial governor. When you add to this the low-level fraud artists, you will understand why the working title for the book was *Clusterf**k: Life in Modern Ukraine*. The publisher suggested its much more presentable title, but clusterfuck remains an accurate description of how events unfolded in a country where the mafia still rules, with the support of the West, and the Ukrainian people are left out in the cold.

Sadly, the thieves have not disappeared from Ukraine. Despite the heroics of the people of Ukraine on the battlefield, their triumphs risk being undermined by corruption. Stories are coming to light of whole freight trains of food and military supplies being shunted onto side tracks to be systematically looted by the local gangsters, and warnings were being delivered from Western military suppliers that 70 percent of the money and material being poured into Ukraine from the West is simply disappearing. The war has not suppressed the corruption in Ukraine. On the contrary, it has led to a feeding frenzy — all without any checks or balances from the West. Ignoring the rampant corruption in Ukraine in the past has greatly harmed the people of Ukraine, who have been the real victims of the gangsterism that has ruled and ruined their country. Continuing to ignore the corruption during and after the war in Ukraine will deprive the Ukrainian people of their future after they have sacrificed so much in blood and tears in their fight against the Russian invader.

CHAPTER 1

UNDER THE SHADOW OF WAR

*It has reached the point where no
one even tries to hide the corruption
anymore. Ukraine is a failed state.*

What I remember most about my last trip to Ukraine, which
took place just a few months before the Russian invasion, was the
meeting with my lawyer, Taras Dumych, at his office in Podil in the old city
of Kyiv.

Taras is a very likeable guy. When he speaks, he looks you right in the eye
and his good nature can be infectious. He is also a person of some standing.
He is the head of the international Wolf Theiss law office in Ukraine, and
all the time, I have known him, he has been a voice of hope for Ukraine.
But this time, his mood was sombre. He said he had pretty well given up on
Ukraine because corruption and political paralysis were killing the country.

We spoke first in general terms of the recent, much-publicized comments
about Ukraine by Mikheil Saakashvili and by Kaja Kallas, the prime minister
of Estonia. Saakashvili, who was then President Volodymyr Zelensky's
reform czar, described Ukraine as a "sump" for Eastern European criminals.
"The criminals know for sure that everyone can be released. Issues must be

resolved — you can hire any police investigator, any prosecutor. . . . You just hire a policeman, and he will dance for any money on your order. The system is deeply sick."

Everyone knew this was the case, but it was startling to hear it from the presidential office. The same week, Kaja Kallas, who was considered one of Ukraine's closest friends, warned her fellow Estonians not to invest in Ukraine because it was almost impossible to get your money back from the crooks who ran the country.[1]

Taras said he didn't really think that Saakashvili was a reliable source for anything, but he agreed with the Estonian prime minister. "Ukraine," he said, "really had become a failed state. And I use that word intentionally. Obviously there is still a functioning economy and a few very basic services to the population, but in a political and legal sense, it really is a failed state."

I was surprised to hear him say this. Taras had always tried to put a brave face on things or dangle some kind of hope. But now he was clear and unequivocal: Ukraine was a failed state and I would not get justice there.

In a strange way, though, the honesty was a nice change from all of the false hopes I had been hearing for years. And it did sum up what I had been seeing in Ukraine for the 20 years that I had been going there. Things had been getting worse, not better, and the people paying the biggest price were not the ripped-off investors like me but the people of Ukraine. While the elites fought about ethnic and linguistic rivalries and East versus West and the names of cities, towns and streets, the people were abandoned to poverty and desperation. And the misery was increasing: the median wealth of its citizens was sinking to around the same level as Nepal, Bangladesh and Cameroon.

So Taras's characterization of Ukraine as a failed state was borne out by the facts. The people were getting fed up but they didn't seem to know what to do. Yet pressure was clearly building. I had read about a Kyiv taxi driver who complained to his American passenger about the economic disaster

---

1   Kaja Kallas, prime minister of Estonia: "I advise citizens: trade with Ukraine, but do not invest. Because you could lose your investment. And we have already had such cases when our people lost their property here. And even having received an arbitration decision in their favour, they could not [recover] their property."

in Ukraine for the ordinary people and the passenger argued with him, defending the imagined advances in Ukraine following the Maidan revolution, the 2014 uprising that brought the nationalists to power. The falsity of the American's praise of the revolution's results so incensed the taxi driver that he pulled over and stabbed the American in the thigh. The people were tired of the apologists for the failed state.

Taras told me that the nail in the coffin for him was a case he had been working on where a foreign investor had had his property stolen by the City of Kyiv, and the city had gone to court and said, basically, that it was the investor's fault because everyone knew Ukraine was corrupt, so the businessman knew of the risk before he invested. "It was more than a little shocking," Taras said, "to hear the state argue this as a fact in their defence for stealing someone's property."

So that's it. Ukrainians were now admitting that they could not help themselves. On my way back to my apartment on Lvivs'ka Square, I realized that Ukrainians were admitting they were like the scorpion in the old fable of the scorpion and the frog. As the story goes, the scorpion hails a frog on the riverbank and asks him to take him across. The frog is suspicious and says, "If I let you on my back you will sting me and I will drown." The scorpion says no, no, he will not sting him because he needs the ride across. So the frog agrees, but halfway across, the scorpion stings him. The dying frog says, "You said you would not do it!" But the scorpion replies, "It's your fault, you knew I was a scorpion when you took me on your back. It's who I am. It's in my nature." That was where Ukraine had arrived by the end of 2021, with even government lawyers telling investors essentially that you deserve to be ripped off by Ukraine because you must have known we were corrupt when you came here. And in the end, both the frog and the scorpion drown in the river.

The country was a basket case. It was the rampant corruption in both the political and economic spheres that left Ukraine outside of the European Union and NATO while its neighbours — Poland, Slovakia, Hungary, Romania and Bulgaria — were all safely within the Western camp. That night, I decided to move all of my remaining Eastern European business interests out of Ukraine and into a much safer harbour in Poland. Like much of the world, I wanted nothing more to do with conducting business in Ukraine.

◇◆◇

Only four months later, everything was eclipsed by the Russian invasion.

I watched from my home office in Kelowna, British Columbia, as missiles streaked across the skies and pounded into neighbourhoods where friends lived and where I had shopped at the markets. I saw columns of Russian tanks moving on Kyiv and Kharkiv, and Russian troops arriving by helicopter at the Antonov International Airport, just 25 kilometres from Kyiv, while the highways leaving the capital toward the west were choked with cars trying to escape. My Skype sounded with three or four calls arriving at the same time.

I took all of the calls from Richard Spinks and ignored the rest. Richard was a friend and business associate who was living in Lviv. Both of us had been involved in Ukraine for twenty years and had many friends, colleagues and employees there. Richard and I would be in almost constant contact over the following weeks as we did what we could to evacuate friends and colleagues to Poland, where I had recently purchased three houses for investment purposes.

To find addresses and contact numbers of my Ukrainian friends I had pulled all of my Ukraine files off my shelf, and they covered my desk. When there was a pause in the calls, I started tidying up my desk and putting the papers and photos back in the files. I noticed one of the photos was of Yulia, my accountant, who we had managed to get out to Poland with her son while her husband was conscripted into the armed defence of Kyiv. She was much younger in the photo, looking happy and relaxed on the day we opened our $28-million grain operation in Shchorsk in the Dnipropetrovsk Oblast.[2] I glanced at the other photos in the file. They were all from that day in Shchorsk, September 7, 2007, which in many ways was the moment in

---

2   Oblast is the regional administrative unit in Ukraine, in some ways the equivalent of a state or province in a federal system. The big difference under Ukraine's centralized state is that the oblast leaders are appointed directly by the ruling party.

my twenty years in Ukraine that I felt the greatest optimism. I believed in the country and its possibilities, and that day had a kind of magic to it. But it also hid the broken bits, the deceptions and the lawlessness that led the country to financial ruin by the end of 2021.

CHAPTER 2

THE ART OF CORRUPTION

*The Golden Key to the most
lawless region of one of the most
corrupt countries in the world.*

T he photo taken in the yard of the new grain elevator complex showed
me with a somewhat surprised look on my face, receiving an outsized
golden key from Yuriy Yekhanurov, the former prime minister of Ukraine,
who was at the time the governor of the Dnipropetrovsk Oblast.

Also in the photo is my business partner, Viktor Fesun, whose claim
to fame was that he went to the same university as Leonid Brezhnev, and
Fesun's attractive daughter, Anna, who is smiling approvingly over my
shoulder. We are surrounded by a crowd of well-wishers in front of the
complex's new office.

I remember the day well. We made the six-hour drive to Shchorsk and
back from Kyiv, where I was living at the time, on the bad Ukrainian roads.
But we were in good spirits. Yulia, my young accountant, was there and the
CEO from my Canadian operation, Cathy Hellyer, and her husband were
along for the ride with my driver, Volodya. We left at sunrise. It was a beautiful late-summer day and we drove miles and miles through the Ukrainian

steppes in the company Audi, past the golden fields of wheat and soybean, the bright yellow expanses of canola and the breathtakingly beautiful seas of sunflowers with large, round brown faces trimmed in gold that followed the movement of the sun across the sky like audiences at a performance.

When we arrived at the Shchorsk facility, we were met under Ukrainian and Canadian flags by a kind of honour guard provided by a group of grain handlers dressed in blue overalls and yellow T-shirts — Ukraine's national colours. When I looked around, I couldn't help feeling a sense of pride in what we had built. The complex included nine new stainless steel grain elevators glinting in the sun, a loading dock, an office building, a gatehouse and a large machine shed. Our company, Unirem-Agro, had been established two years earlier with more than 9,000 hectares (22,000 acres) of growing lands, and the processing complex gave us 20,000 tons of grain storage to serve farmlands in a 50-kilometre radius. A spur railway line entered right into the complex loading area, allowing us to ship grain directly from there to the port facilities we were leasing on the Black Sea.

The business plan called for me to put up 51 percent of the capital to build the complex and purchase the type of modern agricultural machinery that would bring us greatly enhanced yields from the rich Ukrainian soils. Viktor Fesun, the general manager and three other partners were to put up the remaining 49 percent. But that capital was very slow in coming and on that sunny September day I was actually the 90 percent owner of the company and was listed on the company charter as its president.

But this was not a business day. It was a day of celebration, of spectacle, that began when we stepped into the yard. The place was already packed with guests — employees and their families and local dignitaries. I was met by Anna Fesun, who would serve as my translator that day and my guide through the show that her father and his organizers had put together.

We were ushered to a grandstand that had been set up in the parking lot. Within minutes you could hear the thunder of the horses' hooves as a group of Cossacks — strong young men with fur hats, long moustaches, red capes and embroidered vests — entered the yard at full gallop in a cloud of dust. For the next twenty minutes, they displayed remarkable acrobatic riding skills, from standing up on the back of the galloping horse to twisting almost to the underbelly to reach down to pick up flags from the ground, tricks that would have impressed the old North American Indian rodeo performers like my grandfather. They finished the performance with the horses in a circle and I was summoned into the middle, which I did with some concern because I had heard that Cossack initiation consisted of bullwhipping the initiate three times on the back. Fortunately, instead of a whipping, they presented me with the gift of a Cossack sash that resembled the one that the Métis people on the Canadian plains use, making me think again of the similarities between peoples around the world who live directly off the wealth of the land.

After the show, I was led by Anna to the elevator yard where the visiting dignitaries and others were gathering for the ribbon-cutting ceremony. I was handed the scissors by Fesun and we stood by while the former Ukrainian prime minister Yekhanurov spoke in Russian to the smiling crowd with, I could see from the faces that turned to look at me, a few friendly references to me. When he finished, I cut the ribbon. The people applauded warmly, and it was then, with Viktor Fesun at my side and Anna over my shoulder, that Yekhanurov stepped forward to give me the oversized key, and the photo was snapped.

Even now it is hard to imagine a better day than that one. Everyone was very kind to me. They smiled when they caught my eye. They were appreciative of the investment in their community and they applauded warmly while I was receiving the golden key. It was a day of fine words, fine feeling, of brotherhood.

Viktor Fesun introduced me to his father and grandfather, both of whom were wearing serge suit coats with their chests emblazoned with medals from their service in the Red Army during the Second World War.

The company accountant, Lyuba Chernysh, who was a long-time associate of Fesun and who was supposed to invest in the company, introduced me to her husband, Sergey — who I would learn often worked in the shadows with Fesun — and her son and daughter.

I was also approached by a local official from the Dnipropetrovsk Oblast Agriculture Department, who told me through a translator that the construction of these grain elevators and the import of the modern farming methods were important milestones in the development of Ukrainian agriculture and were seen as a great gift to the welfare of the local people. In fact, this type of comment was far more gratifying to me than a golden key because I really liked Ukraine and Ukrainians and the idea that I was making a positive contribution to their country.

The crowd then moved into the bright new employee cafeteria for lunch.

I sat with Yulia, Volodya, my Canadian CEO Cathy and her husband, Greg, and we were served an excellent Ukrainian meal of borscht, varenyky, deruni and cherry nalysnyky. There was a sense of elation around the table. We had built an extraordinary agro-business with a grain elevator linked by rail to a Black Sea port that would bring profit to our company while it enriched the lives of the local businesses and farmers in this colourful and storied land. Volodya, I noticed, was more circumspect, and he told me later that even then, he felt something was wrong. He thought everyone was smiling too much.

People did, at times, seem overly hospitable and sometimes laughed a little too long and a little too loudly at my jokes, but my sense of satisfaction came not so much from the smiling people as from the business plan I had executed. I had done my homework. I knew the operation was solid and would make all of the partners, Ukrainians as well as me, a lot of money. I also liked the idea of making a contribution to the development of Ukraine, which by now had almost become my adopted land. I also noticed that when my partners talked about the business, they spoke with what seemed like a genuine passion and they seemed to know what they were talking about. I knew the fundamentals were all good and if we followed the plan and stuck with it, we would be successful.

After lunch, I went out to look at the farm machinery I had purchased, which was parked at the back of our compound. While I was examining the massive, 374-horsepower grain harvester CX880 I'd bought in Saskatchewan for almost $800,000, I was approached by a young Ukrainian who spoke excellent English. He said he was working in Dnipropetrovsk with a Canadian NGO called Facility for Agricultural Reform and Modernization, and they were looking at our operation as a model for others to follow.

The approach by a Canadian organization didn't surprise me. I was generally aware of the close relationship between Canada and Ukraine — it was the protections included in the Canada-Ukraine economic treaty that convinced me to invest in the country — but at that time I wasn't aware of just how deeply entwined the two countries had become.

Canada, I was to learn, was a major financial and political player in Ukraine, but the influence went deeper than that. It was no accident that when Ukraine broke free of the crumbling Soviet Union in 1991, Ukraine's president-in-exile, Mykola Vasyliovych Plaviuk, was actually living in a Toronto suburb where he had fled after fighting alongside the Germans in the Second World War. Since 1991, virtually every Canadian foreign minister and most of the prime ministers made a pilgrimage to Ukraine, and since 2014 Canada had taken a major role in political, financial and military aid to the country.

This close relationship was reflected that day in that Yuriy Yekhanurov, the guy who gave me the oversized key, had hosted the Canadian trade minister, Jim Peterson, in Kyiv the year before, as well as planning "Canada Days" in Kyiv and Lviv. Yekhanurov was also the guy who replaced the previous governor of Dnipropetrovsk Oblast and current People's Deputy Sergey Kasyanov, who would end up stealing that magnificent property from me. And Kasyanov's usual partner-in-crime, a convicted murderer and bank fraud artist, was a Canadian-Ukrainian citizen who used the Montreal neighbourhood of Westmount as his hideout when things were too hot in Kyiv.

At the time, these men were all respected members of the Rada, the parliament of Ukraine, which is a haven for crooks because parliamentary immunity protects them from prosecution. Being a People's Deputy in Ukraine is better than a "get out of jail free" card, it's a "never having to go to jail" card. So corruption in Ukraine starts at the top. But as I was to learn, it passes through the whole of society. In Ukraine, corruption is an art, as intricate and acrobatic as the Cossack welcome ceremony, where the performance includes everyone from the local notary on the dusty village street right up to the gilded halls of parliament and the presidential palace playing tricks before your eyes.

And nothing is ever what it seems.

CHAPTER 3

BEST MAN

An Okanagan Indian discovers
Україна on a journey that begins at
the Wedding Palace in Kyiv in 2000.

Even today, I am still trying to sort out what was real and what was not in Ukraine. Twenty years later, I am still learning about new deceptions that began in the first days of my life there.

The complex stream of events that led me to the village of Shchorsk on that sunny summer day in 2007, and then headlong into the failed state that was Ukraine in the fall of 2021, began with a phone call to my office on the Westbank Indian Reserve in central British Columbia in 2000. It was from Darrell Michaels, a businessman friend from across Lake Okanagan in Kelowna.

Michaels turned out to be the perfect introduction to Ukraine. I had met him years earlier when he was a Calgary stockbroker and known by a different last name. He'd introduced me to the backers of a Calgary-based bank that I was made a director of when I was still chief of the Westbank First Nation. The bank failed in 1985, at a time when I was embroiled in a national controversy that had nothing to do with him. Even so, I was reluctant about doing business with Michaels afterward, but I also liked the guy. He was a colourful character full of wildly imaginative schemes that I enjoyed hearing about but would not touch with a ten-foot pole. He was an entertaining lunch companion who saw life as an adventure and always had new stories to tell.

At the time Michaels called me in 2000, I was rededicating myself to my business interests after my final two-year stint as chief of the Westbank band, a position I had held for ten years in the 1970s and '80s. Michaels told me he was about to marry what I understood was his fifth of seven or eight wives, and it seemed he was already running out of best men because he asked me if I would do it.

My first thought was, How can you refuse such a request? And before I had time for my second thought — which was that it was an odd request, since we were not that close — I heard myself agreeing.

"There is a hitch," he said. "The wedding is in Kyiv."

I asked him where Kyiv was.

"Ukraine," he said.

After the call, I had to check a map to find out where, exactly, Ukraine was. When I saw it was on the other side of the world, I was not unhappy. I had just escaped from the pressure cooker of Indigenous politics, which had led to a war in the woods with the BC government over logging rights. The idea of slipping away to some far-off place to serve as best man for an eccentric friend's wedding seemed like a welcome escape from the media, the political attacks and the occasional death threat from local rednecks that I had endured over the previous two years.

Because of the great distance — with the numerous changes of planes it was almost 24 hours from my house in the B.C. Interior to downtown Kyiv — I decided I would stay on to explore the place, so Darrell arranged for me to rent an apartment while I was there.

At the time, I was 58 years old and had never shied away from life's adventures. As well as band chief, I had worked as a welder, a rancher, and an entrepreneur and businessman who had amassed one of the largest real estate holdings in the B.C. Interior. Along the way, I'd been the North American champion speedboat racer and had survived both a Royal Commission into my affairs and an assassination attempt by a thug from Alberta who'd been paid off by local trailer park owners. So life had, in many ways, already prepared me for the roller-coaster ride Ukraine had in store for me.

The first part of my preparation came from Michaels himself, who was his own invention. His real name was not Michaels, it was Markowsky. He changed it after he was caught up in a financial scandal in Calgary (not the bank failure — another one) in 1989. By the time he moved to Kelowna in 1991, he had a new company — which eventually also came under investigation by the securities exchange — and a new name.

This colourful character, a cheerful man, a lover of women and a lover of wine, who lived his life along the line separating legality and illegality — often with one foot on each side — was my introduction to Ukraine. He celebrated it as his ancestral homeland, a land of charming people and beautiful women and a delicious cuisine marinated in alcohol and corruption. Michaels blamed all of the traits in himself on his Ukrainian heritage and said that was what drew him back time and again to the country.

This time I would be along for the adventure.

◊◆◊

The customs officials at Boryspil International Airport waved me through with a minimum of interest, and I found myself in a crush of people in the main hall, swarmed by rough-looking guys of all ages shouting about their taxi service to town and lunging toward my suitcase. That was a recurring theme in Ukraine. People were willing to do whatever it took to get a few hryvnia (Ukrainian currency) because they had to or go home hungry. In post-Soviet Ukraine, the oligarchs had already seized most of the wealth, and there were no safety nets. To survive you had to grab the remaining crumbs for yourself and your family.

I was finally rescued from the mob by Michaels, who had come to pick me up. He was happy to see me and I had a sense that he hadn't really believed I would come. I hadn't heard from him for a few weeks so I wasn't sure that he even remembered inviting me. But we both made it and it was with a sense of adventure that we drove into Kyiv.

I would learn quite a bit about Ukraine and its history over the next two decades, but at the time I had read just enough to know that it had been part of the Russian empire for centuries, and then when the Soviets took over it was made a republic within the Soviet Union. When the Soviet Union broke up in 1991, Ukraine made a run for it and managed to break free to become its own country — although for some time afterward it was still within the Russian orbit.

On the road in from the airport, we passed a few shabby-looking villages, then a group of Soviet-era concrete apartment blocks, most with laundry hanging from the balconies, which rose from the dusty, weedy fields on the outskirts of the city. My first look at the city itself came from the bridge crossing the kilometre-wide expanse of the Dnieper River.

What surprised me from the bridge was the beauty. The high cliffs on the other bank were green parkland, and in and around the parks the Byzantine golden cupolas of the Eastern Orthodox Christian churches glinted in the sun; some of them, I was to learn, were a thousand years old. As we crossed the bridge the dominant feature rising above the green ridge of the hills was the giant Motherland Monument, a 100-metre stainless steel figure of a woman in flowing robes holding a sword in one hand and a shield in the other. It was built by the Soviets in 1980 to celebrate their victory over the Nazis, and like virtually all the public monuments in Ukraine, then and now, it would become a source of controversy because many want to tear down symbols of the country's Soviet past. This one survives, perhaps because it provides such a striking entrance to the city.

On the other side of the bridge, even though we were travelling along broad avenues, we were suddenly plunged into the city traffic. Most of the cars were beaten-up old Ladas and Nivas left over from Soviet times, but there was also a surprising number of Mercedes and BMWs. Clearly, someone was making money here.

The apartment Michaels had arranged for me to rent was near the big Bessarabska Market, a large, round, brick-and-glass food market built some time before the First World War. Around the square were dozens of shops, restaurants and takeout stands. My apartment was up a steep hill only a few hundred metres from the square. Michaels suggested I rest for a couple of hours and he would pick me up later for supper.

I took the tiny elevator up to the fourteenth floor to the small but not uncomfortable one-bedroom apartment. From the window I could see across the city, including the golden domes of the thousand-year-old St. Sophia Cathedral and the broad avenues of the downtown area that are characteristic of a Slavic city. I was jet-lagged but happy to be there and looking forward to exploring this strange city that a couple of months earlier I did not even know existed.

I had dinner with Michaels in the old section of the city, called Podil. He said the wedding would be a small one and mentioned that her family would not be in attendance. I was still exhausted from my trip and hardly listening, but I did get the impression that in the months since his call, his enthusiasm for the marriage had dampened somewhat.

The wedding was in the Soviet-era Central Wedding Palace, a strange-looking saddle-shaped building near the railway station. I arrived on my own by taxi. There was a grand entrance of polished black marble that led to an inside set of red and gold carpeted steps up to the grand hall. Michaels's wedding was in the hall to the left, lit by a wall of windows around the high end of the saddle. There was a kind of secular altar at the front and a handful of cushioned chairs on either side. Six bouquets of flowers in giant urns formed an arc around the table.

When I arrived, Darrell and his bride, Olga Rossian, were already there, near the front, framed by the great windows in the near-empty hall and surrounded by a small group of people — maybe five or six of Olga's friends.

That was it. Her family, who were well-off Ukrainians, didn't approve of the wedding and were nowhere to be seen. Olga was not wearing the full flouncy wedding dress and veil worn by younger brides but instead a stylish white dress. No question she looked beautiful, but they both seemed a little lost in this vast wedding palace. In fact, we all seemed lost.

I took my place to the right and slightly behind Michaels, across from a young Ukrainian woman who was the maid of honour. The ceremony took no more than fifteen minutes. The government official conducting the ceremony, a very polished man in a dark suit, spoke Russian in a rapid monotone, pausing now and again to inject an English word or phrase for Michaels and me. On the official's prompt, I handed over the impressive diamond wedding ring to Darrell to put on Olga's finger. She smiled. Not a blushing bride smile but a kind of triumphant smile. They kissed. The five or six people in the room smiled and applauded, a small clapping sound in the vast wedding hall that was finally drowned out by a blast of upbeat Ukrainian music coming from the loudspeakers. And it was over.

Mr. and Mrs. Michaels headed off for their honeymoon on the Black Sea.

◇◆◇

If I had come to Kyiv solely for the wedding, it would have been a letdown. But before I arrived I had already decided I would take advantage of my trip to explore the country.

I began near my rented apartment at Bessarabska Square. The streets were bustling with shoppers and strollers as well as beggars and hungry people. I went into the market, which was decorated on the outside with ornate sculptures of a milk woman and a peasant with an ox. It was dimly lit, but rich in the sound of market clamour in an unfamiliar language and in the smells from the abundant fruits and vegetables, dairy and meat products, various kinds of fish, and red and black caviar, all perfumed by flower stalls. The place had a wonderfully exotic feeling.

Part of this was the strange language with its, at the time, inscrutable Cyrillic alphabet. In Ukrainian, Bessarabska Market was written *Бессарабский рынок*, and the restaurants in the square were all advertised as ресторан. There were a couple of blinking green аптека signs, which I would later recognize as "pharmacy," but then I was completely lost. Until my eyes suddenly settled on a familiar and very welcome sign: Friday's.

This English word in the middle of all the confounding Cyrillics was on the window glass below a much larger neon sign for Фрайдис, which I was to later learn was the Cyrillic phonetic spelling of Friday's. I crossed the street toward the beckoning English word that gave me hope that I would be able to order food.

The smart lunch crowd struck a contrast to the shabbily dressed throng in the square. In fact, it looked like any of the chain's restaurants in Vancouver or Calgary, but of course the voices rising and falling were speaking Russian and Ukrainian. I was greeted and shown a table by a beautiful Ukrainian waitress who instantly sized me up as a foreigner, and to my relief spoke to me in excellent and charmingly accented English.

This, I knew, was the force that brought Michaels back to the country again and again: Ukrainian women. He told me once that on any given day in Ukraine, you can meet the most beautiful, most desirable, warmest and most charming woman in the world, and you think that she is perfect for you, that this is the woman you have been dreaming of all your life! And you spend the most wonderful day and night with her, and the next day it is settled: this is the woman you want to make your life with. But within two days, you meet another Ukrainian woman who is so incredibly beautiful and charming and warm and desirable that she makes you completely forget the previous one. So Michaels was definitely a lover of women, but he was far from anything resembling a sex tourist. Michaels, as his marriage record attested, was looking for love. He fell in love with the women he met and he wooed them and married them. So maybe it was more accurate to call him a love tourist.

But it was also clearly an obsession. Even his son admitted to this. I exchanged notes with Jason Markowsky, a promising young writer living in South America, many years after his father's death. When I asked what drew his father to Ukraine, he spoke frankly: he said this love of women was what "made Darrell, Darrell." Women and wine. That is what lured my friend Darrell (Markowsky) Michaels again and again to Ukraine. And he paid for his passion with trips and gifts and a fistful of diamond rings that in the end he couldn't really afford.

◊•◊

In the crowded Friday's, the waitress brought me an English-language menu and I found all of the usual burgers with fancy descriptions that these types of North American restaurants specialize in. I also noticed an

English-language newspaper, the *Kyiv Post*, on the empty table beside me. The front page was about the mysterious disappearance of a journalist who had been critical of the government, and while I was waiting for my food I flipped through the paper, settling on the classified section. As a real estate investor in Canada, I was interested to see the houses and flats for sale and I made a mental note of the surprisingly low prices for what looked from the photos like substantial real estate investments. I also saw a few ads for people offering their services as interpreters and guides to the city.

When I returned to my apartment, I called one of the numbers for guides. The woman who answered said her name was Helena Konolova, but she told me to call her Lena. Her English was quite good.

Lena, it turned out, was proud of her city and she unlocked the door into Ukraine for me, while simultaneously impressing me with her refusal to be intimidated by police officers trying to extort money from us for this or that phony permission. One of our first stops was the famous St. Sophia Cathedral. We walked up the steep hill from Independence Square to the cathedral gate, a huge white tower topped by a golden dome. On the other side was a grand courtyard with a church and several other ancient buildings.

After my eyes adjusted to the dimness inside the cathedral, I was struck by the spectacular gold-trimmed artwork illuminating the dome above the altar. The walls were decorated with dozens of ancient paintings, some of them part of the thousand-year-old original church and hardly visible now that time had nearly erased them. Others had been added through the centuries, mainly of holy men in robes with a few half-naked angels flitting about to liven things up.

I stayed maybe half an hour. I find that after the initial blast, these places lose my interest. I was happy, finally, to get out of the damp church and back into the sunshine. Lena was obviously proud of her country's national treasures and liked to show them off, so I was always careful to praise them. But after she showed me the third grand church, I told her honestly, that was enough churches! (Although Lena remembers my exact wording as: "No more fucking churches!")

On another outing, she took me up the hill to the Motherland Monument to Ukrainians killed in the Second World War. Lena told me many stories about the brutality the people suffered and how it deeply affected her parents' generation. "Millions of Ukrainians were killed. Every family lost someone," she said.

As we strolled along the lush green parkland, she told me the history was even more complicated because before the war was the great famine that the communists brought to Ukraine in the 1930s. Literally millions starved to death. So for many Ukrainians, the victory over the Nazis was not really a victory but a reoccupation by the Russians.

This complexity is a constant feature of Ukraine's history. Around every corner, there is a confounding fact. Lena mentioned that when the Nazis were at the door, the communist secret police executed Ukrainian nationalists who they said were sympathetic to the incoming Nazis. Later she spoke about a monument in the city that marked a killing field where tens of thousands of Jews were slaughtered by the Nazis a few weeks after their arrival, with the help of the Ukrainian nationalists. The brutality in this country had been on a breathtaking scale, and everyone had their own, often conflicting, story.

But these were the heavier moments from the past and they were only a small part of my exploration of Ukraine. My interest was in the present, and Lena took me to the most amazing food markets with vendors who sold every part of their animals, even the tails, and decorated the stalls with their wares. There were stalls selling incredible-tasting dried berry juices, and I discovered that Ukrainian fruits and vegetables tasted the way fruits and vegetables tasted in my youth, fresh from the tree or garden. With Lena I also began to sample many of the great dishes in Ukrainian cuisine — which after twenty years I am convinced belongs with the great international cuisines. I learned to cook some of my favourite Ukrainian dishes myself, and at one point I even considered putting together a show to be called *Cooking with the Babushkas* to feature this great cuisine for North Americans.

From my first days there, I liked the feel of Kyiv. I had spent a lot of time in Canadian cities — Vancouver, Calgary and Ottawa — and I had a place in Palm Desert, California, where I retreated to escape the worst of the winters, but there was something restrictive in these spaces. Kyiv, with its broad avenues and the solid architecture of its Russian empire roots, is built to a larger scale. At the same time, it also manages to incorporate more intimate spaces, like the winding uphill path I climbed to my rented apartment behind Bessarabska Square, where the sounds of violin music drift from the music academy on the corner.

When I was dropped off at the airport to return to Kelowna ten days after the wedding, I strongly suspected that I would come back to this country. At that first quick glance, it seemed to have much to offer and at the same time needed so much help from the outside. So I would come back. But I did not know that I would be returning so soon.

◊•◊

Darrell Michaels brought Olga back to Kelowna with him and I saw them a couple of times in the fall of 2000. The last time was at Heritage Motors, a car dealership I owned, when Michaels called asking if I had any good deals on a used luxury car. I told him I had some first-rate used Mercedes and BMWs and I would meet him there to show him around.

He brought Olga with him, but I could see from the strained look on her face that life with Darrell was not agreeing with her. When he showed an interest in a late-model used BMW, she actually stomped her foot. She wanted a new car, not a used one. Then she glared at me angrily for taking her husband's side, and I thought that with all the charming women in Ukraine, he had finally found a charmless one. I was not surprised when their marriage barely made it to New Year's Eve, and in mid-January Olga was heading back to Ukraine alone.

That spring, I would be heading back to Ukraine too. With Michaels. When we talked about it in Kelowna, Michaels described a possible trip to Odessa on the Black Sea as a search for business opportunities. I knew I would not in any circumstances go into business with him, but I was interested in seeing more of the country, so I volunteered to go along.

We spent a couple of days in Kyiv before heading south to Odessa. I had expected a kind of Mediterranean-style resort town, but I discovered that the Black Sea was not the Mediterranean. We landed at a small, vintage Second World War airfield with a kind of shed for a terminal. We had left

Kyiv at dawn and it was still early in the day when a taxi took us along the winding, dusty roads into the city, then through the morning traffic jam on narrow streets that passed through the chaos of Privoz Market and then the big Odessa Zoo.

Our hotel in the heart of the city was comfortable enough, but in the Soviet style, which was basically the style of hotel rooms fifty years earlier: radiators, exposed pipes, and old, heavy, and often scratched and chipped furnishings. Michaels was still hungover from the night before in Kyiv when we had stayed late at a club he liked to visit, and he headed up to his room to rest. I decided to explore the area around the hotel.

As I walked along the tree-lined Prymorskyi Boulevard in Odessa, I could feel the cool sea breeze and suddenly came across the broad Potemkin Stairs that lead down to the port. The stairs are one of the best-known features of Odessa, fifteen metres wide and crossing a series of terraces in almost 200 steps, making a dramatic entry to a busy Black Sea port. The harbour was full of ships flying flags mostly from Black Sea countries — many of them with the Turkish crescent — but also from around the Mediterranean, as well as Africa and Asian countries. This was encouraging to me. Even if its current state was a depressed one, Ukraine was still a trading country, and trading countries always have a future.

When I arrived back at the hotel, I was surprised to find Michaels already in the bar. It was obvious that this was not his first drink of the day because he was again in a festive mood, having already drowned the previous night's hangover.

We stayed only a few days in Odessa, but it was enough to time to explore the seaside resort side of town while Michaels filled me in on the country. He seemed to have a great knowledge of the place, especially of the criminal gangs in Odessa, Donetsk and Dnipropetrovsk that ran it.

In Odessa, Michaels said the local boss was Aleksandr Angert, who first made his money selling stolen post-Soviet arms through Odessa to African dictators. Then he became one of the leading figures in the oil mafia, making hundreds of millions of dollars a year stealing Russian oil that was being pumped through Ukraine to the European market, and redirecting it into the Odessa refinery he controlled. Angert would then pump it into independent tankers for sale around the world. Odessa crime groups at the time were said to have up to six thousand "soldiers" not only protecting the illegal oil trade and arms smuggling, but controlling all of the economic activity in the city, including those wasted-looking young women working the street outside our hotel.

Angert, known locally by his nickname Angel, used the usual mafia tools of murder and mayhem to control the city while he was moving most of his money into high-priced London real estate. When international law enforcement threatened him, he cooled his heels in Israel, where there were no extradition treaties. While he was out of the country, he still controlled his empire through the mayor of Odessa, who was one of his gang members.

Over the years I would learn that along with Odessa, all major regions in eastern Ukraine — Dnipropetrovsk, Donetsk, Kharkiv — had their own mafia gangs, which sometimes in co-operated with each other but were more often in competition.

By the time we headed back to Canada, I had developed a full-blown fascination with the country and its slightly madcap reputation. But I was worried about my friend. In both his drinking and his financial scheming, Michaels was on a slippery slope. After we returned from that trip, I read notices in the local paper of stock market regulator investigations into some of his more questionable companies — those that were taking inves-tors' money and using it to live a high life in Ukraine in something that resembled a Ponzi scheme. When I saw him in Kelowna he was looking increasingly haggard.

It was a couple of years later that he told me he had been diagnosed with a brain tumour and the doctors said there was nothing they could do. I tried to get him help from an Arizona Indian tribe that was known for its powerful medicine, but they were reluctant to give their medicine to a white man. Just ahead of the stock market investigators who were closing in on him, and before his sixtieth birthday, Darrell (Markowsky) Michaels exited the world.

A notice of his passing appeared in the paper with the mention of a memorial service to be held in his native town of Vegreville, Alberta, which was known mainly as the home of a giant painted, two-thousand-pound

Ukrainian Easter egg — the largest of its kind in the world. But even with that, I learned that his connection to Ukraine was much less than I thought because his original name, Markowsky, his son Jason told me, was not Ukrainian. It was Polish.

So my Ukrainian friend who had introduced me to the wonders of Ukraine was actually Polish, but had grown up in the town with the biggest Ukrainian Easter egg in the world and seems to have adopted that national identity. This was, in its own way, a perfect introduction to a country where nothing is what it seems.

CHAPTER 4

INTERNATIONAL REAL ESTATE

*Testing the Ukraine business waters,
from real estate to agriculture.
Discovering Canada's prominent
role in the country and the first
of its false promises.*

My business involvement in Ukraine began cautiously. Real estate was an industry I knew well, and after seeing the low prices on Kyiv flats on my first visit, I returned to the country in 2002 to take a more serious look at the market.

I connected with Lena again to act as my guide, and she had a new driver pick me up at the airport. He was in his early 40s and spoke only a little English, but he had a relaxed good humour that put people at ease. His name was Vladimir Marinichenko, but he was known by the familiar version of his name, Volodya.

Volodya was 30 years old when the Soviet Union collapsed and said he liked being a free man. He had his own car — I noticed a religious amulet and rosary beads hanging from the rear-view mirror — and he told me, in halting English, that he was acting as a chauffeur for weddings, corporate parties and the like. Later I learned that after he did his army service, he had studied tourism in Kyiv and took groups of tourists around Ukraine. But his main job was as a driver. He liked his work, but revenues were up-and-down and hard to predict.

Halfway into the city, I told Volodya that I could use a full-time driver while I was in Ukraine. Volodya nodded and thought about it while he drove us through the city traffic. By the time we reached my apartment he accepted the offer. Later he told me it was because he liked the idea of working for a foreigner and getting a steady paycheque, and because he liked me personally. The feeling was mutual. My instincts about Volodya were right. Twenty years later he was still with me as a trusted friend as well as an employee. I later discovered that he was licensed to carry a firearm, so bodyguard was added to the list of services he provided me.

So that was our tiny band. Me, Lena and Volodya. But what I soon discovered was that while post-Soviet Ukraine was in need of almost everything, the one resource it had in abundance was smart, well-educated young people who struggled to find work and were looking for an opportunity to make a life for themselves.

I was first introduced to this fact at the Arizona restaurant, which faced the Dnieper River on Naberezhno-Kreshatytskaya Street in Kyiv. The restaurant had a bright American style — the walls were decorated with old American ads and licence plates and, for some reason, a big Confederate flag — and for most of the day it served a mix of American and Mexican cuisine with specials like deep-fried, cheese-stuffed jalapeños. In the morning, the Arizona also served an excellent North American breakfast with eggs, bacon and toast and a very good cappuccino.

The first morning I walked in with Lena and Volodya, I was surprised to find myself face to face with a life-sized, elaborately painted cigar store Indian guarding the entrance.[1] I saw Lena and Volodya glancing worriedly at the mock-Indian figure and then at me, a real North American Indian.

I could see that they were concerned I might be offended, but I do not offend so easily. I strode over to the figure and embraced it, calling out "Grandpa!"

---

1   Arizona videos showing the cigar store Indian can be seen at https://www.facebook.com/BBQArizona /videos/?ref=page_internal and https://www.facebook.com/150308441734440/videos/347271275371488.

They laughed at this and my Arizona grandpa became a standing joke among us. We ended up eating there almost every morning because the food was good and it was a convenient place to plan our days, which usually began by going through the real estate listings in the local papers. After Lena covered the Russian- and Ukrainian-language papers for me, I would look through the English-language newspaper, reading the political coverage as well as the real estate ads. The country almost always seemed to be in political turmoil.

These were the closing days of President Leonid Kuchma's regime. A tug-of-war between Ukrainian nationalists and Russian-speaking regions was being played out in the press, and increasingly on the streets, with people chanting "Україна без Кучми!" (literally "Ukraine without Kuchma!") In fact, nobody seemed to trust the guy, who had been in power for eight years with his cronies from the Donetsk mafia. Along with rampant corruption, Kuchma was also very likely guilty of ordering the murder of a 31-year-old journalist, Georgiy Gongadze, whose disappearance I'd read about on my first trip. Gongadze's body would be found headless, and someone released a taped conversation between the president and his henchmen discussing the need to silence him. It was almost a decade before they found the head for the headless body. Kuchma was briefly charged for ordering the murder, then had the charges dropped under Ukraine's unwritten Oligarch Protection Act. But the incident would live on as part of the contemporary lore in Ukraine, coming back again and again and never really getting resolved, while Kuchma was restored to official respectability by some magical process that often occurs with Ukrainian gangsters.

Reading the local paper helped me orient myself in those early years in a strange country, as did speaking with as many Ukrainians as I could. At the Arizona, I chatted with the two waitresses, Vika and Yulia, and discovered they were both very impressive young people. The management had them wearing Wild West costumes, short denim skirts and T-shirts with the Arizona logo, but they were serious young women striving to get ahead. Vika was Viktoria Bałenko, a 22-year-old who grew up in Kazakhstan after the Soviets shipped her parents from Kyiv to the far reaches of their empire. As a student, she had returned to study in Kyiv with a major in psychology but then switched to law and began her degree at the university in Crimea at Simferopol. She returned to Kyiv to complete her law degree and was supporting herself by waitressing at the Arizona.

Yulia was a year younger than Vika and came from Nikopol in the Dnipropetrovsk region. She was still studying economics at university with a specialty in accounting. The main fear of the two young women seemed to be that their hopes and dreams and hard work would be for nothing — that they would graduate into a broken economy and a broken country, and never find a job beyond waitressing.

After I came to know them, I told them that when they graduated, they should come to see me and I would try to find work for them. In the meantime, having some idea of how little they were paid, I would leave generous tips. This was not hard to do because the cost of breakfast was so ridiculously low that even with a big tip, the total would be a small fraction of what it would cost in North America.

By the time I returned to Ukraine a few months later, Vika had graduated from law school. She showed up at my door and I kept my promise to give her a job as my legal adviser and administrator. She was a very competent person and twenty years later — with only a short stint in between, when she tried another career path — she was still working for me.

Two years later, when Yulia finished her accounting degree, she also turned up at my door and again I kept my word and hired her as my bookkeeper/accountant. My instincts about her were good because Yulia was also still working with me into 2022 — a loyal and talented employee.

With this small but growing team I made my first cautious forays into the Ukrainian business world through the real estate market. I will not go into too much detail here, because this isn't a story about Kyiv real estate. But my success in the real estate market, and a Canadian government treaty promising to indemnify Canadian businesses against loss to corrupt practices in Ukraine, was what led me down the path to the much bigger investment.

The real estate company was called the International Real Estate Agency, but in truth most of our clients were Ukrainian business people, politicians, government officials, a few soccer stars and people in the entertainment industry, who were looking to buy something chic near the centre of Kyiv.

My specialty was buying old Russian empire or Soviet-era flats and fixing them up. My team included a designer and a couple of contractors who were able to do high-quality renovation jobs quickly and at a reasonable cost.

It was a satisfying experience to take the keys over from an old wreck and a few months later hand the same keys to a sparkling new and modern living space to a new owner. It was also profitable. I would generally buy the place for around $80,000, invest $40,000 or so in renovations, then sell quickly for between $180,000 and $280,000.

As the company developed, I was proud that I'd been able to find success in a place as different and offbeat as Ukraine, even while I was travelling frequently back and forth from Canada. I did have to work extraordinarily long hours, though, because I always kept in touch with my Canadian head office in Westbank, whose hours were from 4 p.m. to midnight Ukraine time. But in the middle of all this I also found time for a social life. It was nowhere on the scale of my friend Darrell Michaels, but I did meet many smart and attractive women in Kyiv and I enjoyed many evenings in their company at some of Kyiv's excellent restaurants, particularly the Karavan, an Uzbek restaurant on Klovskyj uzviz Street, and Da Vinci, a superb fish restaurant in the old city on Volodymyrska Street. If there was a mutual attraction, I found that most women in Ukraine didn't hesitate to act on it. Eventually, one of these pleasant interludes developed into a more serious long-term relationship with Susana, a psychologist with a thriving practice in Kyiv who became my companion for almost ten years while I was in Ukraine.

◊•◊

I was finding my way in business there. Along with real estate, I was briefly associated with agriculture when a Canadian, Robert Morrison, contacted me in Westbank about the possibility of investing in his company, Greenlab Agronomics. Although it came to nothing, it did have me look at the Ukraine agricultural sector, and I discovered just how ripe it was for development. International studies spoke glowingly of potential that had never been properly exploited during the Soviet years or properly capitalized afterward.

Agriculture was something I had an immediate interest in. I had grown up on a small farm on the Westbank Indian reserve in the British Columbia Interior — the community where I would serve as chief for a decade — and farming was in my blood. My first memories were from when I was three or four years old, squatting in the onion patch beside my mother as she picked onions. Later in life, when I worked as a welder in B.C., I saved every penny I made until I had enough to purchase a small ranch with a few cows. I then worked my butt off as a rancher until I had 750 head of cattle and two ranches to run. Finally, it was the sale of those two ranches and the cattle that earned me my first millions, which I then invested in real estate and other entrepreneurial ventures. So agriculture was actually at the base of my fortune.

In Ukraine, part of the problem in investing in agriculture, or anything else for that matter, was the continuing political upheaval in the country as it struggled to break free of the Russian orbit that still held sway over the country's social and economic life. That struggle had once again poured onto the streets in what has become known as the Orange Revolution, which was set off by the November 21, 2004, presidential election. The vote was seen as fixed in favour of Kuchma's successor, Viktor Yanukovych, who was believed to be part of the Donetsk mafia, against his nationalist opponent Viktor Yushchenko.

In the wake of the allegedly stolen election, there were massive protests in Kyiv, with thousands of protesters demonstrating daily. Nationwide, the protests were highlighted by a series of acts of civil disobedience, sit-ins and general strikes organized by the opposition movement. The protests succeeded and the results of the original run-off were annulled; a new vote was ordered by Ukraine's Supreme Court that was set for December 26, 2004. It was won by the nationalist Yushchenko with 52 percent of the vote. Peace was temporarily restored in the country the next month when Yushchenko was sworn in as the new president, but the tug-of-war between the two political forces in the country would continue throughout the decade and into today, often with dramatic consequences. One thing that remained stable was the corruption, which dominates the country's economic life and limits any possibility of political reform.

I was in business class on the last leg of the flight from Amsterdam to Kyiv and began chatting with the businessman across the aisle. His name was Aleksei Gershun. He was from Dnipropetrovsk and he was going back to visit his parents who lived near there. He said he'd been living for many years in Connecticut, where he worked as an engineer with Prestone, a subsidiary of the Honeywell corporation. (When he found out I was Canadian, he said he loved Canada and he'd heard that Canada's Chinese woman president had been in Ukraine a few weeks before. Only later would I find out what he was talking about.)

Gershun told me he was involved in an agricultural project in the Dnipropetrovsk region, and we spoke about the rich farmlands in Ukraine. He said the problem was that the country was still technologically backward and, despite having some of the most fertile lands in the world, the yields were pathetic because of the lack of investment in modern equipment.

I knew what he was saying, about both the richness of the land and the underinvestment, was true. So I listened. Gershun mentioned a friend, Viktor Fesun, who was looking for investors in his agricultural operation to raise his production to a much higher level. He wanted to know if I would be interested in investing. I told him no, I wasn't, I had a real estate company in Ukraine and more than a dozen businesses in Canada under the RMD Group umbrella. I was not looking for any more.

When we were approaching Kyiv's Boryspil airport, he leaned across the aisle and handed me his business card and I handed him mine. He was in Kyiv often, he said; maybe we could meet for a drink.

I said sure, why not.

Gershun called me a couple of weeks later. He was in Kyiv, heading back to the United States the following day, and asked if we might meet for dinner. It was a friendly encounter. He talked a lot about himself and his work as a research fellow at Prestone, with a specialty in engine oils and lubricants — apparently he had dozens of patents. But he also often brought the conversation back to his friend, Viktor Fesun, and his small agricultural company near Dniprodzerzhynsk, an industrial town on the Dnieper River.

He said Fesun had been trying to find investors for the last five years, and Gershun himself had invested a small amount. He again asked me if I would be interested, and I again said no, thanks.

We spent the rest of the meal talking about Ukraine, its huge potential and its many assets for developing businesses there — bright and well-educated young people, access to the Black Sea, decent climate, fabulous growing lands, and the fact that it was close to Poland, Czech Republic, Slovakia and Hungary, all of which had been admitted into the European Union the previous year, giving Ukraine an excellent trading position. He was happy that I spoke well of Ukraine — and especially when I remarked how much I liked Ukrainian cuisine — and we parted almost as friends.

It would not be the last I'd hear from Gershun or about Viktor Fesun. When I was back in Canada, I received an email from Gershun with a Canadian government document attached. It was entitled *Agreement Between the Government of Canada and the Government of Ukraine for the Promotion and Protection of Investments* and covered a 1994 treaty between the two countries.

I read through it with interest. Article IX of the treaty guaranteed Canadians' investments in Ukraine by promising any investor "repayment of loans related to an investment; the proceeds of the total or partial liquidation of any investment" as well as "any compensation owed to an investor."

This document was important for me because it told potential Canadian investors that they would not be left swimming with the sharks in Ukraine. There was a Canadian lifeboat nearby to pick up survivors.

With the Orange Revolution bringing the nationalists to power in Ukraine in 2005, Canadian engagement with the country was expanding rapidly. Canada sent a massive team of 463 observers to the December 2004 presidential election, headed by former prime minister John Turner, who hailed Yushchenko's election as "enhancing in a remarkable way" Canadian involvement in "sponsoring democracy" in Ukraine. Turner said he hoped a "new era" would now begin.

To show this closer relationship and Canada's support of the path Ukraine was on, the Paul Martin government sent Governor General Adrienne Clarkson to Kyiv to attend President Yushchenko's inauguration. Yushchenko showed his appreciation of Canadian support by seating Clarkson beside his wife at his swearing-in ceremony and then right beside him at the inaugural lunch. (Only later did I realize that Clarkson was who Gershun meant by "Canada's Chinese woman president.")

With this level of Canadian-Ukrainian friendship, and especially with the promises in the 1994 economic treaty, I thought that maybe I could at least listen to Gershun and his friend to see what they had to say.

It was only later that I learned that Canadian promises about fighting corruption in Ukraine were always empty. The embrace of Ukraine had nothing to do with a desire to help the people of the country, but had everything to do with the million-plus Ukrainian votes in Western Canada that were badly needed by the Martin minority government — and later for pursuing foreign policy interests. Promoting investments in Ukraine was another sop to the politically powerful Ukrainian community in Canada, but there would be no real follow-up. And if your boat were sunk, I was to learn, Canada would indeed leave its citizens to the sharks in the waters.

Those sharks were already making a home within Yushchenko's Orange Revolution. It turned out to be as welcoming to the oligarchs and gangsters, who had been robbing the people of Ukraine since independence was declared in 1991, as the previous government had been. While the Ukrainian government and its backers were announcing the country was preparing to set sail for a new and better tomorrow, the Ukrainian ship of state would remain grounded on the rocky shoals of corruption while the sharks continued to control the seas.

CHAPTER 5

BIG BANG: COLLAPSE OF AN EMPIRE

Ukrainian corruption — the origin story.
The gangsters rising from the rubble
and Gershun, Fesun and the Chernyshes
scrambling for their share.

Canada was there, front and centre, at the beginning. And by the beginning I mean the immediate aftermath of the big bang: the collapse of the Soviet Union, which cleared the way for an independent Ukraine after more than seventy years in the Soviet orbit, and before that, hundreds of years in the Russian empire.

When Ukraine emerged from the smoky ruins of the Soviet Union in 1991, the pro-Western leader Boris Yeltsin was in control in Moscow, and Ukrainians flooded the streets demanding independence from a reemergent Russia. Leonid Kravchuk, who had been third in line in the Ukrainian communist leadership, joined the people in the streets and declared Ukraine independent. Presidential elections were hurriedly organized for December 1, 1991, and Kravchuk, a man who was said to be so quick and cunning that he could slip between raindrops in a rainstorm, was elected president on the promise of independence, freedom and prosperity for Ukraine.

What is telling is how at this early date, Canada was already deeply involved in Ukraine. It was no accident that Canada was the first country in the world to recognize an independent Ukraine and that an actual Ukrainian president-in-exile, Mykola Plaviuk, had been living quietly in a Toronto suburb for more than 40 years after fleeing to Canada with the wave of Ukrainians who had fought alongside the Nazis in the Second World War. On August 22, 1992, a year after Ukraine successfully broke away from the Soviet Union, president-in-exile Plaviuk flew from Toronto to Kyiv for a ceremonial session of the Rada, where he officially handed over the state regalia of the Ukrainian People's Republic to President Kravchuk, along with a letter stating that the independent Ukraine proclaimed on August 24, 1991, is the legal successor of the Ukrainian state that existed for less than two years after the First World War.

As part of the ceremony, Canada's Governor General Ray Hnatyshyn was invited to address the new Ukrainian parliament. Hnatyshyn, who was of Ukrainian descent, also visited his father's native village of Vashkivtsi in the Bukovina Oblast, and local people from there and surrounding villages spent hours waiting for the arrival of the man they called "the King of America." According to his friends, Hnatyshyn considered his official visit to independent Ukraine, the first by such a high-level Western office-holder, "the most outstanding moment during his time in office." One of his activities at Vashkivtsi was to formally open the Diaspora of Bukovina Museum of Local Lore, and he was accompanied in this by Ukrainian-Canadian artist Pavlo Tsymbaliuk — the creator of the world's largest monument to Ukrainian pysanka (Easter egg) in Darrell Michaels's home-town in Alberta.

Addressing the Ukrainian parliament, Hnatyshyn said that "we must not forget the suffering of the people that we are witnessing" and spoke about "the brave Ukrainian and Canadian soldiers who kept the peace across the world in zones of conflict and unrest." This last reference was a little delicate because the previous day in Kyiv, there had been a massive march by Western Ukrainian veterans of the Second World War who had fought, not alongside Canadians and the Allies, but as volunteers with the German army and Ukrainian SS units.

By August 1991, Kravchuk could claim that he had indeed delivered on the promise of independence, but the promise of freedom was a little more iffy, and prosperity was definitely not in the foreseeable future for the country.

Instead what independence brought was complete economic collapse. And nowhere was it worse than in the Dnipropetrovsk region, which was the heart of the Soviet Union's space and military rocket program and one of its biggest chemical and steel suppliers. Tens of thousands were thrown out of work as the big factories suddenly shut their gates. This devastated not only workers but the technical class of engineers, like Viktor Fesun and Aleksei Gershun. And even for those few who held jobs, their wages plummeted while the price of everything skyrocketed.

In the turmoil that followed, the only people who flourished were those who could turn the lawlessness to their advantage. Ukraine quickly became, in a very real way, a gangster state where the most corrupt members of the old system used violence and intimidation to seize control of former state assets.

For the average person, life became a waking nightmare of struggling just to find enough food to sustain themselves. If you wanted to buy milk, you had to wake up at 2 a.m. and stand in line until noon. Meat became outrageously expensive. Alcohol all but disappeared, and when any turned up there would be fights between alcoholics desperate for a drink. Families sold whatever they had to survive another day: silverware, old toys and used clothes were carted off on buses to Romania, where people still had a little money to buy things. Farmers from the south of Ukraine headed north more than a thousand kilometres to Moscow, where they could get higher prices for their fruits and vegetables.

But without work and without money, thousands were driven into crime, and more criminal organizations began to appear. In fact, what was left in virtually the whole economy was run directly by the local mafia or indirectly through extortion rackets; a study showed that 85 percent of the legal businesses at the time were paying protection money to the criminal gangs. The rivalry between the gangs led to spectacular contract killings and machine gun battles in broad daylight in major cities. In the city of Donetsk a year after Ukraine's independence, police identified 2,186 criminal groups, which were committing thousands of murders, robberies and cases of extortion a year. This in a city of less than a million people.

It was in this cauldron of violence that the hidden structure of Ukraine was established by the emergence of regional mafias. The most powerful were in Donetsk, Dnipropetrovsk and Odessa, and together they would control not only the heights of the economy but also the two main political parties: the Donetsk mafia controlled the Party of Regions, and the Dnipropetrovsk gang controlled Yulia Tymoshenko's Fatherland Party.

The chaos continued into the mid-1990s, and the mafia divisions were overlaid by the country's serious ethnic divisions. These were apparent from the first parliamentary elections in 1994, when the largely Russian-speaking population in the east of the country and Crimea voted overwhelmingly in referendums for more autonomy within an independent Ukraine, and closer ties to Russia.[1] While the western part of the country elected strong nationalists who had been persecuted under communism, the east elected a majority of pro-Russia communists. The great ethnic divide was already baked into Ukrainian society.

Still there were attempts at reform. Among the most useful was in the agricultural sector. In the first part of the decade, agriculture had been just as crippled in Ukraine as every other sector. Despite its incredibly rich growing lands, it was difficult for Ukraine to provide food even to its own population after the big Soviet collective farms had been abandoned. The local agriculture that replaced it, lacking capital and machinery, struggled to feed the people of Ukraine, let alone regain the export market it had during the Soviet Union's existence. What replaced it was a kind of certificate-of-possession system: between 1994 and 2002, seven million people received certificates for land, which they could farm or lease but not sell.

Even here a Canadian was in a leading role. From 1996 to 1999, Bohdan Chomiak, the uncle of future deputy prime minister Chrystia Freeland, developed agricultural markets after returning to Ukraine from Canada, where he was born. Bohdan Chomiak's father had immigrated to Canada

---

1   "Voters Support Crimean Republic's Further Moves Toward Autonomy," *Ukrainian Weekly*, April 3, 1994, http://ukrweekly.com/calendar/TOC/94/14.htm.

after the war, which he spent working with the Nazis in Krakow, Poland. Bohdan studied and taught at an Alberta agricultural college, then returned to the land of his parents after the fall of the Soviet Union. He would become one of the founders of the Grain Association of Ukraine and would remain in the country working as the director of the USAID branch and then as an agricultural consultant.

One thing that I was already familiar with in Ukraine was the land-lease certificate system. It closely resembled the certificate-of-possession system that was used on our Indian reserves, where land could not be sold outright to outsiders but only leased. I understood the system and had made money out of it by renting to trailer park owners, then used the capital this generated to invest in new ventures.

◊•◊

It was in this grey area between communism and capitalism that modern Ukraine began and our cast of characters emerged. My future business partner Viktor Fesun, who had studied engineering at Dniprodzerzhynsk State Technical University, the same school attended by the city's most famous hometown boy, Leonid Brezhnev, was thrown out of work like everyone else after 1991.

Fesun, who had a physical resemblance to Brezhnev but without the heavy eyebrows, first emerged from the chaos in 1994 a few months before his fortieth birthday. He was listed as the founder of his first company, called Bikita, located at the same address on Bolshevik Lane where we would meet a dozen years later to confirm our deal. Bikita was chartered to "rent and operate, own or lease real estate (primary industry)" as well as to operate "ancillary ground transportation services," which I took to be a taxi service, probably with Fesun's own car. Not a great business for a family man — his daughter Anna would have been eight years old at the time — with an engineering degree. His partner in the company was his bookkeeper, Lybov Chernysh, whom he would continue to work with in all of his successive businesses.

Bikita quickly disappeared, but in the following year, 1995, Fesun launched another company, Algol Ltd., this time with my friend Aleksei

Gershun, at the same address on Bolshevik Lane. The board of Algol Ltd. also had some familiar names. Along with Fesun and Gershun, it included the Chernyshes, both Lubov and her husband, Sergey. The fifth partner was a major investor who was supposed to be the controlling partner, a South Korean identified as Ro Hang Duk.

The Algol Ltd. registration lists Gershun as a U.S. resident, so by 1995 he had already broken free of Ukraine. But he was still keeping himself in the circle of corruption. And with his 25 percent share, he was likely the ring-leader — or at least the talent scout who brought in Ro Hang Duk.

Originally, Algol Ltd. was devoted to growing cereals, legumes and oilseeds, but as it evolved it began to list its operations under the catch-all "non-specialized wholesale trade," making it a vehicle for whatever schemes they came up with.

When my researcher translated the first company profile from the business registry, I read it with great interest. Apparently the model of Algol Ltd. was the same one they used on me a decade later, with me playing the Korean's role.

The difference in the outcome was that Algol Ltd. never went anywhere. It was a low-grade operation intended to fleece a few hundred thousand dollars from a foreign investor. In Unirem-Agro, we built a world-class facility that would triple in value within three years and it was this, finally, that brought the bigger, more dangerous sharks into our waters.

CHAPTER 6

DOWN THE RABBIT HOLE

*Visiting the rusting ruins of
Dniprodzerzhynsk. Doing the deal
on Bolshevik Lane and gaining
full control of the company.*

A few months after my dinner with Aleksei Gershun in 2005, he was back in touch suggesting a meeting with Viktor Fesun in Kyiv. By this time, I had not only read the 1994 Canada-Ukraine treaty that promised to protect Canadian investors in Ukraine, I had checked up on Gershun and found he was indeed who he said he was — a research scientist at Prestone Products living in an upscale home in Southbury, Connecticut, with several patents for engine and radiator coolants.

Of course I was still leery about investing directly in any partnerships in Ukraine, but my positive experience in Kyiv real estate, along with what I believed was the backing of the Canadian government, suggested it was possible to swim in those waters. So I'd reached the point where I was at least willing to listen to what they had to say.

The meeting took place in my real estate office in Kyiv. It was there I was first introduced to Fesun, his daughter Anna and Lyuba Chernysh, the bookkeeper. Viktor had what you could call a classic eastern Ukrainian face, with slightly high cheekbones and broad features over his stocky frame. Anna was in her late 20s and had similar facial features, but her most useful attribute at the time was that she spoke very good English.

Lyuba Chernysh, the accountant, looked the part. She was in her late 30s, with a businesswoman's cropped haircut and a few extra pounds, but with the quiet self-assurance that people who keep the books always seem to have — probably because they know where all the bodies are buried.

On my side, I was there with Vika, who was acting as my interpreter and as a help in reading the room. As it turned out, Vika had more time to do the latter than expected because while Gershun ran the meeting, Anna stepped up and did most of the interpreting.

It was a friendly enough get-together. Fesun spoke about a major agricultural endeavour, leasing thousands of hectares of prime growing land and investing in the type of modern agricultural equipment that was still rare in Ukraine.

They had been testing their idea by leasing 200 hectares for the past year and said they were getting good yields, but with the right equipment and a dramatic expansion, they could turn the operation into a major international agro-business. The numbers they were batting around were certainly ambitious: they were looking to lease up to 10,000 hectares, which amounts to almost 25,000 acres, or ten times the size of the average Canadian farm.

When I had looked into Ukraine agriculture with Greenlab, I'd seen that the problem was not only backward equipment and facilities, but they were also way behind North America in agricultural methods, particularly in what is known as low-till or no-till farming.

As someone with agriculture in his blood, I'd noticed that in Ukraine, they were still using traditional farming methods. In the spring, the earth is plowed to a depth of twenty to thirty centimetres, with three passes over the field before planting takes place. And three passes on 25,000 acres takes an enormous amount of time and fuel. In no-till, two of the three passes are dispensed with. Instead, planting is done in one pass, right through the residues of previous plantings with a device (usually a coulter) that cuts a slot several centimetres wide, followed by equipment that places the seeds and closes the trench.

This one-pass tillage saves enormous time, equipment and fuel, but the benefits are even greater than that. No-till increases yield because of higher water infiltration and storage capacity, and less erosion. Another benefit of no-till is that because of the higher water content, instead of leaving a field fallow, it can make economic sense to plant another crop.[1]

For an operation of the size they were proposing, I knew they would also have to build their own elevators and crop drying tanks, allowing them to keep these much higher yields in grade-A condition right through to the final sale. This was a struggle for many Ukrainian grain producers, who only had access to what were basically storage barns for their crops.

Lyuba Chernysh provided some accounting numbers, which I didn't pay much attention to because at this stage in a project, they are always based more on wishes than facts. But I was interested in Fesun's enthusiasm, which was obvious while he spoke. To me, this was central to any new venture. If it didn't excite the people involved, it probably wasn't worth doing.

When I spoke to Vika afterward she had the same generally positive feeling about the meeting. Fesun did seem authentic, although she also thought he didn't really sound like an engineer — he had a rough rural accent when he spoke Russian — while Gershun was a polished performer. She liked Lyuba, who she said came across as the type of solid administrator, with a couple of school-aged kids, who did the task that she was asked to do without fanfare.

By the end of the meeting, Gershun and Fesun were trying to gently nudge me into committing to join them. I was still not convinced and to put them off, I said I would have to see the operation on the ground first. That was exactly what they were waiting to hear, because they instantly invited me down to Dniprodzerzhynsk to check things out myself and suggested that I come in September so I could see the value of the land during harvest season.

Telling myself that there was no harm in looking — and that travelling in Ukraine was always an adventure — I said okay. Everyone was very pleased to hear this and the meeting ended on a cheerful note.

---

1   The difference in the results of these agricultural methods in Canada and Ukraine couldn't be starker. Canadian agriculture, even today, is twenty-three times as efficient as Ukraine's. In Canada, labour productivity is $124,000 per person employed, while in Ukraine it is around $5,500.

In retrospect, I see that this was actually the point when I stepped through the looking glass. By agreeing to travel to Dniprodzerzhynsk, I was about to enter the Ukrainian wonderland where the local collection of Mad Hatters, Knaves of Hearts and Cheshire Cats would be waiting for my arrival.

◊•◊

I travelled to Dniprodzerzhynsk (which is as unpronounceable as it looks) in September 2005 with Volodya and Vika, and like all good Ukrainian adventures it included an excellent meal. We stopped on the way at the Кафе У сестер / Two Sisters Café, a highway restaurant that is always packed with people. After a plate of cabbage rolls, pork and potato, and varenyky washed down with a glass of sweet Ukrainian fruit juice they call kompot, we headed off for the final hours on punishing roads that passed through vast grain and sunflower fields. Finally we crested a hill and below was the kilometre-wide expanse of the lower Dnieper River near Dniprodzerzhynsk.

Near Dniprodzerzhynsk the river was behind a hydroelectric dam that had created a kilometre-wide riverine lake. We drove along a seawall for twenty minutes before the smokestacks of Dniprodzerzhynsk, a former Soviet industrial powerhouse, came into view. When we crossed over the hydroelectric dam bridge into the city you could see the neighbourhoods of what looked like modest housing for workers that was ringed by massive industrial plants, some spewing smoke through their stacks, others cold and rusting. Then we descended into the heart of the city, which was coated in smoke from the remaining industries.

From close up, everything about Dniprodzerzhynsk seemed to be falling apart. We passed city parks where someone had brought a few cows to feed on the overgrown grasses. As we drove toward the centre we passed dozens of abandoned industrial and residential buildings, which made the area look like the site of a natural disaster that everyone had fled from long ago. There was more life closer to the centre, but even here everything, including the pedestrians, seemed covered by a layer of soot. On a closer look, you could still see some of the previous architectural grandeur in some of the buildings, but these, too, were crumbling and covered in soot.

Volodya, with that sixth sense he seemed to possess in finding his way even through unfamiliar cities, wound through back streets and pothole-filled laneways, where local dogs positioned themselves on the narrow roadways and stared at us intently as we approached, then chased our car for a couple of blocks as we passed. Dogs chasing cars were another thing that reminded me of life on the reserve.

The address Fesun had given us was for his office on Bolshevik Lane. We passed through a set of rusted blue gates into a dusty parking lot. The company office was in a small, dirty, two-storey brick building with three unmarked entrances.

Viktor Fesun and his daughter Anna, Aleksei Gershun and Lyuba Chernysh were waiting for us inside. The office was sparse and they had to bring in a few folding chairs to seat us all, but they greeted us warmly. Vika chatted with them in Russian while they smiled and nodded at me, and after overcoming the shabbiness of the place, I had a generally positive feeling about the meeting. One simple reason was the fact that Fesun involved his daughter in the company — as the father of a daughter who happened to be around Anna's age, I could not imagine ever getting her involved in anything illegal or below-board. Gershun's presence was also encouraging because I had checked and I knew that he was who he said he was — a very accomplished technical fellow at an important American Fortune 500 company.

My confidence increased when we went to lunch at a restaurant called The Dacha, just off what was still called Lenin Square. This was a modern building and a surprisingly comfortable restaurant, with a menu heavy on traditional Ukrainian dishes. We were met there by the mayor of the city, who said they were happy to have North American investors in the region. "Ukraine has tremendous potential," he said through Anna's interpretation. "And with the help of people like you, who believed in us, we can become like other Europeans."

Then he promised me that he and his staff would do anything necessary to assist me as a full partner in our deal.

This, too, was encouraging. Surely, I thought, the town mayor would not be openly involved with local fraudsters? Looking back, this was a colossal mistake. In Ukraine, it is most often the mayor and other politicians, from the local councillor to the government leaders in the national parliament, who are working with the gangsters, or in some cases were themselves gangsters — as I would soon find out. But at this point I still had not fully grasped this.

After lunch, Volodya drove me and Vika the 50 kilometres from Dniprodzerzhynsk to the village of Shchorsk, where the farmlands were.

As soon as we left the city, we were in the midst of endless wheat, soybean and canola fields that felt very much like the Canadian Prairie. But these familiar scenes were broken up by the contrast between beautiful sunflower fields and devastated villages. Like parts of the city, the villages looked like they'd been hit by some unnamed disaster many years earlier and still had not recovered. There were no new buildings, and the ones that were standing had fallen into disrepair. People in raggedy clothes carrying heavy sacks walked on the dusty shoulder with the measured steps and downcast gaze of people on a long journey, taking produce to the local market or returning with foodstuffs they had bought or traded for. I saw only the rare car in the villages and only a few people had bicycles.

Then in the middle of nowhere, we passed a large, crumbling walled complex of a dozen or so buildings — barns, rotting wooden grain storage facilities and machine shops, and enclosures full of rusting equipment that Volodya identified as an abandoned collective farm.

After half an hour on the bad roads we passed through the town of Krynychky, which was distinguished by a giant Soviet war memorial overlooking the fields below. It was a six-metre pillar, a kind of totem pole, with faces of soldiers, grieving mothers and children carved into it. The pillar was surrounded by a wall that still had large gold medallions of Lenin and the CCCP insignia engraved on it.

In the impressive monument and empty, windswept collective farms, it was as if the ghosts of the Soviet Union lived on. All during the trip we saw such ghost land, and the only things touching on modern Ukraine were the national blue and yellow colours that someone had half-heartedly slapped on the big Soviet-era signposts in front of the villages.

I had read reports that people in the countryside were much poorer than they had been in Soviet times. Fifteen years later, agricultural production had still not caught up to the Soviet standard of living. By 2003, Ukraine's beef and pork production was less than one-third what it had been in Soviet times, grain production had dropped by as much as 50 percent, and 40 percent of agricultural land had been abandoned. Ukraine also had just 20 percent of its former sheep and goat population.

The picture of agricultural employment was even worse. About a third of the country's 46 million people lived in rural areas, and in 2005 there were fewer than 800,000 jobs in agriculture, leaving millions of people who had worked the collective farms unemployed. In Ukraine as a whole, 26 percent of people were living below the very low poverty line of 430 hryvnia (UAH), a mere CDN$60 a month. In rural areas like the one we were driving through, it was more like 40 percent who were below that $2-a-day poverty line.

We stopped briefly at another abandoned collective farm at Adamivka. This was a facility that Fesun wanted to purchase to house and maintain our farming equipment. The Adamivka farm had been one of the largest collective farms in the region with some twenty buildings of all shapes and sizes — from machine shops to livestock and chicken barns — in various stages of disrepair, and behind the buildings was a large lot filled with broken and rusting equipment. Anything useful had long ago been picked over and taken by the local people, and every single window in every single building was broken. All that remained from the collective farm was a large agro machinery dump.

We drove on to Shchorsk, ten kilometres up the road, and arrived in a kind of economic dead zone. As we passed through the town, we saw people shuffling along the roadside in rotting shoes. Everything around us seemed to be falling apart; there were only two significant buildings in town still in use. One was a large cultural centre in the middle of what looked to have been a park but was now an overgrown weedy field. The centre itself was badly in need of paint and the concrete steps were beginning to crumble. The other was a small technical school, with an iron hammer and sickle over the gate. Across the road was the bust of the first man in space, cosmonaut Yuri Gagarin, on top of a large plinth. There was another large concrete building at one end of town that was difficult to define, because the windows were broken and the insides had been stripped out. Once again, the only sign of independent Ukraine in the village was the blue and yellow paint, the national colours, that someone had painted over the Soviet monument.

We then stopped at another facility made up of several empty buildings. This one had a railway spur line that ran from the middle of the complex to a port on the Black Sea. This was the future site for our grain elevators and grain-drying operation.

It was a hot afternoon, so we stopped off at a small, decrepit-looking grocery store in the centre of town to buy some Cokes. It was dark inside, with a dank smell of damp concrete, and the shelves were mainly empty. The store had only a few canned goods, potato chips and, in front of the cash register, a display of sorry-looking sausages. Behind the counter was a woman in her 30s with a two- or three-year-old boy in her arms.

"Beautiful child," I said in English.

The woman stared at me, not comprehending.

"Красивый ребенок," Vika translated.

The woman smiled, revealing two rotten front teeth.

The people here, I realized, really had nothing and received no help from anyone. There was not even a dentist in town, so they would go through life without ever visiting one.

Although I was struck by the devastation that was still visible in the Ukrainian countryside, I was not frightened away by it. In fact it looked somewhat familiar to me — like a big Indian reserve where the light of economic activity had been snuffed out. But as chief in the 1970s, I had inherited a community that was one of the poorest in the country and, for all intents and purposes, bankrupt. I helped turn it into one of the most prosperous reserves in the country, increasing reserve revenues by 3,500 percent. As we drove back through the grain and sunflower fields, and through the poor villages, I began to see this as a project where I could not only make money — I could also make a difference.

If I did invest, I told myself, I would be able to contribute to the local economy. I could give good jobs to these people with tattered clothing and rotting shoes and rotting teeth, and maybe even build in some social programs for them and their families. Maybe build a preschool so that employees with small children could work while their children were being taken care of and receiving an early education. And maybe start a few businesses, like a bakery, that the town seemed to lack, and try to bring in a dentist.

This is what I was thinking as we headed back to Dniprodzerzhynsk. We arrived at dusk, entering the city from the northern hills, and drove down the long broad avenue. The city centre lay below as we passed the statue of Leonid Brezhnev at the Premier Hotel near the bottom.

Inside the hotel entrance was not the lobby but a large, completely empty ballroom. A lone security guard pointed to an elevator in the corner that took us up to the lobby. It was a decent place, but the rooms still had the old Soviet hotel features of ancient radiators and exposed pipes, heavily painted over, in the bathroom.

My room overlooked what was still called Lenin Avenue, now called Freedom Avenue, and a city square with some kind of gold statue on top of a large concrete plinth. I couldn't tell what it was but it was obviously from the earlier era. I lit up a cigarette and smoked while darkness descended over this strange city suspended between worlds.

By the time I finished the cigarette, I knew that I was in. Against my better judgment, I was going to invest in Ukrainian agriculture. My strongest argument to myself was that I knew if we invested in the right equipment and facilities and used modern farming methods, we could all make money and grow the operation into an important international grain company. All of the pieces, from some of the world's best growing soil to access to the direct rail link with the Black Sea ports, were in place for success. But I was also thinking that I could help these people out of the economic mess they were in, just as I had helped my own people on what had been our dirt-poor reserve.

The deal was done the following day at Viktor Fesun's office on Bolshevik Lane. Fesun and his gang had registered the company, Unirem-Agro, in Dniprodzerzhynsk in February 2001 and leased their first few acres of growing land the following year. They had paved the way for my entry into the company at a meeting two months earlier when Fesun, Lyuba Chernysh and Aleksei Gershun increased the authorized investment capital limit to UAH 3,787,500, or roughly US$750,000. As the meeting minutes explained, "The increase of the authorized capital is due to the acceptance into the membership of the new members and the direction of profit received in 2001 to increase the authorized capital."

The eventual capital required would be many millions of dollars, but I was glad they had started low.

At the September meeting, I was presented with this set-up and initial proposal. I would be joined on the board of the new company by Viktor and Anna Fesun, Chernysh, Gershun and Vika, who would keep an eye on my interests and have access to all of the documents.

Initially, my investment was supposed to be 40 percent of the total authorized capital, which started out as UAH 1.5 million, or CDN$200,000. So my share was only $80,000, while Fesun would also invest 40 percent and Chernysh and Gershun 9 percent ($18,000) each. Anna and Vika would both invest 1 percent ($2,000) to complete the capitalization. (I was paying for Vika's 1 percent share because I wanted her included in the deal.) According to plan, I was elected as company president and I appointed Viktor Fesun to a five-year term as the company's executive director.

One of the keys to this arrangement was a single word they had chosen. They identified me as company президент (president) and not председатель (chairman). That simple distinction would have important implications in what followed. But at the time, I was satisfied with the deal. I knew that agriculture, if done right, could yield real profits, and in producing something as fundamental as food, there was an additional pleasure. To do all of this and help people in my newly adopted country of Ukraine improve their lives felt good all around.

According to the deal, we were all supposed to make our payments by October 10, 2005, and we set the next meeting in Kyiv for October 12. This meeting would include only Fesun, Chernysh, Vika and me, and would involve the approval of a new version of the charter drafted at our September meeting. The updated version included a resolution to raise the authorized capital of the company to just over a million dollars Canadian, allowing us to begin implementing the business plan, which in the end was estimated to cost $10 million in equipment and construction costs.

Everything seemed to be in order — with one glaring gap. Neither the Fesuns or Chernyshes, or Gershun for that matter, had made their agreed-upon payment into the company, and I was beginning to suspect that they didn't actually have the cash resources to do so. Still, I transferred my 40 percent share of UAH 3.9 million (roughly $420,000) into the company account to start things moving, but I insisted we insert a clause in our agreement that stated that my share of the company would be increased to the level of my contribution. So my ownership was immediately increased from 40 to 51 percent, while Fesun's dropped from 40 to 35 percent and the Chernyshes' dropped from 9 to 6 percent.

A few alarm bells did go off after this meeting, when their capital was still slow in coming, but at the same time, the fact that my ownership had nudged up over 50 percent meant that now, if worse came to worst, I could shut down the company and pay myself back the capital I invested. I was now in majority control. With the 1994 Canadian-Ukraine treaty in place I could exit with my money at any time, or so I was assured by the treaty.

I met with Fesun and Chernysh one last time in 2005, in mid-December. We raised the authorized capital again, to UAH 39,678,562 (about CDN$9 million), to cover the coming purchases and construction costs. To level the playing field, it was acknowledged that deposits by members of the company could include cash, buildings, facilities, equipment and other tangible assets, securities, and rights to use land, other natural resources and intangible assets, and other property. We also passed a resolution:

"If the participants during the first year of the partnership did not pay the full amount of their deposits, the company should declare a reduction of the authorized capital and register the relevant changes to the charter or liquidate the company. Participants have the number of votes in proportion to their contribution to the authorized capital."

I was now in complete control of the company — in principle my investments were fully protected — and we were launched on our journey together.

CHAPTER 7

LAUNCHING THE OPERATION

*Putting the machinery in place for
a successful operation, while the
Ukrainian partners work behind
the scenes to kill the goose before it
can begin laying the golden eggs.*

For an entrepreneur like myself, there is little that is more satisfying than building a company from scratch. I have done it many times in many different industries. The Ukraine operation was one of the greatest challenges I had faced and, initially at least, one of the most gratifying.

We purchased our facility in Shchorsk on December 8, 2005. Six months later, we purchased the complex of buildings in Shchorsk with the railway spur line at a public auction. The following year we acquired the Adamivka facility, the former collective farm, which was then owned by the village council of Adamivka.

Fesun and the Chernyshes went to work on securing the land. In their small operation they were leasing a couple of hundred hectares from the local people, but our operation would require up to 10,000 hectares that was then in the possession of 1,200 local peasant farmers, who lacked the equipment and capital to properly farm it. So Fesun and the Chernyshes had their work cut out for them: they had to track down the local leaseholding farmers and negotiate the transfer of their leases to our company. The farmers would then work for us on the land with our equipment and financing.

While the land package was being assembled, I set out to acquire the machinery. I spoke to international sellers and manufacturers about their latest technology and found that the best deal for me was in Saskatchewan, where a farm machinery company on an Indian reserve could sell me, as a status Indian, the equipment tax-free. So I purchased it in Saskatchewan and shipped it in containers to the Black Sea port, where it was put on the local freight train and shipped right into our facility at Shchorsk.

After I bought the first few machines, the Saskatchewan guys got greedy and increased their prices, so I went looking for better deals on the international market and found them in Italy, where I purchased the rest of the equipment. In the end, I spent close to $2.5 million for state-of-the-art agricultural machinery.[1]

The massive equipment arrived at Odessa and other Black Sea ports and was loaded onto railcars for shipment to our facility in Shchorsk, arriving at our door like giant versions of the farm toys that I'd had as a kid.

In the meetings with my partners, you could feel the excitement as they realized that yes, indeed, we were going to do what we set out to do, to install on Ukraine's rich farmlands the most advanced cultivation and processing operation that the country had ever seen. When the construction of the elevators began, we agreed to once again raise the level of the company's authorized capital to purchase a prefab warehouse and administrative office, allowing us to run the grain-drying facility as a separate business.

This was decided at an April 18, 2006, meeting in Kyiv. With my purchases and investment, my controlling interest in the company had now reached 70 percent of the shares and Fesun's had dropped to 20 percent. But in fact the worth of his shares had dramatically increased. In the beginning he had 40 percent of total assets that were worth at most $100,000. But now

---

1   The machinery I purchased included a New Holland TJ 425 tractor, used in 2003 ($211,947); New Holland TJ 425 tractor, used in 2002 ($180,774); the 5710 Bourgault Air Hoe Drill, used in 2005 ($123,031); a new 6450 Bourgault Air Seeder seed drill truck ($72,036); Sprayer SP 2010 SprayAir Trident Sprayer, new 2005 manufacturing ($200,174); Model 8810 Bourgault cultivator, used from 1997 ($48,968); two new grain harvester CX880 (374 hp) with chopper combine harvester ($816,000); the 2005 LM445A Telehandler loader ($90,100); Bourgault grain cart 1100 storage bin in 2003 ($58,200); and the Phoenix 2436, Westeel grain-drying tanks and construction equipment ($1.3 million).

Fesun had 20 percent of an asset that, with the farming equipment, the grain elevators and the acquired land leases, had a value of around $8 million. So the value of his shares had gone from $40,000 to $1.6 million in a single year, without any investment from himself. This operation promised me a very good return on my capital, but for Fesun it could bring an exponential return that would only increase in the years to come.

This is really the most important thing to understand about everything that happened in Ukraine. If we worked hard and smartly with this operation, all of us — but especially my Ukrainian partners — stood to make a lot of money, more than they ever dreamed of. At the time, I thought all of them understood this, so my confidence in the deal and the company reached its high point. Why would the scorpion sting the frog and cause its own death in the process? This was something I was about to find out.

When I visited Shchorsk with Fesun later that spring and saw the construction was underway on the grain elevators and our now jointly leased lands were planted, I think for a moment even he felt pride at what we had done. Fesun had signed up the farmers and overseen the initial construction. It was, of course, all with my money, but for him it was his first real success in life after all those miserable years scratching about after the fall of the Soviet Union. He had a right to take pride in this accomplishment and he could have looked forward to a bright future. But finally he and his country seemed unable to travel the high road to success: when presented with the option at the fork in the road, they inevitably opted for the low road toward calamity and failure. It might sound harsh to say, but check Ukraine's development over the past thirty years and you will see that they have, as a society, made disastrous choices every single time.

I was back in Dniprodzerzhynsk in December 2006 with all of the stockholders to review the year and look ahead to our first complete season with our new equipment and facilities. With Gershun and Vika now present, it was the first time that the whole company had gotten together for a year. Vika had actually already moved to a new job, but she was still listed as an investor in the company and I valued her input, so I continued to keep her informed about the company's activities.

When we reviewed the ownership of the company, which was roughly based on our financial contributions, it was distributed as follows:

Derrickson R.M. (70 percent of votes)
Fesun V.V. (19 percent)
Gershun A.V. (4.5 percent)
Chernysh L.P. (4.5 percent)
Balenko V.A. (1 percent)
Fesun A.V. (1 percent)

According to Fesun's report, we had a very promising first year, which would provide us with the baseline for future years when our operation was fully underway. All of our three main crops of wheat, sunflowers and canola had years that were better than expected, and big increases were expected for 2007.

At the December 7, 2006, meeting, Fesun also described how we would have a big tax liability when the grain elevators were operating because as it stood, we were profiting from considerable tax exemptions because our activities were listed as purely agricultural. Our grain elevators and drying facilities would put us in a much higher commercial tax category and we would lose our agricultural tax break. The solution was to create a new entity, Unirem-Oil, to operate our elevators and our machinery separately, so our purely agricultural activities in Unirem-Agro would continue to be taxed at the much lower rate.

The way it was set up, I would hold 51 percent of the new Unirem-Oil shares, and Unirem-Agro (of which I owned 70 percent of the shares) would hold the other 49 percent, so my actual ownership interest in the new entity was 85 percent. The authorized capital would start low, at only $500,000, and my share to pay was $255,000, of which I had to pay half up front.

During the discussions, Fesun suggested that we also move the newly acquired Adamivka property, the large collective farm we had purchased, into the Unirem-Oil company to give it an asset it could use for future borrowing. So the property was removed from Unirem-Agro and was to be added to Unirem-Oil — although I would later learn that this was never done.

From what I knew at the time, everything was in order. I had brought the Unirem-Oil documents back to Kyiv with me and sent them over to my notary, Sabrina, for checking. When she approved them I signed off on the deal and paid my $125,000. On December 10, I headed back to Canada to spend Christmas with my family and planned to take some time off at my place in Palm Desert, optimistic about the future of the Ukraine operation.

On the flight from Kyiv to Amsterdam, I reviewed our expansion plans for 2007 and 2008. We foresaw the 100 percent utilization of our grain-drying facilities and an increase in outside contracts, with the company employing twenty people there and our crop production employment expanded to fifty people. So we were offering tangible benefits to what had been a depressed part of the country ever since the fall of the Soviet Union.

I caught the 4 p.m. flight out of Amsterdam, and after a good business class meal, I slept soundly for most of the transatlantic flight.

What was missing in my bliss was information — most pointedly regarding two visits that Fesun and Chernysh had made to their friend Yulia Polansky, state notary at the First Dniprodzerzhynsk Notary Office in the old Soviet municipal building on Petra Kalnishevskogo Square. The first visit had been in August, when they brought the minutes of an August 4 meeting that I, the major shareholder, had not been informed about, to be officially certified.

While I was relaxing in California after the December 7 meeting, on December 19 Fesun made another trip to his friend Yulia to certify the December 7 meeting minutes. But they were not the ones I had signed.

All this was hidden from me at the time. A more immediate issue arose when US$560,000 suddenly disappeared from our bank account. Fesun and Gershun informed me that the accountant, Lyuba Chernysh, had discovered that the tax authority had withdrawn the money, without warning. Gershun said this was an illegal move by the Dnipropetrovsk Oblast and my partners were immediately filing papers to claim a value-added tax (VAT) refund and demand the return of the money. But this came at a time when they were in urgent need of funds to complete the construction of the elevators, so they asked me if I could transfer the missing $560,000 to Unirem-Agro with the condition that the company would return the full amount to me after VAT reimbursed it — which they assured me would be the case.

So I transferred the money and hired lawyers to make sure I got it back. When I kicked up a fuss about the $560,000, local officials responded by quietly contacting the RCMP and Canadian Security Intelligence Service to see if I had any charges or accusations they could use against me. So I wrote a letter to Viktor Yushchenko, the "reformist" president who was strongly backed by Canada and had given the Canadian governor general a place of honour at his side at his inauguration, to ask him to intervene directly to ensure my money was returned.

I began by praising the Orange Revolution that brought him to power, then got to the point. I told him I had invested almost $10 million in the country by this time, in the form of a modern agricultural business, only to have $560,000 illegally seized from my company's accounts. Unless it was immediately returned, I wrote, "I will be forced to stop any investment activity in Ukraine, to remove imported and customs cleared equipment from the country, to break off land rent contracts with 1,200 owners of land plots and to sell a newly constructed elevator. This frustration would also lead me to inform Canadian and international media so as to prevent further investment in Ukraine."

I signed the letter "President of Unirem-Agro LLC," and we continued in our court case against the local officials who had removed the money from our account.

◇•◇

While troubling, these things still only rose to the level of background noise — certainly a concern but not alarming. At the time, I could still see the beauty in the operation. Especially in the early summer of 2007, a couple of months before our grand opening, when I flew over our lands in an old Soviet Antonov 2 aircraft.

We had hired the plane to fertilize our nine thousand planted hectares from the air. The Antonov 2 itself was something of a wonder, a Soviet biplane from the 1940s that was probably comparable to the Canadian de

Havilland Otter, although its biplane wings gave it an antique look. Its powerful engine started with a roar and a cloud of smoke, letting you know you were in for an extreme flying experience.

The Antonov 2 cost us $100 an hour, but it was more than worth it and the former Soviet air force pilot flying it was friendly and efficient. On his fertilizing runs, he could take on a load and spread it and land again every seven minutes. He could do two thousand hectares in a day, so he would start the operation on our fields on Monday morning and finish on Friday — a job that would take weeks for several men on several expensive spreader machines to complete.

The pilot took me for a bit of a tour after one of the runs and I was struck again by the rich possibility and sheer beauty of this land — the steppes on the gently undulating lands of southeastern Ukraine. Large sections of it had reverted to native grasslands after the collapse of the Soviet Union, but gradually those lands were being cultivated again and displayed the straw-coloured wheat, the greenish yellow of the soybean and the reddish yellow of the canola. From the biplane circling Shchorsk, I could see thousands of hectares of some of the best growing lands in the world.

My thrill at the beauty of the operation pushed back my gradually growing concerns about the irregularities I had noticed in the company management. The upbeat mood held throughout the summer and into our September 2007 official opening with the Cossack show and the golden key.

When the former prime minister of Ukraine and current governor of the Dnipropetrovsk Oblast cut the opening ribbon with me, I felt we had an unbeatable formula. News of our success even reached Canada when Karin Briere, a reporter from the Regina-based *Western Producer*, toured our operation and wrote: "In August, it was full of rapeseed, most of which had been sold and shipped through the Black Sea by the end of October. The sunflower harvest was underway, however, and those seeds were filling up bins."

She visited the facility with Sergii Vladimirovich, who told her that he was the company's deputy director, and quoted him extensively in the article. When I saw it, I had no idea who he was until I realized that Vladimirovich was his patronymic and it was Sergii Chernysh, Lyuba's husband, who had been closely tied to Fesun's shady deals in the past. I wasn't aware Fesun had made him "deputy director" of our operation, although I noted they had at least identified me to the reporter as the company president.

Immediately after the grand opening I kept the promises I made to myself during my first visit to the region. I had the company set aside a monthly amount to run a daycare. Then I bought, from my own account, state-of-the-art bread-making ovens from Sweden and had them shipped to the company to open a bakery for the workers and the community. And, remembering the young woman with the rotting teeth, I set aside funds to bring a dentist to the Shchorsk for one day a week to look after people's teeth. I was pleased to be able to do all of this as part of the project.

That fall continued as a high point in my dealings in Ukraine when I was invited to my accountant Yulia's wedding at the upscale Dykan'ka restaurant in Kyiv on the east side of the river. The restaurant had a large, elegant dining room surrounded by a number of small terraces with exclusive dining huts, and waitresses and waiters wearing traditional Ukrainian embroidery. It was a lively affair and Yulia said she was very happy that I came. Most North Americans, she said, would have hung back and their distance would have felt like disapproval to the people there. But she said I wasn't like most North Americans, that I seemed to feel things more deeply, like Ukrainians.

It was a great party and I did my part by paying for the liquor. Although I did not know beforehand the quantities that I would be expected to consume. There were fireworks at 11 p.m. and after that, I headed off wobbly-legged to bed. On the way out, I apparently gave the wedding singer a $100 tip because I was profusely thanked for it the next morning.

The party was still going on, and in fact would last two more days. Gallons of vodka were consumed and I have blurry recollections of chatting and joking with dozens of people, all of whom insisted that we exchange contact information and actually got in touch with me later. I was reminded that at the social level, Ukrainians are among the most likeable people in the world.

While I was enjoying my life in Kyiv, the low-to-medium-level thievery was continuing in Dniprodzerzhynsk as Fesun and Gershun began to feed off the cash flow. The biggest theft came from Fesun using the company accounts to pay off Gershun for bringing in my initial $5.75-million investment. Gershun's backroom deal with Fesun for landing me was 10 percent of every dollar I invested, and this was acknowledged in a secret promissory note between them signed on April 14, 2007. The first of these secret payments was made in late 2007, drawn from company accounts without the board's approval or knowledge, and was for $205,357.

The initial outflows to Gershun were easy to hide at first because the contested $560,000 VAT payment had been quietly returned to the company by the tax authorities in the fall of 2007, although I was not told about it — despite my agreement with Fesun that I was to be repaid the money as soon as it came in. And they were doing this just as our operation was getting into full swing.

CHAPTER 8

SUSPICIONS RAISED

*My kleptomaniac partners: stealing
from the dentist, from the daycare
and from the bakery. But mainly
stealing from their own future.*

When I was a kid and someone was caught cheating at a game, we
would chant, "Cheaters never prosper!" I don't know where the
saying comes from or even if it is true in all things, but the phrase did
come back to me when I was thinking about the high cost of corruption in
Ukraine. It has brought and, in the shadow of war, continues to bring ruin
to the country and the people.

It turns out there is even a scientific basis for the saying. It is shown in
an experiment that involves two people who are given the option of putting
a coin in a machine that then pays out three coins to the other person.[1] The
other player is then expected to put one of the coins in the slot on their side
and the first person gets three back, and so on. But each player also has the
option of cheating at any point — not putting in a coin for the other person
while they continue to do so for you.

---

1 https://ncase.me/trust/.

In the experiment, five different strategies are tested — someone who cheats all the time; someone who co-operates all the time; the grudger, who starts with co-operation but who if cheated against will start to cheat all the time; the detective, who keeps testing the waters and, if the other side cheats, will cheat all the time too; and the copycat, who will do whatever the other person does. In the immediate term, the always-cheat does fairly well, but then very quickly is surpassed by every other strategy, except always-co-operate. And once always-cheat eliminates the always-co-operate player, all the other strategies beat the always-cheat. In the game and in economic systems, always-cheat is preprogrammed for failure because everyone else quickly avoids doing business with them and stops putting coins in the machine for them to reap. The strategy that comes out on top is actually the copycat — the person who always starts out co-operating, but if you cheat them they will do the same to you. Ironically, it's this "do unto others as they do unto you" approach that is the winning economic strategy in the game as it is in life.

For Ukraine, always-cheating has been devastating for the economy. Denys Shmyhal, the current prime minister of Ukraine, calculated that rampant corruption had cost Ukraine a trillion dollars in GDP over the past decade. That is about half of the country's wealth. Ukraine's reform czar, Mikheil Saakashvili, estimated that because of Ukraine's rampant corruption, foreign investment in the country has fallen from a meagre 2 percent of GDP to a ghost-like 0.02 percent.

The numbers are even starker when you compare Ukraine to neighbouring Poland, as Ukrainian economist Alik Kokh has done. He has pointed out that both Poland and Ukraine gained their independence from the Soviet orbit around the same time and had the same degree of freedom of speech, free elections and economic development, and they had human capital of about the same high quality. The territory and climatic conditions are also about the same with, if anything, a slight advantage to Ukraine. But in 2022 Poland's GDP was US$586 billion and Ukraine's was US$130 billion. So Poland's GDP was four and a half times greater than Ukraine's. That is another measure of what corruption has cost this country.

In Shchorsk, and throughout most of the Ukrainian economy, the always-cheats were firmly in control. Fesun did not repay me my $560,000 VAT payment, as we had agreed, or even let me know that it had been returned to us. Other money was also being siphoned off from the company bank account in small amounts. I would learn that at this point, he had already pilfered $200,000.

The insane part of this was that he had a 20 percent share of a company that at that point was valued at well over $15 million. If he had been even a modestly honest man, or even a modestly smart man, instead of stealing a couple of hundred thousand from the company, he could simply have sold his share to me for $3 million at that point — and I would have been happy to buy it from him on the spot because the company was rapidly increasing in value. Fesun could have then walked away richer than he had ever been in his life. In fact, far richer than he ever *would* be in his life. This was the self-destructive Ukraine at work, the one that moves in the shadows to destroy what others have created, but in the end succeeds only in destroying itself.

By this time, I was becoming increasingly uneasy about the operation and my doubts increased when I received an official government letter addressed to the president of Unirem-Agro stating that the company had been charged with seventeen violations of the law, mainly in not paying salaries to the employees.

I had been working in Ukraine for seven years at this point. I knew how things were done and one thing for sure, I told Fesun, was that you had to pay your damn employees. The conversation took place over the phone with an interpreter and I could sense him sulking in silence while I spoke. As the one-sided conversation progressed, I had a sinking feeling. I knew things were about to get worse. Perhaps much, much worse.

◇•◇

But in 2008, while Fesun and his associates were playing these destructive games, I was focused on other things. Back in Canada, my major new purchase was an eighteen-hole golf course with a restaurant and very elaborate clubhouse. The guy who was running it had somehow mismanaged it into bankruptcy, so I purchased it for $3 million. I rechristened it the Two Eagles Golf Course and installed a pair of $60,000 eagle totem poles at the entrance.

Ukraine faded for a few months as I focused on upgrading the golf course. I added a golf academy and a first-class restaurant, the Okanagan Grill, as well as a $1.5-million maintenance shop so all of our equipment — from heavy machinery to golf carts to irrigation pumps — could be maintained and repaired on-site. I also made arrangements for the Marriott hotel chain to build a hotel on the golf course lands. This is the type of thing I like to do — acquire a marginal operation and make it into a first-class one by investing in upgrades.

The golf course made money every year, but I didn't take a cent out of it — all of it was reinvested into improvements to the point where today it is worth many times what I paid for it because I built real value into it. This is what I was also willing to do in Ukraine: build a world-class agricultural operation that would give us a good return on our investment while it contributed real value to the Ukrainian economy. In the case of the golf course, I would sell the whole expanded operation a dozen years later for $50 million.

I didn't realize it at the time, but looking back, part of the pleasure of building the golf and country club complex was that it allowed me to escape what was becoming unpleasantness in Ukraine. As part of my golf course renovations I built my corporate office overlooking the fairway and filled it with one of my passions, Indigenous art. The collection grew piece by piece and even I didn't realize its full extent until an art dealer told me that over the past twenty-five years, I had been the biggest purchaser of Indigenous art in Canada. Things were running smoothly in Canada and I was finally ready to get back to Ukraine to give a much greater degree of oversight to my business there when I was blindsided by the global economic meltdown in 2008, the huge financial collapse brought about by corrupt mortgage-lending practices in the United States.

I was forced to work full-time trying to save my properties in Canada from banks that were suddenly calling in loans and using every tool they had to withhold previously promised financing. By the end of the summer, the massive U.S. investment bank Lehman Brothers went bankrupt and the whole international financial system was teetering on the brink. Governments around the world began to desperately shovel cash bailouts into the major banks and lending institutions to keep them afloat.

It was amid this financial chaos that I made a few sporadic attempts to get a handle on what was happening in Ukraine. And there were more troubling signs.

First, Fesun was not providing me with proper balance sheets or income statements, but only optimistic "projections" that were not being realized. In one of these projections, I noticed that our landholdings had been reduced by a thousand hectares.

At the same time, Fesun was demanding more investment to complete subsidiary construction on the elevator facility. When I saw this, I wrote to Vika to let her know that things were not adding up. She was working with the insurance company at the time, but I wanted to keep her in the loop. She said she would do whatever she could to help. In the meantime, when I was back in Ukraine, I decided to make an unannounced visit to Shchorsk to get a better sense of what was going on.

◇◆◇

It was July 2008 when I got up at dawn one day and Volodya met me at my Darvina Street flat for the trip to Shchorsk. After the six-hour drive we arrived in the village at lunchtime, but I didn't go directly to visit the operation. I had Volodya take me to the dentist office that I had been told was staffed one day a week by a visiting dentist from Dniprodzerzhynsk, at a cost that the company was subsidizing. This was obviously false, because the "dentist office" that I was told was functioning was a boarded-up storefront. The village preschool/daycare we were funding for children of our employees was not operating, either. When we arrived at the grain elevators I passed by the loading docks and found the expensive, stainless-steel bakery equipment that I'd purchased in Sweden and had shipped to Shchorsk to provide the town with fresh bread was still in its containers. It had been sitting there for months, even though Fesun was reporting to me that the bakery was up and running, and all of these non-existent activities were showing up on Fesun's sporadic accounts.

I have a hard time expressing the depth of my anger at that point. I had discovered beyond any doubt that my partner was a liar and a thief, and the fact that he was stealing bread, child care and medical services from his own people made me understand that I was dealing with a stupid, heartless person.

I would like to say I had never, in the forty years or so I'd been doing business, met anyone like Fesun. But that was not the case. I'd had crooked partners and thieving employees before. That's how it is, and you learn how to cope with it, to clear out the sludge and restart an operation from scratch, if necessary. It would be more complicated in Ukraine because I was in a foreign country, but if my only problem had been Fesun and his little band picking my pockets, things would have been solved quite quickly. On paper, I had all the tools to get rid of Fesun.

But what was coming would soon eclipse Fesun's disorganized crime. Because Ukraine's much more devastating organized crime, led by corrupt members of parliament, was already then circling in the shadows like wolves ready to pounce on unsuspecting prey. When it was time to strike the gang would include everyone from the lowly paid clerk working out of a tiny stucco building in that dusty village all the way up to the officials working in the gilded halls of parliament. In a mafia state, the criminals don't break the laws, they make them.

These were threats that you could not call the police on, because the culprits controlled the police; threats that you could not take to court, because they controlled the courts; and threats you could not counter by pleading for support from the government, because they were, in fact, the government. They were not threats that I could call on Canada to help me with either, because in Ukraine, Canada was, objectively speaking, in bed with the crooks.

My only hope in facing these threats was to sell the company before it was targeted. Which I was already determined to do.

I would not be entirely alone in this. While I was looking to escape from the mess in Shchorsk, I found two important allies — one a foreigner, a British citizen, and the other a Ukrainian. Both would become trusted friends as well as allies in my struggle ahead.

The Ukrainian friend was Oles Kopets, who would play an important role in everything that followed, from the assault rifle phase through the courts and beyond. The Brit was Richard Spinks, who became the company's prospective buyer in 2008 and would become a business partner and friend.

I met Richard Spinks in Kyiv in 2007. He had been introduced to me as someone who was also in the agricultural business in Ukraine. We were from very different backgrounds and even generations — he was only 42 years old at the time — but it seemed we shared a similar outlook on the world and got along well from the very first meeting. I was also interested in Richard's achievements. With his partner Glenn Tempany he had put together Landkom LLC in western Ukraine, at the time the largest agricultural company in Europe at 126,800 hectares.

Richard was also interested in what I had built in eastern Ukraine with our grain elevator and drying facilities and direct spur line to the Black Sea ports. When I met him again a year later, he expressed an interest in buying our operation and I said I was open to an offer.

This was the break I was looking for. A way to get my money back and get the hell out of the deal with Fesun and his gang. Richard said he would do his due diligence and get back to me with a price.

Despite his relative youth, Spinks was already an old hand in Eastern Europe and was known as a kind of take-no-prisoners entrepreneur. After a stint in the British army serving as a radio operator in the Falklands, Spinks turned up in Poland after the fall of the Soviet empire and was involved with a steady stream of business ventures there and elsewhere in Eastern Europe — ranging from running a network of pool halls in Warsaw to buying former Soviet fighter planes in Azerbaijan and selling them to wealthy Americans as corporate jets. This venture had him answering some hard questions from the CIA when it was discovered that some of the planes were landing in Miami with their Soviet air-to-surface rockets still attached to the wings.

It was while he was based in Poland that Richard met a charming Russian-speaking Ukrainian woman, Tanya Volodchenko from the Donetsk region, who had moved to Warsaw in search of work in the wake of the Soviet economic collapse. During the late 1990s, her city had been reduced to a gangster-ridden wasteland, and after her youthful marriage broke up, she left her daughter with her parents and emigrated to find work to feed her family.

Spinks, who was already fluent in Polish, learned Russian with Tanya. He was eventually drawn to Ukraine by a quite remarkable agri-business opportunity. After receiving an economic tip, he began researching growing lands in the Lviv region in western Ukraine and found that, as in the eastern part of the country, the once vast collective farms had been chopped up into small plots of land that were not really suited for modern farming production — which required expensive equipment to operate — so much of the land was sitting idle, with local people holding deeds without the means to seriously cultivate it. So with his partner Glenn Tempany, he began buying up leases and Landkom was born.

In April 2007, the company received funding of US$13.8 million from Credit Suisse, which was used to dramatically expand its holdings as well as purchase modern equipment, high-quality seed stock and fertilizers.

In a short time, Spinks and his team were able to amass the largest single agricultural territory in Europe: 126,800 hectares of prime Ukrainian growing land, with the acquisition of almost 500,000 signed leases from local landholders. By 2008, Landkom had 10,000 employees and was one of the most important employers of local people in the economically depressed region.

When Spinks learned about my operation in Dnipropetrovsk, he saw it as a natural fit for Landkom because it would expand their production into the rich growing lands of the east and, more importantly, provide them with a direct rail link to the Black Sea. While I was waiting for his offer, I sought my own independent evaluation of my company by hiring Aleana, an auditing firm from Dnipropetrovsk, so I would have a number to base the sale price on.

Aleana came back with a very encouraging valuation of US$22 million for Unirem-Agro and Unirem-Oil if sold as a unit, but noted that even this was not taking into account all of the companies' considerable growth potential. I decided then that if Spinks could meet or beat that, I would sell it to him.

But while I was pleased with their evaluation, there was a disturbing note in their audit. Unirem-Agro had declared zero profits for the year because, as Fesun told them, there had been bad growing weather. Aleana found this odd because when they checked with other agricultural companies in the region, they reported that it had actually been a good weather year, and they all had bumper crops and declared significant profits.

◇•◇

My Ukrainian friend in the battle ahead, Oles Kopets, was a sharp-witted and straight-talking young consultant with strong business sense who was working with international investors in Ukraine.

Oles had heard about me from one of his business associates who had met Fesun at a grain conference at the beginning of 2008. Fesun told him there was a Canadian investor in "his company" that he was "looking to replace." That is how Fesun described me at the time. So Oles called my office to ask if I might want his services in finding investors to buy me out. I agreed to meet him at the Premier Palace Hotel bar on Taras Shevchenko Boulevard, just up the hill from the Bessarabska Market, to discuss the possibility.

Despite his youth, Oles had a pretty impressive resumé. Born in 1977, he was in his early teens when the Soviet Union collapsed, which meant he grew to adulthood during the harsh times immediately afterward. But he was resilient and bright. He enrolled in Lviv University when he was only seventeen years old and graduated five years later with a degree in international relations. Like so many Ukrainians of his class, he had his own Canadian connection. In his last year at university, he won a student competition to take part in a Ukrainian-Canadian parliamentary exchange program where he was sent to Ottawa to work as an assistant to a member of parliament.

When we got down to business, he asked me if I was looking for other investment opportunities in Ukraine. I told him I wasn't — I was only looking to sell my controlling interest in Unirem-Agro and Unirem-Oil. I told him the businesses were up and running and fully capitalized with a valuation at US$22 million. A new owner could simply step up, put his own people in place and start taking the profits.

Oles said, "Okay, hire me and I can help you sell it."

"Why should I hire you?" I asked.

"Because I can get you the best price," he said.

For me, his arrogance was not a negative. It is a quality I am often accused of having myself, and one that I find is often associated with success, which first and foremost takes a profound belief in yourself. That, and a sense of humour, will get you far in life.

Oles's plan at that point was to bring in an investment fund that would buy me out and Fesun would stay as the local partner. I was sorry about one thing — that my plan to help the local community had failed — but the situation, I knew, was unsalvageable. I told Oles that I didn't care what happened after I was out. I just wanted out. I told him that Richard Spinks from Landkom was thinking of making an offer, but I was open to any offers he could get for me.

Oles then agreed to head down to Shchorsk for a modest fee to take a look at the operation and to take some photos for a promotional package.

I said fine. "Let me know what you think when you get back."

Oles, I learned, was someone who pays attention to detail, and the sales package he put together was excellent. It was titled "International Investment Opportunity. For Sale or Partnership Shares: Ukrainian-Canadian Agricultural companies Unirem-Agro and Unirem-Oil." The cover had images of state-of-the-art machinery working wheat fields, massive sunflowers, and a world symbol flanked by the Canadian and Ukrainian flags in the bottom corner. Among other things, he sold the operation as a place "Where Bio-Fuels and Agriculture Meet a Growing World Demand." The brochure went on to tell the story of Ukraine as "an emerging market" with vast resources that was "poised to become not only an asset but also a key player in global economic profits and solutions."

Oles put our no-till techniques front and centre as "not only safe and efficient, but nurturing of the soil," while saving both time and energy. For Unirem-Oil, he underlined our 20,000-ton Westeel grain elevator, the ten 2,000-ton silos and 60-ton scales, as well as grain-drying equipment and licensed laboratory with a total capacity of 150,000 tons per year. He also made much of our on-site railway for fast shipments to Kherson, Mykolaiv and Odessa on the Black Sea. For the asking price, we agreed on US$25.5 million.

It was a good package, but what also interested me were Oles's impressions of the operations in general and of Fesun in particular. At our meeting to review the promotional package, Oles said he stayed at the Premier Hotel in Dniprodzerzhynsk, the same one I stayed in on my visit there, and Fesun picked him up in his Freelander Land Rover to take him to Shchorsk. He said he found Fesun "a rural type, small-minded and limited." He realized this when he was at our facility in Shchorsk and noticed that, in a back corner of the yard, Fesun had workers making cinder blocks using the company cement mixers and reinforcing steel scavenged from abandoned mills in Dniprodzerzhynsk. Fesun was doing this as his own side business, and Oles said he found it foolish for someone responsible for a company valued at $22 million to be wasting his time trying to earn a few dollars on the side making cement blocks with company personnel and equipment.

But this, I was to learn, was the essential Fesun and the essential Ukrainian problem: so obsessed with making a few dollars for themselves, by any means, that they overlook the fortune before their very eyes. So obsessed with finding a way to cheat the system that they are blinded to the fact that if they work it honestly, it can take care of all of their needs and even help them thrive. Forever stuck in the always-cheater role and in the end only succeeding in cheating themselves.

◊•◊

The stage was set for my first direct confrontation with Fesun and Chernysh, and in October 2008 I called them in to read them the riot act. It should have been the last act in this drama, but instead was the opening shot in a war that would involve people much more powerful than them.

I waited in my Kropyvnyts'koho Street office with Yulia and Volodya for more than an hour and had almost given up on their appearing when there was a knock at the door. It was Lyuba Chernysh, the accountant. Alone.

She looked around fearfully, as if she expected someone to leap at her.

"Where's Fesun?" I asked as she sat in one of the chairs across from my desk.

"He's very sick," she said. "He's in the hospital in Dniprodzerzhynsk. He can't even get out of bed."

She spoke hurriedly, the way people do when they have over-rehearsed a lie. But I didn't challenge her on that. I told her I knew Fesun was lying about everything and stealing from me, and I wanted a full accounting of the business from the beginning and tried to get her to come clean. "I know you are running two sets of books," I said, "but if you don't give me the real figures within a week, I will go to the police and have you and Fesun arrested and put in jail."

She didn't know that I didn't have enough proof to go to the police, but I could see by the frightened expression on her face that she was taking me seriously. So I pressed on.

"Time is running out for you, Lyuba," I said. "I am selling Unirem-Agro and Unirem-Oil to a guy with a lot of experience in Ukraine. He's going to come in to clean house. If you don't—"

I noticed from the corner of my eye that Volodya, standing by the window, was trying to get my attention.

"What is it?" I asked.

He came over to me and, with his back to Lyuba, whispered, "Fesun is outside sitting in the car."

I looked at Lyuba and said, "So you were lying about Fesun, too. Why don't you just come clean? Look at how he is using you. Why are you defending that crook? He's setting you up to go to jail for this."

Lyuba lowered her gaze.

"Come on, Lyuba," I said, "why don't you work with me and we can fix all of this? I'll get a new manager and you can help me rebuild the company."

There was a long moment of silence. Then she looked up. "I am not going to turn on Viktor," she said. "We have been working together for thirteen years. I am not going to turn on him." Her voice was trembling with emotion. She then left, and I watched her from the window as she crossed the street and got in the car with Fesun to take the six-hour drive back to the smoky ruins of Dniprodzerzhynsk.

At the company's $22 million valuation, Fesun would have made a profit of $4.4 million on his zero investment if he had simply sold me his share and walked away. He would have been set for life in Ukraine, which was one of the most inexpensive places to live in Europe. But instead, he'd decided to play out his always-cheater hand.

CHAPTER 9

THE DNIPRO MAFIA

*The People's Deputies arrive on the scene:
Ukrainian-Canadian bank fraud artist
and serial murderer Alexander Shepelev,
company theft artist Oleg Kryshin, and
land theft and bank fraud artist Sergey
Kasyanov, the former Dnipropetrovsk
governor. And the games begin in earnest.*

In the spring of 2009, it seemed like I was winning against small-time crooks like Fesun, but I would soon find out that I wasn't truly aware of what game I was playing. By then, a much more elaborate plan to seize my $20-million-plus agri-business was being put in place by much more powerful gangsters who were in fact part of the Ukrainian government. Fesun would simply become a pawn in their game, and I was about to get a behind-the-scenes glimpse at the reality of Ukraine, where gangsters are lawmakers and lawmakers are gangsters.

The next level of crooks had actually been awakened by the success of Richard Spinks's Landkom in securing the multimillion-dollar loan from Credit Suisse, and locally by the publicity of my operation in Dnipropetrovsk. Suddenly it registered with the Ukraine mafia that there were enormous possibilities for lucrative frauds in the agri-business, and many of Ukraine's leading oligarchs entered the game with their own agri-businesses.

Chief among them was the People's Deputy and former governor of Dnipropetrovsk, Sergey Kasyanov. My impression of him is coloured by my dealings with him, but even when I first saw him I thought he had oddly porcine features — a meaty face with small, widely spaced eyes and pointy ears. The perfect face for the greedy politician/gangster who owned a pig farm and played the major role in the theft of my property. Kasyanov, it would turn out, was also a near-perfect representative of the businessman/politician class of gangster who had ruined Ukraine and finally gave it the pariah status that kept it out of the EU and NATO.

Kasyanov's trajectory was a familiar one for the Dnipropetrovsk mafia. He was born in 1966 in Kirovograd, a city about 240 kilometres west of Dniprodzerzhynsk. Like most of the local thieves I would encounter, he trained as an engineer in Soviet times but in his case was still studying at the Dnipropetrovsk Civil Engineering Institute when the Soviet Union collapsed. He graduated in 1992 and there were no jobs. According to his official bio, he made money importing items like light bulbs and electric motors from Bulgaria and reselling them in Dnipropetrovsk. In the mid-1990s he somehow gained control of a former Soviet chemical plant in Kharkiv and, with the help of Turkish capital, began to produce cheap Ukrainian knock-offs of European household cleaning products. In 2002, he sold the company to the American multinational Procter & Gamble for a significant profit — although it is uncertain how much, if any, of the profits made their way back to his Turkish investors.

Kasyonov's further economic rise was fuelled by his political rise, in the Ukrainian way of using his newfound wealth to move into the political sphere — where among other things he would have immunity from criminal prosecutions for his economic activities. To prepare the political ground he followed the Ukraine playbook in launching the Future for Social Development charitable foundation in 2000. The foundation included the launch of vote-getting local programs, with names like Happy Pension, Clean City and Youth Sport, that put a priority on "assistance to the most vulnerable segments of the population, educational programs, assistance to youth sports."

In 2002, Kasyanov was elected a deputy in one of the districts in the Dnipropetrovsk region, and like oligarchs everywhere, his political loyalties were determined by his own immediate economic interests.

Until the victory of the Orange Revolution in 2005, Kasyanov was closely aligned with Viktor Yanukovych's corrupt Party of Regions. Like most of the Ukrainian criminal class, Kasyanov changed his political stripes as often as necessary, but he was apparently loyal to the political boss who really mattered in Dnipropetrovsk, the regional crime lord Igor Kolomoisky, probably best known in the West for stealing US$5 billion from Privatbank when it was under his control and for bankrolling Vladimir Zelensky's rise to power. Kasyanov would soon follow Kolomoisky into bank and stock fraud operations, but in 2005 both of them switched their political allegiance to the Orange Revolution and Viktor Yushchenko at the last moment. Yushchenko knew how to repay a favour and appointed Kasyanov governor of the Dnipropetrovsk Regional State Administration a month later.

But the local people were not so easily deceived. As even one of his media supporters admitted, "The appointment of S. Kasyanov as governor was perceived very ambiguously in the region."

In fact, the population rose up to oppose him, holding rallies at the regional state administration denouncing him as one of the local crooks who ran Dnipropetrovsk. There were popular demands for his immediate firing by Yushchenko. The police tried to brutally suppress these protests, which turned violent. Within weeks of Kasyanov's appointment as governor, he was forced to resign.

This did not end his political career, however. In 2006, Kasyanov was elected as a People's Deputy of Ukraine in Constituency 37, Dnipropetrovsk, with 33 percent of the vote, which was split between nine candidates. This time he sought to give himself maximum flexibility on choosing sides by running as an independent.

It was his re-election to parliament that allowed Kasyanov's criminal career to really take off because it brought him into an alliance with a gangster politician from Donetsk, Alexander Shepelev, a dual Ukrainian-Canadian citizen who by 2006 had already left a trail of bank fraud and murders in his wake. He would soon become Kasyanov's partner-in-crime and, in true mafia style, their alliance would be cemented by intermarriage between their children.

◊•◊

Today Alexander Shepelev is one of the few Ukrainian political criminals who actually sits in a jail cell, and if you were writing a novel about Ukrainian gangsters it would be hard to invent a more colourful one than him. After beginning his career as a money-launderer for the Donetsk mafia in the early 1990s, Shepelev was implicated in the murder of one of his rivals. In 1995, he fled to Montreal and bought a $1.5-million house at 41 Surrey Gardens Avenue in Westmount, just up the hill from the Mulroneys and down the street from Senator Leo Kolber's mansion. Shepelev would get his Canadian citizenship in 2001 and Canada would henceforth serve as the family's comfortable refuge when he had to flee from the frequent bank fraud and murder investigations in Ukraine.

By 2003, Shepelev was back in Ukraine. We know this because on January 21, 2003, another local rival, Sergei Kirichenko, manager of the Avtoraz bank, was murdered, left with fourteen stab wounds on his own doorstep in Donetsk. Court documents stated that it was a contract killing done by two local teenagers who had been hired by Shepelev's personal driver, who was convicted of organizing the murder for US$40,000 in cash payments from the Doncreditinvest Bank. Two years later, in 2005, the name of Doncreditinvest was changed to the much more impressive-sounding European Bank of Rational Financing (EBRF). Eventually this bank would become the KSG Bank, controlled by Sergey Kasyanov and his wife, Ksenia, with Shepelev retaining a 16 percent share. By then the combined Doncreditinvest, EBRF and KSG bank operations had laundered an estimated US$4 billion in crime proceeds.

But the biggest scam would take place a few years later when Shepelev, with assistance from Kasyanov, took down the Rodovid Bank. Until Igor Kolomoisky's US$5-billion theft from Privatbank, the Rodovid bank fraud was the biggest in Ukraine's history. Tens of millions of dollars went missing and a couple of additional murders and attempted murders were left in its wake. But more on that later.

Like Kasyanov, Shepelev had purchased a seat for himself in parliament in 2006. In Shepelev's case, his parliamentary immunity helped him get away with murder yet again when a police colonel in his pay, who was asking for more protection money, was taken for a ride and killed and buried on the outskirts of Kyiv.

It was around this time that the Ukrainian gangsters were alerted to the financial possibilities in the agricultural sector by Landkom's US$13.8-million loan from Credit Suisse, and Sergey Kasyanov's KSG holding company launched KSG Agro and began vacuuming up a series of small agricultural operations.[1] This allowed him to gain control of local leases, which he in turn re-leased back to local growers without any investment of his own. The prize he was aiming for, I would soon discover, was my operation, with its almost ten thousand hectares, grain storage facilities and spur line to the Black Sea ports.

But of course he had no intention of actually purchasing it. He would simply steal it. What he needed, though, was a middleman, someone who could work with a dullard like Fesun to seize the property, cover up the theft through the corrupt courts, then deliver it clean to him for a fee.

But where, you ask, would they find the corrupt middle-man who could handle this? If you have to ask this question, you have not been paying close enough attention. The obvious place to find a low-life crook in Ukraine is the national parliament. By this time Kasyanov and Shepelev were both People's Deputies, and they turned to a third member of parliament, Oleg V. Kryshin, to engineer the theft of my $28-million operation.

Kryshin was a mid-level player in the Dnipropetrovsk mafia who, as a politician in the corrupt Batkivshchyna (Fatherland) party, was still a couple of ranks below the top of the Dnipropetrovsk crime syndicate that was headed by Igor Kolomoisky. But he had all the tools needed to engineer the theft, for a fee, for Kasyanov.

Kryshin's corruption was mainly at the level of using his fish cannery in Kerch, Crimea, to buy expired food for pennies and sell it as fresh for full

---

1   Among these were Scorpio Agro LLC, Soyuz-3 LLC, Goncharovo Agricultural LLC and Pivdenne Agricultural LLC.

market price, and selling cigarettes with counterfeit tax stamps and pocketing the tax amount. Kryshin also ran a successful US$21-million loan scam targeting Expobank, a private lending institution from the Czech Republic, with his Volnogorsk Glass company. The glass plant was located in the village of Volnogorsk, just twenty kilometres from my Shchorsk operation.

So this, finally, was the team I would be playing against. The mafia did not have to break the law, or even the rules, because all of them — Kasyanov, Shepelev, Kryshin — were lawmakers in a government led by the Orange Revolution leader who the Canadian government was hailing as the great reformer in Ukraine. Fesun would be a mere water boy in these big leagues and his reward, finally, would be infinitely less than if he had simply done the honest thing and sold me his shares.

CHAPTER 10

THE $28-MILLION SOLUTION

*Showdown. Confronting Fesun
and Chernysh and the Fortune 500
snake in the grass. A race against
time to save my companies.*

By January 2009, I still hoped to make a quick exit from Ukraine. It looked promising when Richard Spinks came back to say he had completed his valuation of Unirem-Agro and Unirem-Oil and made an offer to purchase them for US$28 million, conditional on seeing the books.

It was an excellent offer and I was happy to accept it. With his background as a smart and tough entrepreneur who spoke the Russian language, he also had the capacity to clean out the nest of crooks in Dniprodzerzhynsk and get the company running profitably.

But I was frank with Richard. I told him that Fesun was skimming the cream and he would have to deal with that at the outset, and I assured him I would get the real numbers for him before the deal was finalized. Then I invited him to a company board meeting set for March 23 in Kyiv, where I would formally dismiss Fesun and Chernysh and clear the way for Richard to put his own people in place.

Aleksei Gershun flew in from Connecticut two days before the meeting, and I told him that I was getting out and had a buyer from Landkom, Richard Spinks. Gershun had been acting as if he, too, was appalled by Fesun's and Chernysh's behaviour and said he would absolutely support the sale of the company to Richard.

I did not know that everything I was telling Gershun was getting directly back to Fesun and through him to Kryshin and his crooked lawyers.

The meeting was set for 1 p.m. in my Kyiv office. When Fesun and Chernysh arrived, I was there with Gershun, my assistant Yulia, my personal notary Sabrina Sibiga and, as a precaution, two armed members of a security firm. Richard was supposed to join us for the last part of the meeting when I would formally appoint him to take on Fesun's duties until the sale was final.

This time, with the help of Kryshin's lawyers, Fesun didn't have to hide in the car to avoid the meeting. Instead, he arrived with a bulky legal dossier and told me, "I will not stay because this is not a legal meeting."

He handed the dossier to Yulia, who looked through the files. "They are all signed by Fesun, Lyuba Chernysh and Anna Fesun," she said.

"What do they say?"

She began to read them:

> The notification of the received on March 5, 2009, at 10 a.m., by a private notary finds that the Extraordinary Meeting of Unirem-Agro on March 23, 2009, does not conform to the requirements of the acting legislation of Ukraine on the following grounds:
>
> 1. The notification from March 5, 2009, does not include the agenda, that provides a detailed list of questions, that are to be considered at the general company meeting;
> 2. The notification about convocation of a general company participant meeting, both ordinary and extraordinary, is to be made not less than 30 days prior to the convocation of the general meeting.

According to the laws of Ukraine, you may only call an emergency
meeting if the company is in danger of insolvency.

This last item involved a degree of chutzpah because, as I was soon to
discover, Fesun and Kryshin were at that very moment working feverishly
to bring that insolvency about.

At the time, I was surprised by the move. I didn't think Fesun had
the smarts for this, which he didn't, but I still wasn't aware Kryshin and
Kasyanov were in the picture. My immediate concern was to prevent Fesun
and Chernysh from leaving before Richard arrived. So to create a diversion,
I began confronting Fesun about some of the side issues. I told him I had
just received the report from Aleana and they had said his contention that
there were no profits in the past year because of low yields caused by bad
weather was a lie. It was a better-than-average year for crop yields in the
region and others were making money. I then went right into the infamous
US$560,000 that had been returned from the tax grab and had still not been
repaid to me. Finally, I told him I had information that he had been holding
participants meetings without me and making decisions during these meetings that he had no right to make.

Fesun reddened and began to sputter. He insisted, with his voice cracking,
that the poor yields were the fault of the workers, and he had not returned
the money because he needed it to invest in production — to purchase diesel
fuel, fertilizer and seed.

Then he turned his attention to the presence of the notary, Sabrina
Sibiga, in the room. She should not be there, he said. The company charter
said outside officials were not allowed in participants meetings. We went
back and forth on this a few times before I said, okay, Sabrina could leave
the room.

When she was gone and the security men stepped outside the door, I told
Fesun that I was waiting for Richard Spinks to arrive to start the meeting.
We then got into a bizarre conversation where Fesun insisted we could not
sell the company because it was profitable, in effect completely reversing his
position of a few minutes earlier.

That was enough for me. I told him he was not to interfere with the business any longer and I was removing him from his position. Fesun looked like he wanted to spit at me, and Chernysh said, "You have no right to do that. Viktor is the director!"

"I absolutely have the right," I said. "I control 70 percent of the shares and I am going to replace Viktor with Richard Spinks as company manager until the sale goes through — then Richard will take over as president and owner and appoint his own manager."

It was then that Fesun and Chernysh got up to leave. "This is not a legal meeting!" Fesun said in a voice choking with emotion.

From the window, I watched them walk to their car, Fesun gesturing wildly as he spoke to Chernysh.

I was not at all happy with how things had gone. I sensed I was missing something. Fesun had obviously lawyered up before the meeting, so I knew I was not fighting him alone. And whoever it was, they seemed to be trying to buy time with this illegal meeting crap. So what was their plan? I turned to Gershun, who seemed to be watching for my reaction.

"I don't like the way this went," I said.

Gershun shrugged. "At least now he knows he is finished with Unirem-Agro."

"I don't know what he knows," I said.

But Gershun, who was the front man for that gang of thieves, knew everything. And it is one of my biggest regrets in all of this that I did not see that. I was blinded by the fact that he was a respected engineer and entrepreneur with a Fortune 500 company. With my experience with crooked white businessmen in Canada, I should never have fallen for that — confusing corporate credentials with honesty and integrity.

Richard arrived at 1:30 p.m., only five minutes after Fesun had left. He had taken the night train from Donetsk with his lawyer, Oleg Kusiev. We called Sabrina back in to notarize the proceedings. With Gershun acting as secretary we continued with the participants meeting, making Richard a member of the board of directors and formally replacing Viktor Fesun as general manager. At the end, Gershun and I signed the minutes of the meeting.

When it was over, I felt even less satisfied. I was sorry about the project — one that had begun so promisingly but fizzled out because of a stupid crook. With Spinks's offer to purchase, Fesun could have made even more money than before by selling his share legitimately, but remained just a frightened small-time crook on the run who'd been caught in the web of a much higher class of criminals — the People's Deputies Oleg Kryshin and Sergey Kasyanov. Fesun had been skimming the cream from the operation, but Kryshin and Kasyanov were determined to walk off with the whole dairy and all of the cows. What little money Fesun gained from them, he would fritter away in bribes trying to keep himself out of jail.

After the March meeting, it took me some time to decide what I should do next. I spent a couple of weeks in discussion with Richard about the sale of the company, and at some point we both decided that we needed a forensic audit to see what, exactly, had been going on at the ground level.

For this, I wasn't sure about who I could turn to. If I used an off-the-shelf Ukrainian company, I would never be sure who they were working for when they got back to me. So I decided to call the young guy who had worked with me on selling the company, Oles Kopets.

Oles seemed happy to hear from me. I suggested we get together for dinner at Da Vinci's and he agreed. I didn't know it at the time, but we were about to enter the AK-47 period of Ukrainian business negotiations.

CHAPTER 11

THE DISAPPEARING COMPANIES

*Mafia black magic in Ukraine.
Using the courts to make a company's
assets disappear, then suddenly reappear
in someone else's portfolio. And poof,
the original company then disappears
entirely — as if it never existed.*

Da Vinci's was one of the best restaurants in Kyiv and, like most of the expensive establishments in the city, it was run largely as a money-laundering operation by the gangsters controlling the commanding heights of the economy.

As is often the case with the mafia, they spared no expense on decor. Da Vinci's was known not only for its superb seafood dishes, but for the ornate gold and red furnishings and expensive antiques. One of its special features was that like all good gangster restaurants, it provided private rooms for its clients where they could have discreet meetings away from the prying eyes of their Kyiv business and political associates, or, perhaps even more often, from people who knew their wives.

I met Oles in one of those private rooms, and we began by talking about Ukraine and Canada. It was, after all, the powerful Ukrainian diaspora that had brought him to Ottawa when he was a university student, and he'd been fascinated by Ukraine's long-standing connection to Canada.

Canada's special relationship with Ukraine actually began with the tens of thousands of Ukrainians who flooded into the Canadian prairies at the beginning of the twentieth century. The country was generously giving away to the white immigrants the vast lands they had stolen from the Plains Cree, the Saulteaux, the Kainai, northern and southern Piegan, Siksika, Dakota, Lakota, Nakoda, Assiniboine and Métis nations after the federal government had followed a conscious plan to starve the people into submission — in fact, to institute a Canadian holomodor on Indigenous peoples.[1]

Attracted by the now "free" Indigenous lands, the Ukrainians arrived in droves and it is no accident that today you find the world's biggest Ukrainian Easter egg in Darrell Michaels's Vegreville, the world's biggest perogy in Glendon, Alberta, and Ukrainian Orthodox churches throughout Saskatchewan and Manitoba. Most of these Ukrainian immigrants came to Canada from Lviv Oblast in western Ukraine.

Another big wave arrived from the same region immediately after the Second World War: people who had fought for or been allied with the Germans, including many thousands who joined the special Ukrainian SS units. This group of immigrants included Michael Chomiak, the grandfather of Canada's current deputy prime minister, Chrystia Freeland, and who had edited a Nazi propaganda newspaper in Krakow during the war. At the beginning of the Cold War immediately following the German surrender, Canada allowed so many of these German-aligned immigrants into the country that noted Canadian historian Irving Abella pointed out in an interview on the TV news show *60 Minutes* that it seemed that one sure way for a Ukrainian to get into Canada after the Second World War was "by showing the SS tattoo."

The Canadian motivation for hosting Ukrainian Nazi collaborators seemed to be along two related tracks. Domestically, they could be set against the largely left-wing, even pro-communist Ukrainian organizations that had been formed in Canada in the 1920s, and the extreme Ukrainian nationalists would be useful tools in the Cold War battle that was shaping up against the Soviet Union.

---

1   John A. Macdonald's Indian agents explicitly withheld food in order to drive bands onto reserves and out of the way of the railroad. A Liberal MP at the time called it "a policy of submission shaped by a policy of starvation." James Daschuk, *Clearing the Plains: Disease, Politics of Starvation and the Loss of Indigenous Life* Regina: University of Regina Press, 2013).

There were also political benefits for the Liberal government of the time in welcoming the new Ukrainian refugees, because by this point the community had significant political clout — its large and growing population gave Canada the third-largest Ukrainian population in the world, after Russia and Ukraine itself.

It was the large Ukrainian-Canadian community that arranged for Ukrainian students to come to Canada under the student parliamentary program. When he arrived, Oles was assigned to work as an assistant to Liberal MP Benoit Serré. This gave him hands-on experience with North American life, and in the fall of 2000 he enrolled in the master's program at Harvard's Kennedy School of Government.

So when Oles returned to Ukraine in the early 2000s, he brought with him international connections and a strong sense of how the Western world worked, and was determined that his generation had to fix Ukraine. "We are still Soviet people," he said. "We are still fighting to escape that."

Oles says that even with his experiences in North America, he was still trying to break through the Soviet mentality of always looking for someone above you to take responsibility. Or looking for a line to get in to get your share from the state, rather than going out and building a life where you could take care of yourself and your family by your own means. Even the Ukrainian gangster class had settled into a rigidly hierarchal system: every city and oblast had their Mr. Big who controlled the local criminal activity, which entailed most of the economic activity, in one way or another. It was, he said, the Soviet model, but instead of the Communist Party directing political and economic life, it was the local mafia.

As we ate the excellent Da Vinci's lobster frittata, I finally got down to business. I told Oles about Richard Spinks's $28-million offer. But I had concerns about how the business was being run in Shchorsk and I needed someone to look at the books, to dig down a couple of levels to see what was really going on so we could make sure everything was in order before the sale — or at least before Richard completed his own due diligence.

Oles was astute enough to know what was being asked without my drawing a detailed picture. "Sure," he said. "I sometimes work with a lawyer who is good at these sorts of things. I'll bring him with me."

"You would go down there with a lawyer?"

Oles smiled. "Working in Ukraine without a lawyer is like walking a minefield without a minesweeper."

This seemed reasonable, but to be honest, I was still hesitant — and this is always the dilemma in Ukraine. Even after you identify who is stealing from you, you are never sure the people you enlist to help you are actually working for you or are snakes in the grass.

For all I knew, Oles would go down to Shchorsk and he and Fesun would drink vodka and sing sad Ukrainian and Russian songs for a few days, then Oles would come back with Chernysh's doctored books and tell me that everything was fine. That was a risk I had to take. But in this and every other case, Oles would prove his loyalty.

Oles and his lawyer friend went down to Shchorsk in early June 2009 and worked for five days going through the books. This time, Fesun disappeared before Oles arrived, so he and his lawyer had to work only with Chernysh.

It was an unpleasant task. Chernysh was determined to make their stay there as fruitless and miserable as possible. From the beginning, she insisted they could not take any documents off the site and refused them the use of the photocopier. That meant they had to write down the long list of numbers that she was feeding them with a minimum of explanation.

One of the things this accomplished, however, was to confirm to Oles and his partner that they really were in a forensic audit situation and dealing with people who had something to hide. So they trusted nothing that she said and asked for backups on all of her numbers — receipts, invoices, bank statements, cancelled cheques — trying to follow the trail of each transaction.

Oles remembers that the days with Chernysh were long. They were buried under files containing government paperwork and poorly identified cheque stubs while Chernysh hovered nearby, simmering with resentment. On the way back to his hotel in Dniprodzerzhynsk, Oles noticed the Brezhnev statue on Lenin Avenue and was thinking of how the Soviet Union had ruined his people. Seventeen years after its fall, they were all really Soviet citizens trying to make it through a changed world that they did not really understand. So they clung to the corrupt ways they'd learned from the old regime. Like Chernysh struggling to use all the paperwork to cover the crime, because in Soviet times, if you had the paperwork in order, the crime did not exist.

It was on the third day that Oles found what he was looking for. It was staring him in the face on the income statement that I had never been able to see. Everything was in order at the top and bottom of the page, and the value of the company was unchanged. But what was balancing everything was not in the assets section but in the receivables. When Oles questioned Chernysh about it, she seemed to suggest it was for grain that had been sold and not yet paid for, but when Oles dug deeper, it was obvious it was for the grain elevators themselves. They had disappeared from the assets line and reappeared, as if by magic, in the receivables line.

Chernysh would give no explanation, and it would actually take almost two years before we could understand what, exactly, had happened. By then, Unirem-Agro and Unirem-Oil had also disappeared down the dark hole of the Ukrainian legal system. People's Deputies Kasyanov and Kryshin were masters at this kind of corruption. They had the ability to make companies disappear, then magically reappear in their portfolios, then disappear again while they pocketed their value. And all of this they were able to accomplish not only in the view of their fellow lawmakers and Ukrainian law, but with their active protection.

◊◆◊

After the March 23 meeting with Fesun and Chernysh in my office, when I announced that I was going to sell the company to Richard Spinks and relieved them of their duties, the raiding plan had been launched with lightning speed — even though the plan was a complex one involving transferring or selling assets to phony companies for receivables that were never paid. Then the corrupt courts were used to award my assets to those companies, which then transferred them to a new entity, and the intermediate companies were stripped of their assets.

From a distance, all I could see was a shadow puppet show on the wall. Vaguely familiar shapes were moving through the darkness, but it was impossible to understand what exactly was happening behind the screen.

In the broadest sense, Oleg Kryshin, with Fesun as his little helper, had consolidated all of my assets in two new companies with similar-sounding names to mine — Unirem-Service Plus and Unirem-Agro Plus, with Kryshin controlling 85 percent of the assets and Fesun 15 percent. Kryshin then moved to bankrupt my two companies, like a pirate who scuttles captured ships after he empties them of treasure, by forcing the original Unirem-Agro and Unirem-Oil into bankruptcy.

The scheme had a certain genius to it, and for those who are interested in how these Ukraine mafia schemes work in general, and the particulars of the theft of my companies, I have set out all of the details in Appendix III. It allows you to follow assets through their "sales" to numerous phony companies set up by Fesun or associates of Kryshin to their final resting place in Kasyanov's pocket, and to get an idea how this veritable raiding industry works in Ukraine.[2]

At the end of this process in November 2009, the deck was cleared. There was nothing left of my companies or the intermediate companies that my assets passed through on their way to the control of People's Deputy Kryshin. The initial stage of the scam was now complete, and my properties under another name were ready for the final stage of the fraud — turning them over to Sergey Kasyanov's KSG, with a multimillion-dollar fee paid to Kryshin for his work. For that relatively small outlay, Kryshin and former governor Sergey Kasyanov had a $28-million asset that he would soon, through a stock market fraud in Warsaw, turn into a $40-million one.

It was only later that I learned that this criminal raider scheme was not a brilliant ploy by Kryshin and Kasyanov. In fact, these types of legal raids were so common in Ukraine that there were actually mafia-affiliated lawyers who specialized in them, like lawyers specializing in real estate or employment law. When the local oligarch or mini-garch, as local oligarchs like Kasyanov were often called, wanted to steal a business, he called the

---

2   If you are foolish enough to even consider investing in Ukraine (perhaps you skimmed the book so far), Appendix III is a must-read.

raider lawyers, paid a retainer, and a lawyer went to work arranging the theft. From the shoot-'em-up street gangs of the 1990s, Ukraine had evolved into a sophisticated criminal enterprise.

But as I was to soon learn, the men with guns still had a role to play.

CHAPTER 12

THE AK-47 GAMBLE

*The Ukrainian business solution to men
with guns: more men with bigger guns.*

In the end stages of the fraud, I was already in court fighting to block the liquidation of my companies. But my ad hoc team of lawyers could not even get full standing in the case. I remember the lunch with my legal team after a morning in court when they told me we were at the end of the line.

"What do you mean the end of the line?" I asked. "They stole my companies. There must be something you can do."

The young lawyer shook his head sadly. "We can't do anything more to get your companies back because they no longer exist."

I think even more than what he was saying, the fake sadness made me want to throw my cabbage rolls at him. He was telling me that because the thieves had received the stamp of approval on their fraudulent paperwork from a corrupt judge, there was nothing more to do. Everything was in order.

After the lunch, and the firing of that half-hearted legal team, I met with Oles to ask his advice on what to do next.

I knew Oles had come of age during the gangsterism of the 1990s and he understood that was where much of the power lay in Ukraine. He helped me get my initial lawyer, but he told me that in the crooked system, where judges were usually on someone's payroll, I would need much more aggressive moves to get my property back.

"What do you mean by aggressive?" I asked.

"Men with guns," he said.

I could see he was serious. "Doesn't Kryshin already have men with guns down there?"

Oles shrugged. "More men and bigger guns. This is Ukraine. It is how things are done. Like everywhere, possession is 90 percent of the law and in Ukraine you sometimes have to provide your own law."

I told him I would think about it.

◇◆◇

I would like to say that I was astounded by having gunmen on your payroll in Ukraine — and it certainly was not the way I wanted to do business — but violent attacks arising from business deals was not entirely foreign to me in Canada, where I had been on the receiving end of an actual assassination attempt. But that had as much to do with old-fashioned Canadian racism as it did with business.

It happened in 1982 while I was band chief. I had worked hard to promote the economic development of the community, and I was successful in launching a number of new band businesses and ensuring that we received fair market value for the reserve lands we were renting out to a group of white trailer-park owners. At the time, they were paying us a pittance and making a bundle of money on our land, and I renegotiated the leases to a value much more favourable to us. The idea of paying a fair premium to Indians outraged these local redneck trailer-park owners, and on August 21, 1982, I answered a knock on my door and was met by a stocky young stranger wielding a sharpened bar, a two-foot-long piece of steel with a sword edge.

Instantly blows from the bar were raining down on my head with murderous intensity. Blinded by my own blood, I managed to get a couple steps upstairs and kicked him in the face, then ran up to my office, pulled a revolver from my desk drawer, and shot the attacker in the shoulder. He spun around and faced me. Realizing that he had brought a sword to a gunfight, he got up and stumbled back down the stairs. I looked through the upstairs window and saw he was pulling out a sawed-off shotgun from the trunk of his car, and I shot again. He turned and looked up at me for a moment, then leapt into his car and drove away.

I followed him outside but collapsed in the driveway, bleeding profusely. By a miracle, my fifteen-year-old son Doug came up the hill from where he was living with his mother and found me. I was taken to hospital and received an immediate blood transfusion and 285 stitches in my head and arms where I had fended off the blows.

Later that afternoon, a local motorcycle cop heard my assailant's description on the radio and captured 25-year-old Richard Cooper, a hired thug from Edmonton, in his motel parking lot. Cooper was preparing to flee back to Alberta, with my bullet still lodged in his shoulder.

This was beyond anything I had imagined. But I knew, instinctively, where it came from. The rage behind this attack had not originated in the mind of a small-time Edmonton hood. I knew with certainty that it came from somewhere within the association of trailer-park owners who had been denouncing me to the local politicians and in the press with ever-growing intensity. Charges were laid against the clearly guilty plotters, but they were white and they got off. The only person convicted was a Chinese-Canadian trailer-park owner who was actually the only one who had nothing to do with it. Cooper went to jail and served a few years, then disappeared. If you are an Indian in Canada, you are familiar with violence and injustice. So I was not as shocked by Oles's suggestion — or by the aftermath of the assassination attempt — as I might have been.

◇•◇

I thought about Oles's proposal long and hard that night. The idea of getting involved in some kind of crazy shootout in Ukraine was the last thing I wanted to do. But lying in the dark smoking a cigarette while I listened to the sounds of the city — Slavic cities go to bed late and Kyiv can be a noisy place at night — I realized that the last thing I wanted was not that. The last thing I wanted was to walk away without a fight and leave the crooks with my $28-million company. So the next day I called Oles.

"Let's try it the Ukrainian way," I said.

When we met to discuss the details, Oles told me he had already taken this route himself once. He had learned through experience that Europeans who come to Ukraine knowing its Wild West reputation were sometimes only too willing to play the corruption game, believing that in such a lawless land they can stiff the locals and then bribe their way out of trouble. These people seriously misunderstood the rules of the game in Ukraine.

This had been the case with one of Oles's recent partners, a German-based international cement group, whose management decided that because it was Ukraine, "they could cross the street on a red light."

"What?" I asked.

"They decided they could do what they want here, so they tried to cheat me and my associates out of our 10 percent ownership in the company."

So Oles went to ask for help from the mayor of Dnipropetrovsk, who was known to have his own gangster army at his disposal. He discussed the matter with the mayor, a price was agreed to and the Germans were visited by the type of guys who don't knock before they enter. The mayor's boys kicked down the door of the German CEO's house and began negotiating with him on Oles's behalf — with their guns drawn. Within a few minutes, the negotiations were successfully concluded and the German paid Oles the money they owed him, and Oles handed over the agreed-upon percentage to the gunmen.

Oles told me that to have a hope of winning, we would also have to take back control of my properties while we were in the courts. Possession was, indeed, nine-tenths of the law in Ukraine, and it would put the judges on notice that we had our own gangster friends.

Our move would be complicated by the fact that Kryshin and Kasyanov already had their security in place, so it was important that they would be instantly outgunned, and then to send the message that we were back at the Shchorsk complex for the long haul. Oles told me that the mayor of Dnipropetrovsk had the firepower to get the job done, but warned me that it would be expensive and we would have to play the long game, because as soon as our guys left, Kryshin and Kasyanov would have their people back there.

So Oles went down to Dnipropetrovsk to negotiate with the mayor, who agreed to take on the job, but said it would cost a hell of a lot because the raiders were People's Deputies and had government connections. He said it would take a minimum of a half-dozen guys with AK-47s guarding the place full-time. But the mayor would start the operation as soon as I transferred $100,000 to his bank account in Dnipropetrovsk.

While the operation was going on, I was in Kyiv waiting for the call from Oles, who was on the site.

◇●◇

It was a cold, sunny morning in January 2010 when three black SUVs passed through the gate at the grain elevators in Shchorsk. Six young men got out of their vehicles and opened the hatchbacks to take out their automatic weapons.

All activity stopped. Kryshin's lightly armed and badly paid security people froze. They knew that an AK-47 can empty its thirty-round clip and cut a man in two in about five seconds, so after a brief conversation, Oles's guys escorted them from the facility, which was now under our control.

Oles then went to speak to the managers. They were, understandably enough, very worried by these mercenaries toting automatic weapons in their midst. Oles told them not to worry. These guys were working for Ron.

He told me the relief was palpable. "As soon as I told them the guys were with Ron, they relaxed."

They didn't like Fesun because he was always trying to screw them out of what he owed them. But when I had heard of his labour board infractions and withholding of payments to the employees, I'd raised hell and Fesun was forced to pay up. They knew I supported them and cared about what happened to them. They told Oles that Fesun was always bad-mouthing me, but the employees didn't believe him. They liked me.

They were happy I was back, even if it meant having to work with my security people guarding the gates.

One immediate benefit of our repossession of the facility was that we acquired some of the old financial papers that had been left behind. And it was then, finally, that I learned that Aleksei Gershun, the Fortune 500 engineer with impeccable credentials, was also in on the fraud. Proof came in the form of a receipt from a US$205,000 payment Fesun made to Gershun for bringing me in as a target of the scam, with further payments of US$295,000 to follow. This would amount to a 10 percent payoff for the first US$5 million I invested, taken out of my company without my knowledge. Of course I felt foolish for having trusted Gershun. But the proof was there. It seemed, with this final confirmation of betrayal, that everyone in Ukraine was in on it.

I took a bit of revenge by making copies of the receipts of payouts to Gershun and sending them to the U.S. Internal Revenue Service to suggest they might check if he paid taxes on this ill-gotten foreign income.

My own money was headed out the door by the shovelful during this period, however, and not only to the gangsters. I was also paying tens of thousands of dollars to my half-hearted lawyers without even being sure they weren't secretly on the payroll of my opponents.

When I discussed this with Oles, he said he knew another lawyer, Nikolai Orlov, who had the type of connections that could help us reverse the decisions going against us. I said okay, let's go with him, but when I found out the "security" and legal fees I was being charged, I told Oles, "These guys better be able to deliver. Fast."

The legal fees alone came to an astounding $24,000 a month. Eventually, I would come to the realization that I wasn't sure who Orlov was working for, either, but initially he seemed to be making all the right moves.

First, he pressured the Ukrainian government's financial investigators to open a criminal case against Viktor Fesun. The state investigator, O.V. Protsenko, actually did a pretty good job in gathering the basic facts. He noted that Fesun, who was listed as a director of both Unirem-Oil and Unirem-Agro, had let the court put my companies into bankruptcy without any contestation on his part. He also pointed out that as a result of the insolvency of the two companies, Fesun and his partner in Unirem-Oil Service had ensured that there would no longer be any entity that could claim the elevator and other property from them. Protsenko also noted that with the liquidation of Unirem-Agro and Unirem-Oil, the majority of the corporate and business documentation of the companies was destroyed.

Protsenko even found a paper trail in the legal filing of the minutes of the companies' meetings. One from March 18, 2008, had my forged signature on it. The meeting was said to include only me and Fesun, and there were two items on the agenda: the first was about increasing the capital of Unirem-Oil, and the second was "Approval of the revised Articles of Association of Unirem-Oil." It was noted that these new articles strengthened the role of the executive director in selling the property. The phony minutes were registered by the state notary, V.Y. Zhidkov, on April 15, 2007.

In addition, Protsenko noted that local authorities from the village level up to the national parliament, where Kryshin was sitting as a People's Deputy, were implicated at various stages in the fraud, most notably judges and other court officers.

With these findings, I thought I was on the road to getting my property back. This hope was bolstered when Orlov had us recreate Unirem-Agro and Unirem-Oil as they had been at our March 2009 meeting, when I put Richard on the board and relieved Fesun as the director. As far as we were concerned, everything that Fesun did after that was illegal and therefore invalid. Orlov also asked us to add an associate of his to the board, P.A. Oliynyk. Things seemed to be moving in the right direction.

Another positive development was that Vika came back to work with me. She had been away for several years, having gotten married and had a child, and she came back just in time because Yulia, at that moment, wanted to reduce her hours leading up to her own maternity leave. So Vika and Yulia did some job sharing for a few months, until Yulia went on leave and Vika returned full-time.

Richard Spinks was also on the case, helping whenever he could. At this point he was already suspicious of my new lawyer, Orlov. He thought that our opponents might have gotten to him.

As I would later learn on several occasions, Richard's instincts tended to be right.

CHAPTER 13

GUNMEN ON THE DOORSTEP

*Face to face with People's Deputy Oleg
Kryshin. Then, People's Deputy and
former governor Sergey Kasyanov
emerges from the shadows.*

One evening when I arrived back from dinner, I noticed a black Jeep parked thirty metres from the door of my apartment on Darvina Street. Darkness was falling but I could make out the shapes of two men slouching down in the shadows. When I got inside my fifth-floor apartment, I didn't turn on the lights right away. I went over to the window and saw that the Jeep had a direct line of sight to my window. I turned on the lights and waited ten minutes before I checked again. The Jeep was gone.

I awoke early, before 6 a.m., as I generally do. When I looked out the window the Jeep was back, parked in the same spot. And I could see that there were still two men inside.

I made coffee and waited. I had no way of knowing if they were there for me, but I also knew that if you put automatic weapons in play on your side, like we had done at the grain elevators, you have to expect that the other side would do the same. At 8 a.m., I called Vika and asked her to call the police and tell them that two armed men were parked outside a building on Darvina. The police arrived a half an hour later and pulled up behind the Jeep.

I had been guessing at the "armed" part, but when the two cops arrived and checked the back of the Jeep, they pulled an assault weapon out of a duffle bag. They had the two Jeep occupants out of the vehicle to check their identification, and there was a long discussion while one of the cops stood with what looked like a Kalashnikov rifle cradled in his arm. I assumed they were about to arrest the two when, to my great surprise, the cop put the assault weapon back in the gym bag and returned it to the back of the Jeep, and the two men then drove off.

I could not be sure who these men were or what they wanted, but that morning I asked myself: What the hell was I doing in the middle of all of this? I could be back in the B.C. Interior, sitting at my desk in my office over-looking the golf course and putting together the financing for a shopping centre development I was working on, then heading over to the clubhouse restaurant for lunch. I was here to build a state-of-the-art grain operation, not play around with a bunch of Ukrainian gangsters. I decided I needed to have another chat with Oles.

But the next time I spoke to Oles, he had such positive news that I didn't raise any questions about gunmen. He told me that Orlov was arranging his own meeting with People's Deputy Kryshin in his office in Kyiv, and we might be able to settle this thing quickly.

On the surface, it did seem like a breakthrough. Maybe Kryshin was going to ask for a small face-saving payment before returning what was mine. But when I thought more about this, I had trouble imagining Kryshin shaking my hand and apologizing for stealing a $28-million company from me and giving me back the deed to a business that I had already seized back with armed mercenaries. Or maybe he would be declaring war against me and threatening to lead a counterattack with a bigger group of mercenaries against the property in an all-out, grain-elevator shooting war, while he sent assassination squads after me. The gunmen on my doorstep were then part of his warning to me. If these were the only possibilities, I feared it was more likely to be the latter than the former.

But it turned out to be neither. I arrived early at Orlov's office on

Tarasivska Street, which was just a twenty-minute walk from Bessarabska Square. Kryshin entered the room like the third-rate politician/con artist he was, smiling and shaking hands and then talking expansively about wanting to settle things with the Canadian in the spirit of mutual respect. He sat across from me. He had a smooth face but small eyes behind a pair of wire-rimmed glasses. His gaze flitted between me and Orlov, who was translating his words. Kryshin told me he was very sorry to hear about the falling-out between me and my Ukrainian partners, but said he'd been dealing with the company in good faith and had spent a lot of money purchasing the assets of Unirem-Agro and Unirem-Oil in the hope of keeping the companies alive until they could be sold to another agricultural business, one that had the industry experience to run them.

In reality, of course, he had spent nothing because he'd scuttled my companies with his meagre payables still on their books.

He kept smiling and now he was looking directly at me as he was talking. Kryshin said he had only been caught in this unfortunate situation because he'd spent millions of dollars of his own money acquiring the assets, much more than he could afford to lose. So he was sure Mr. Derrickson would understand that he would have to be compensated for at least part of the losses he incurred in purchasing the property in a completely legal fashion from the company director, Viktor Fesun. He emphasized again that all of this had been done completely legally, and he had the court-approved legal paperwork to prove it.

But he hoped it would not be necessary to go through the courts. He wanted to settle the matter right there and then with Mr. Derrickson, in a friendly manner.

Orlov nodded. "And what were the terms of the proposed settlement?"

Kryshin kept smiling. "I am asking Mr. Derrickson to meet me 50-50 on this. I have spent US$8 million on this deal, but I am only asking that Mr. Derrickson compensate me for half that amount."

So that was it.

The People's Deputy Kryshin, who hadn't spent a cent of his own money on my properties, was asking that I make a $4-million extortion payment to get them back — at a time when those assets were being held by armed guards who I was paying a fortune for. Equally ridiculous was the idea that I would trust this man enough to make any kind of deal with him.

I glanced at my lawyer, expecting to see the same disgust on his face that I felt at this brazen extortion attempt. But Orlov was impassive. And I wondered if he, too, was in on the deal. Maybe he had discussed it with Kryshin beforehand and they decided Kryshin would ask for $4 million, Orlov would get me to accept and then Kryshin would walk with $3 million and Orlov would get paid a $1-million commission.

This is how the mind works in a den of fraudsters and thieves. This is what business in Ukraine is reduced to. My only thought then was to get the hell out of there. But I was not going to let any of them know what I was thinking. I thanked Kryshin and Orlov and said, "You have given me something to think about."

The wisdom of not haggling with Kryshin was confirmed later when I put together the final timeline and realized that at the time of Kryshin's offer, he had very likely already turned my assets over to Kasyanov, the ultimate beneficiary. The $4-million offer was simply a new scam. I would have been paying Kryshin for assets he'd already delivered to their final destination, his colleague Sergey Kasyanov.

But the meeting with Kryshin did give me a lot to think about. I was caught now in a web of gangsters and con artists and paying $24,000 a month to a lawyer when I did not know if he was working for me or my opponents. I was paying tens of thousands of dollars more a month to my gunmen occupying the grain elevators, who were either keeping the elevators in control for me or simply extorting a monthly fee from me, or a little bit of both.

It was in this moment that Oles called me up and asked to meet me at a restaurant in the old town. Over lunch, I told him about the meeting with Kryshin in Orlov's office and said I was beginning to have my doubts about Orlov, too.

Oles was sympathetic. He could see, he said, what a fuck-up Ukraine had become for me. At times like this he was embarrassed by his country. But it was the way the game was played here.

I reminded him that I didn't come here to play games, I came to build a business that would be good for me and good for Ukraine.

He nodded. "But I think now the only way to get back to that is to ride out this wave." Then he told me he'd been speaking to his associates in Dnipropetrovsk, the ones that were providing the armed force securing the grain elevators.

"They are not satisfied with only providing security," he said. "They have offered to help by putting pressure on Kryshin directly, to make him see reason."

I knew better than to ask Oles how they proposed to accomplish that and instead asked, "How much do they want?"

"They are asking for a million dollars."

"Jesus," I said. "And do they guarantee they will find a way to solve the problem?"

Oles shook his head. "No. They are confident they can solve the problem. But they cannot give a guarantee."

"And if I don't pay?"

"They said they would have to withdraw their people from the grain elevators. Security personnel like that are in high demand."

"This sounds like a shakedown," I said.

"I know, I know," Oles said. "But I think you need to keep these people in play. Without them, Kryshin will move back in."

I told Oles I would think about it, but my mind was already made up. I simply could not throw a million dollars at these other Ukrainian gangsters without a guarantee that they would get my property back, or that they would do this without killing people. I was already being bled by lawyers and I was not going to start handing over a million dollars a year to local thugs, because in the end I would not be solving my problem but doubling my losses.

When we finished eating, I told Oles, "I'm not paying anyone a million dollars. It just doesn't make sense. If you tell me they can get my assets back, maybe — if they can do it without shooting up the place. But a million dollars is a lot of money to spend on a wish and a prayer."

"Yes, it is," Oles said. "But it might be the only way."

What Oles predicted would come to pass, came to pass. My automatic weapon–toting security detail was withdrawn from Shchorsk, driving their black SUVs out of the gates and back down the road to Dnipropetrovsk. Within twenty-four hours, Kryshin's gunmen, or perhaps by this time Kasyanov's, were back at the elevators in bigger numbers and with bigger weapons.

Orlov said he would continue to work through the courts, first with a criminal case against Fesun that might nullify all of his initial manoeuvrings and fraudulent paperwork that permitted the sale to Kryshin. But I was back to square one.

And it was at this point that Sergey Kasyanov emerged fully into view.

I first read about his involvement in the financial press, in the brief "Sale of Assets" section:

> Object of the transaction: over 50 percent of the authorized capital of LLC "Unirem-Agro Plus" (Dnepropetrovsk region) and LLC "Ukrainian agro-industrial holding" (Kyiv).
>
> The selling party: LLC "Ukrainian Agro-Industrial Holding" — LLC "Unirem-Agro Plus" — Dnipropetrovsk corporation of the integral property complex people's deputy from Dnipropetrovsk Oleg Kryshin.
>
> Acquired party: KSG Agro of Sergey Kasyanov.

The article that followed provided some telling details. It described the purchase of my properties as turning Kasyanov from a dabbler in agriculture into a serious player. It also alerted me that the end-game for my assets was a stock fraud on the Warsaw Stock Exchange.

"Last week, the Cyprian company KSG Agricultural and Industrial Holding (KSG Agro) announced the receipt of control over two Ukrainian agrarian structures: Unirem-Agro Plus and the Ukrainian agro-industrial holding. According to the owner of KSG Agro, the former head of the Dnipropetrovsk Regional State Administration Sergey Kasyanov . . . the new acquisitions are explained by his plans to expand his presence in the agrarian market. . . . The ex-governor of the Dnipropetrovsk region . . . also announced the intention to conduct a private placement of shares on the Warsaw Stock Exchange."

So this was the ultimate destination of my assets. The "ex-governor of Dnipropetrovsk" — who had been thrown out of office for corruption, had specialized in bank fraud and would soon be charged with attempted murder — was moving my assets into his stock fraud.

For me, the "businessman" Sergey Kasyanov is the perfect example of the ruling class of modern Ukraine — a political shapeshifter with a taste for luxury whose wealth was built on violence and fraud and who, in a corrupt system, a criminal state, could act with impunity and as a People's Deputy.

I was now in a battle whose rules were still unclear, but I finally understood who my opponent was.

CHAPTER 14

KASYANOV: THE HIDDEN FACE OF UKRAINE

*The wonders of business in Ukraine:
Unirem-Agro disappears into KSG
Agro, passes through Luxembourg and
turns up in Poland as part of
a $40-million stock fraud.*

Sergey Kasyanov emerged on the national scene in Ukraine during the presidential campaign in 2005, making what seemed like a surprising switch from supporting the corrupt Party of the Regions to the incoming Viktor Yushchenko regime, which had a reformist reputation. Along with a huge donation to the Yushchenko campaign, the move earned him the appointment as Dnipropetrovsk governor.

Kasyanov's change in parties was part of the standard Ukrainian mafia playbook — the oligarchs position themselves to work with, and eventually absorb, any political movements that arise. The mafia kingpin in Dnipropetrovsk, Igor Kolomoisky, was a master of this. A long-time member of the corrupt Fatherland Party, he also switched to Yushchenko's Orange Revolution movement, along with Yuri Bereza, the man responsible for his security and a close associate of Kasyanov. All of them would quickly switch allegiance again when Petro Poroshenko came to power, and would then seamlessly emerge as supporters of the new "reformer," Volodymyr Zelensky.

But as we have seen, what distinguished Kasyanov from the rest of the Dnipropetrovsk gang was his second affiliation. That was with the Donetsk crime family of Mikhail Friedental and the mercurial Ukrainian-Canadian Alexander Shepelev, who was on his way to legend status among Ukraine gangsters with his murder and bank fraud rampage. Kasyanov would be involved with Shepelev in both these activities — the massive Rodovid Bank fraud and the attempted murder of one of Rodovid's inconvenient bank executives.

The Rodovid Bank fraud, led by Kasyanov's Ukrainian-Canadian associate, was the biggest bank takedown in Ukrainian history — until Kolomoisky surpassed it with his own PrivatBank fraud a few years later — and it tells you all you need to know about how the criminal class works in Ukraine.

This one was a Ukrainian classic. It began with the initial collapse of the Rodovid Bank, one of Ukraine's largest, in early 2009. It turned out that the bank's original owners had embezzled some UAH 220 million (US$35 million) from its coffers, and the bank failure threatened the savings of thousands of bank customers. The corrupt government of Yulia Tymoshenko decided to nationalize and refinance the bank with UAH 315 million (US$50 million) in state funds, and the person who they put in charge of ministering Rodovid back to health was Alexander Shepelev.

Shepelev was head of Ukraine's banking committee — a position he had been given after serving as a bagman for Tymoshenko's party — and gleefully took on the role. He set up an office inside the bank and quickly began embezzling the tens of millions of dollars that the state had just invested to refloat the defrauded bank.

One of Shepelev's deals was with Sergey Kasyanov. Shepelev had the bank lend KSG Agro millions of dollars to what was in fact a non-existent property owned by one of Kasyanov's newly acquired agricultural companies, Soyuz-3. As soon as Kasyanov had the money in his account, he transferred ownership of the phantom Soyuz-3 property to an unrelated company that he himself owned, called Business Management Group Inc. Then Kasyanov did to Business Management Group what had been done to my companies the year before: he liquidated it, making it disappear, after he had transferred the Rodovid money to his other companies. So Kasyanov had the money and the bank had no collateral to back it up. This was just one of many Shepelev-managed scams to clean out the tens of millions the state had invested in the bank to engorge himself and his crime associates.

While he was working with Shepelev on the Rodovid Bank fraud, Kasyanov was also moving on his scheme to turn my stolen properties into ready cash. This time with a stock fraud.

On April 15, 2011, Kasyanov announced in the Ukrainian business press that he was preparing to list the properties on the Warsaw Stock Exchange with the posting of an IPO for 33 percent of his agricultural holding for US$40 million. As soon as I read about this deal, I sent for a copy of the IPO from Equity Trust, the Luxembourg company that was handling it.

KSG's offering was for up to 15.5 million shares. According to the prospectus, Kasyanov was limiting trade on the stock from my property to the Warsaw exchange, probably because he did not want to have the scrutiny of the American regulators that issuing stock on international exchanges would entail.

To prepare for the IPO, Kasyanov seems to have drawn on his Donetsk criminal connections by bringing onto his board two Luxembourg-based operatives, Jacob Mudde and Gwenaëlle Bernadette Andrée Dominique Cousin, who were also on the board of the Donetsk businessman Viktor Vishnevetsky's Coal Energy Holding Company, which was also launching an IPO on the Polish exchange.[1]

In response, I moved to inform everyone involved that they were dealing with stolen property and that by participating in this IPO they were working with a criminal enterprise. The person to help me with this, I knew, was Richard Spinks. He had lived in Poland for almost a decade and he knew all of the players there. Spinks had also been hounded by gangsters and attempted raids on his holdings in the Lviv Oblast while he was building Landkom, so he knew the lay of the land.

At the time, Richard was living in Donetsk, where his wife, Tanya, had grown up. He'd laid down roots in the city by building a fabulous multi-million-dollar home, while Tanya fulfilled her lifelong dream by opening

---

1   Vishnevetsky was known for both his coal holdings and for funding the pro-Russian Union of Orthodox Journalists, and both companies ended up with their head offices at the same address in Luxembourg.

an antique shop on Pushkina Street, the upscale commercial street in Donetsk. They were living an ideal life when I visited them there. But of course this was Ukraine, where the world could turn upside down with amazing speed. And in their case it certainly did three years later with the Maidan revolution.

I flew to Donetsk with Vika and we arrived at the Sergei Prokofiev Airport in a steady rain. The terminal dated from the early 1970s, when the Soviets were still rebuilding infrastructure destroyed in the Second World War, and the lousy weather probably made everything look more shabby than it actually was.

So that was my impression as we travelled along the rough provincial roads at the edge of the city. But by the time we arrived downtown, the dark cloud had passed and there were sunny breaks in the sky. The main streets were clean and bustling with odd-looking trolley cars, and the city centre was full of flowers. Vika and I were staying at the very comfortable, five-star Donbass Palace Hotel. While we were checking in, Vika mentioned that the hotel was owned, like everything else of value in Donetsk, by the gangster Rinat Akhmetov, who today remains the most powerful oligarch in Ukraine.

Richard picked up Vika and me at the hotel. He told me he had come to really like Donetsk, the centre of a coal-producing region, saying it reminded him of northern England with its majority of hard-working, predominantly blue-collar workers and a strong regional identity. Most were ethnic Russians who had a strong affinity for Russia and often a nostalgia for the Soviet Union. In Ukraine's first parliamentary elections in 1994, after the Soviet collapse, the region held its own referendum and voted 90 percent for keeping close ties to Russia and elected a majority of communist deputies. At the time, in the late 2000s, these feelings were mostly underground, but they would erupt again in 2014 and contributed, with Putin's Russia fanning the flames, to a brutal break between eastern and western Ukraine.

We stopped off to pick up Tanya at her antique shop and headed to their stunning house in the heart of Donetsk, near a lake in a private community in a section of parkland. Tanya gave me a tour. The place was very large — five bedrooms and six bathrooms, with two balconies overlooking the beautifully groomed properties. It was furnished in the finest antiques, chosen by Tanya herself. Everything was impeccable.

After meeting Richard's family, his sons and his daughter, we went down to his ground-floor office. I had already told Richard about Kasyanov's plan to cash in on my property by using it to raise capital on the Warsaw Stock Exchange, and he had put together a list of everyone in Poland, in the stock exchange and the Luxembourg Equity Trust company that was shepherding the deal, who we should contact to warn that they were dealing with stolen goods.

Richard had a large number of contacts in Poland that he could draw on, and his list included everyone from a former prime minister who was a member of the Warsaw exchange to officials and regulators he'd met in his own business dealings.

So we drafted the warning letters together and we didn't mince words. We made it clear to them that Kasyanov was, in effect, trying to use the Warsaw Stock Exchange to fence stolen goods. We said that in accepting Kasyanov's money, the Warsaw exchange was partnering with organized crime.

We also discussed my case in the Ukrainian courts. I told Richard that the criminal investigation was still proceeding against Fesun, but I couldn't tell if the way it was moving was two steps forward and one step back, or one step forward and two steps back.

Richard said he was not that optimistic about justice in Ukraine. But I had no choice. I was not going to simply walk away from a theft of $28 million. But I was going into the next phase with my eyes wide open.

In the end, the Polish authorities were of no help.[2] We received only a form letter in reply from them. Then the firm hired by KSG to oversee the launch of the IPO told us, in legal language, to fuck off. The only response we

---

2   I later learned that the stock exchange also had a record of screwing Canadian grain companies out of money. A decade earlier, the Saskatchewan Wheat Pool had decided to become a player in the international agricultural business by arranging to take the leading interest in building a CDN$77-million grain terminal in Gdansk to bring Ukrainian grain to the market. They sunk CDN$38 million into the project before it collapsed into a series of bitter lawsuits between the partners, and SaskPool finally walked away with nothing. The 150-metre-long storage building and handling equipment of the EuroPort was left half-completed on the edge of the Baltic Sea. SaskPool's stock price then collapsed on the Toronto exchange to $2.32 a share from a high of $24.20. So looking to Poland to right a Ukrainian wrong was probably a bit optimistic of us.

received from our letter to Kasyanov's KSG, which warned them we would take them to court if they proceeded with the IPO, came from Kasyanov's right-hand man, Sergey Mazin, who replied that after conducting a "rigorous review" of the allegations made in the letter, he saw "no legal grounds" to reverse the "sale."

When the press challenged Kasyanov about the validity of the IPO that contained my stolen properties, he acknowledged having received my letter but said he purchased the majority stake "at market price after conducting due diligence in strict accordance with Ukrainian law." He went on to state that the audit had been done by the major European accounting firm BDO International, based in Luxembourg, so he said everything was in order, although he did not mention that he had quietly put two of the employees of Luxembourg's Equity Trust on his board of directors for the period that the IPO was being launched.

In the end, my property was the gem in Kasyanov's IPO and it netted him US$40 million from the initial public sale of one-third ownership.

◇◆◇

The bank and stock fraud schemes were making for high times for People's Deputies Shepelev and Kasyanov, but witnesses to their crime spree were having mysterious accidents. In the fall of 2011, Hennadiy Piskun, the only Rodovid Bank official who had direct oversight on Shepelev's manoeuvres at the Rodovid, mysteriously fell out of his seventh-floor apartment window while he was said to be fixing his air conditioner on a cold November day. Shortly after this, the head of Rodovid Bank's legal department, Olekshandr Ivakhnenko, "slipped in the bath" and received serious head injuries, which seemed to have the effect of making him forget everything he had seen at the bank when he was interviewed by police.

But there were more challenges ahead. In 2010, Shepelev came into conflict with Yulia Tymoshenko and was ejected from the Fatherland Party. He quickly joined the competing gangster party, the Party of Regions, but failed to get re-elected in 2012 and suddenly found himself in the dangerous position of having lost his parliamentary immunity. So he did what he usually did when he was having trouble in Ukraine — he headed to his other home in Canada to let things cool down while he worked on new schemes.

While Shepelev was in Montreal, I had another Canadian moment when Bohdan Chomiak, the uncle of Chrystia Freeland and the editor of the leading grain investment newsletter, UkrAgroConsult, gave backing to Sergey Kasyanov's KSG Agro stock on the Warsaw Stock Exchange. Chomiak was born in Canada but moved to his parents' country, Ukraine, shortly after the fall of the Soviet Union to work in the grain business. I was troubled by Chomiak's support of Kasyanov's criminal activity, although I later heard he had a change of heart about Kasyanov and saw him for the fraudster that he was. But at the time, I didn't know what to make of Bohdan Chomiak. I met him once and all I remember is that he looked like a college professor and seemed to be interested in getting some sort of contract from me. But I also knew that as the organizer of the annual UkrAgroConsult grain conferences, he had hired my previous lawyer Nikolai Orlov as the in-house legal counsel. This made me more than a little suspicious of him because, at the time, I was convinced that Orlov, too, was working with the thieves.

I had reasons to believe that Orlov was meeting in private with Kryshin without telling me, and when I did some checking, I found out that the fellow who Orlov insisted I put on the board of the reconstituted company, P.A. Oliynyk, had been associated with Viktor Fesun. I went to Orlov and demanded an explanation. He tried to throw me out of his office. I told him I was firing him. I had just made a retainer fee payment of US$36,000 to him and I demanded it be returned to me since he would no longer be representing me. He refused.

So I launched a lawsuit against Orlov to get my $36,000 back, and to do this I needed to hire and pay yet another lawyer. This of course was only a small part of my herculean battle with the Ukraine justice system, which at the time was taking up more and more of my time and money. The morass seemed endless and it seemed that the more I struggled, the deeper I sank.

CHAPTER 15

THE INJUSTICE SYSTEM

*Back and forth in Ukrainian courts and
the spectacular arrest of Kasyanov's
Ukrainian-Canadian partner on
murder and bank fraud charges.*

I t was Oles who best described the Ukrainian justice system to me.

He said the corruption of today was rooted in Soviet times, when the judiciary was directly controlled by the Communist Party. In those days, decisions would be delayed until judges had political direction from party officials.

"Today you have the same delays, but instead of direction from the party, judges wait for the local crime boss to tell them what to do. Or the more independent ones will wait to see who will make them the best financial offer before deciding which side to take."

One of the ways this functioned, Oles said, was that the courts took what he called a "formalistic approach," where all they demanded was that the paperwork was in order for them to proceed. Justice was not, in itself, at issue. It was all in the packaging.

On the face of it, he said, it was obvious to all that your assets were stolen and then the fraudulent paperwork was put together to cover it up.

This fake paperwork itself was central to the fraud. "Everyone can see that the whole thing looks like shit and smells like shit. But if you wrap it up and label it as chocolate, the court will accept it as chocolate — as long as the paperwork says so. Everyone can still smell the shit, but if the paperwork is in order, the court will declare that it is, legally speaking, chocolate."

So with that dispiriting news, I went in search of another lawyer. I ended up hiring Viktor Mokritskiy, a tough-looking 45-year-old who could have passed for a crime boss himself, but who had a reputation for taking on the mafia when they tangled with his clients.

Mokritskiy was not only suing Orlov for me, he took over Orlov's litigation against the front-line thieves, Fesun and Kryshin. When he first looked at the case, he said he was impressed by the heavyweight lawyers that Kryshin and the crooks had lined up against me. Kryshin's legal team was led by Viktor Bogun, who was also head of the Department of Civil Law at Dnipropetrovsk National University. Bogun's reach increased considerably when he was appointed to the board of Ukraine's supreme financial auditing institution, which under the Ukrainian constitution had control over use of funds in the state budget. So parliamentary gangsters like Kryshin, Kasyanov and Shepelev had connections right into the government budget office.

This made it tough for my lawyers to fight back, especially since they were forced to litigate on two fronts — in the commercial as well as criminal courts. Mokritskiy, who was charging me US$21,000 a month, was working with a specialist in commercial crime, Sergey Tarasov, who had degrees in both business and law. Sergey was young but he had the right experience for the case. He had started out working in the government's economic affairs department with a specialty in analyzing bankruptcy cases, then went out on his own as a business and legal consultant in forensic investigations. He was just coming off a successful case for Ernst & Young: there was a US$700-million fraud involving construction contracts that the government said were rife with theft and corruption, but in the end it was shown that it was the state officials themselves who were stealing the money, and the government was forced to reimburse Ernst & Young. So despite Oles's warning, Sergey offered a slim ray of hope that the system could be beaten.

When Mokritskiy contacted him for advice on my case, Sergey was immediately interested because it was "one of the most complex cases" he had ever seen — two businesses stolen and actually liquidated. So it would take some extraordinary legal manoeuvrings to get them back on the court docket. But he told me that it was, in the end, winnable.

In Sergey's analysis, the first thing that had to be done was to follow up on restoring the two bankrupt companies, Unirem-Agro and Unirem-Oil, and proving in court that they had been liquidated under a fraudulent scheme. From there, we could fight the fraud from the position of the legal owners of the companies that had had their assets stripped from them by Fesun and Kryshin.

Mokritskiy was impressed enough that he offered Sergey a job as case manager, even though he had not yet been called to the bar in Ukraine. I was also impressed by the enthusiasm of the young lawyer.

This was the beginning of our one-step-forward moment. Sergey continued pushing both the civil and criminal cases, and for a brief period he seemed to be forcing some reluctant judges that it was indeed shit and not chocolate under Kryshin's and Fesun's gift-wrapping.

Sergey began by compiling a list of all of Fesun's documents — bills of sale and minutes of meetings — that were obvious forgeries. There were minutes from meetings that I reportedly attended and signed off on, even though I could easily prove I was in Kelowna at the time. The most important of these were the minutes from a March 2007 founders meeting, where the company constitution was changed to allow the company director, Viktor Fesun, to sell huge parts of the company without the approval of the board.

Sergey then took all of our documents, including the contracts for the sale of the company, to the Dnipropetrovsk Scientific Institute of Court Expertise to review them and determine if all of the paperwork and signatures were legitimate. After an extensive review through most of 2012, the institute came back with a judgment that the deals made by Fesun and Kryshin were frauds and many of the signatures were forged.

I was in court several times a week during this period, so the process was a costly one. Not only was I paying the lawyers, but my time away from my businesses was also costing me. But Sergey was getting results.

He found an area where the courts themselves had tripped up when they had permitted the farm equipment I imported in 2006 to be sold off by Fesun in 2009. When I had brought them in duty-free in 2006, it was under the condition that they could not be sold for five years. The 2009 sale had therefore been illegal.

Sergey and Mokritskiy seemed to catch the Ukraine injustice system off-guard with this new wrinkle and the Dnipropetrovsk institute findings. When he took them to the commercial court in Kyiv, the court agreed to freeze all of my assets that were controlled by the Warsaw-listed KSG Agro in a judgment that, without accusing Kasyanov, declared that all of the fixed and movable property within Unirem-Agro and Unirem-Oil had been fraudulently taken from me.

Kasyanov's lawyers fought back, but the court confirmed the freezing of my assets in two additional rulings while the bigger case to get them back was being prepared.

There was another quick victory when the court reversed the bankruptcy proceedings for the two companies and disallowed their liquidation. This allowed me to reconstitute them and I held a board meeting with Vika, Richard Spinks and my lawyer Viktor Mokritskiy to reactivate the companies as a first step in getting their stolen assets returned.

In early spring 2013 I met a young guy in the Dnipropetrovsk prosecutor's office, Anton Makashov, who seemed to be taking the case seriously and let us know he was close to having enough evidence to arrest Fesun. This was also encouraging, and with things moving forward we decided to press our advantage by going public. On May 23, 2013, I called a press conference that was carried live on Ukrainian TV and let the government know that I would not stay silent in the face of the thievery. With Mokritskiy and Spinks at my side, I told my story:

> I came to Ukraine in 2000 for the wedding of a friend and invested
> in agricultural businesses called Unirem-Agro and Unirem-Oil in
> Shchorsk, Dnipropetrovsk Oblast. Shchorsk was a dying city, just
> about every store on the main street was closed. I thought if I
> built a grain elevator, which will have all the equipment at a very

modern level, and provide modern technology, it will in some
way contribute to the development of the economy. And when I
invested in Shchorsk, I also built social programs for the employees.

  I told the press about the preschool and dental office I had funded and
underlined the fact that all of the funds in the company were my direct
investments. No one else invested and we did not borrow from any banks,
so at the time the company had no debts to anyone except me.

  I explained that after a year of operation, I noticed some irregularities.
I investigated and found out that the dental office, clinic and bakery were
closed. It was then that I decided to sell the company.

  It was at that point, I told the press, that I discovered the fraud. My
partners had falsified a lot of documents and put my counterfeit signature
on them while I was in Canada. Then I used the services of a law firm and,
after some time, discovered that this firm also received money from the
opposite side, which paid them even more so that the results would not be
in my favour.

  Then I made a direct plea to the Ukrainian president:

> I now hope that Viktor Yanukovych will keep his promise that
> he made at one summit in Europe when he said that he would
> make every effort to protect all foreign investment and foreign
> investors in Ukraine. I am an honest businessman, I have not
> deceived anyone in my life, I have always honestly conducted
> business and in my [employ] there are 250 employees. And most
> of my employees work with me for twenty to twenty-five years. It
> was most unpleasant that in this case my Ukrainian partners were
> involved in the bankruptcy scheme.

  The press conference was followed by a flurry of activity as the business
press immediately focused on the role of Kryshin and Kasyanov in stealing
my assets. But when reporters questioned Kasyanov, he was quoted as saying
the rulings freezing my assets under his control would have a negligible effect
on his farming operations since the frozen assets involve "only a warehouse

and other properties not central to his business." He also denied that he was using our farmland for his own operation. Both statements were lies.

The Ukrainian press also went after Fesun and Kryshin, pointing out that the companies had been sold to Kryshin at the November 2, 2009, meeting of Unirem-Service without the deal having been approved by the Unirem-Agro and Unirem-Oil majority shareholder. Which of course was me.

When the press contacted Kryshin, he strenuously denied involvement in the fraud. He said the companies he once controlled that were connected to the now-frozen assets "were bought and sold legally," adding that he had the documents to prove the legality of transactions. He said he spoke once to me regarding my concerns, after which he said "Derrickson indicated he was satisfied with the outcome" of the exchange, which was nonsense.

Kryshin then added that he would file a countersuit against me should his "clean reputation" be harmed and for any moral damages. He dismissed the accusations against him as "black PR" and threatened to sue the press for libel if the case wasn't "reported on objectively."

I told the reporter I would love to meet Kryshin in court and I was certainly not backing down against Fesun, who had been a key player in the theft. About Fesun I said in the press, "We could've made more money together than [he could] having it stolen. It was greed to the highest degree you can imagine; it's not so much the money I'm after, it's the principle. I'll spend all the money I have [to get my assets back] for as long as I'm alive. I've never cheated anyone in Ukraine."[1]

I was glad to finally have my say in a public forum and to be able to denounce the thieves and the corrupt system. At that point, things did seem to be moving forward. We were getting our message out to the press and we were, against all odds, advancing our case in the courts.

But once again our opponents were busy behind the scene, calling in favours, paying off officials and manoeuvring to get the case back before mafia judges and on-the-take prosecutors.

The first shot in the next battle came in July 2013, when Senior Police Lieutenant M.A. Osyka of the Dnipro Police Department released her

---

1   Mark Rachkevych, "Tangled business dispute involving Canadian in court," *Kyiv Post*, April 19, 2013.

pretrial investigation report. It began by accurately tracing the main elements of the fraud, but then in the middle of it — you could almost see the envelope of money arriving on her desk — she drastically changed course and pointed out that Fesun's paperwork was in order and the shit was, indeed, chocolate.

Osyka echoed Kryshin's and Kasyanov's lawyers by characterizing the whole thing as a misunderstanding between partners, me and Fesun, and she closed the criminal investigation against Fesun because, according to her, no crime had been committed.

This took some mental gymnastics because it was glaringly obvious that I was by far the majority shareholder in a company that had been sold and then liquidated without my approval and without me receiving a single penny in compensation. How could that possibly be anything else than a major fraud?

But Osyka's report was only part of a co-ordinated counterattack. As soon as it was out, Kryshin's lawyers were back in court in front of one of their pay-to-play judges and quickly managed to get the criminal case against Fesun dropped and the commercial law judgment freezing my assets reversed.

And that is how it went. One step forward, two steps back. Whenever we made headway in one case, the decision was reversed by a corrupt judge in another court. This pattern would continue for years.

◊◆◊

While he was battling me in court, Sergey Kasyanov was having legal problems of his own.

On July 4, 2013, Ukrainian news was dominated by the dramatic arrest of Alexander Shepelev in Hungary for criminal activities that Sergey Kasyanov had also been involved in. An arrest warrant for Shepelev for bank fraud and murder had been filed in Ukraine while he was still hiding out in Canada. When Shepelev left Canada, he didn't return to Ukraine but instead set up shop in Budapest and ran his Ukraine operations from there with a fake Hungarian passport using the name Shevchenko.

While he was still in Hungary he had the ownership of his Doncreditinvest Bank, which he had renamed the European Bank for Rational Finance in 2005, quietly transferred to the control of Sergey Kasyanov and his wife, Ksenia, who renamed it the KSG Bank. Shepelev kept 16 percent of the shares for himself and a further 32 percent of the shares in the control of his companies Ukrmegaeco (8.072% of shares), Ecogroup (8.205%), Donelitprom (8.088%) and Regoptpromsbyt (7.991%), all of which today are in the name of Shepelev's Canadian-born son, Michael.

Just as he was leaving Ukraine for Canada in January 2012, Shepelev arranged for the murder of Sergei Dyadechko, the Rodovid Bank vice-president who some said was involved in the original theft of the bank's assets but was also on hand to witness Shepelev's theft of the state assets that had been sent in to refloat the bank. By Ukrainian standards, it was a run-of-the-mill hit. Late in the evening of January 19, 2012, in the Kyiv suburb of Sofievskaya Borschagovka, Sergei Dyadechko's driver slammed on the brakes about a hundred metres from his house because someone had put a row of large boulders on the road. As soon as the car came to a halt, two gunmen sprayed twenty-six bullets into the car from their VZ-58 assault rifles, the Czech version of the AK-47, and sped off. Miraculously, Dyadechko, who had back problems, had his seat reclined when the bullets struck the car. His driver was killed but he escaped unharmed.

In August 2012, when Shepelev was still in Canada, five suspects were arrested, among them Vasily Danyliv, who was closely connected to him from his Donetsk days. Shepelev was suspected of ordering the hit from the very beginning, but he would only be put on the Interpol wanted list in December — after he lost his immunity with his defeat in the parliamentary elections.

The failed hit on Dyadechko was perhaps the biggest mistake in Shepelev's life. Dyadechko was also from Donetsk and was known as the banker and money launderer for President Viktor Yanukovych and his gang. Shepelev also had ties to the political party of Yanukovych's rival, Yulia Tymoshenko, so he was now a marked man in Kyiv power circles.

He compounded his error when, during secret discussions with the Ukrainian prosecutors to try to "fix" his legal problem in Ukraine, Shepelev offered to give them information on the criminal activities of Fatherland Party and Party of Regions officials in exchange for dropping the murder and fraud charges against him. When this information passed through the various connected officials in the prosecutor's office, the order to stomp on Shepelev came down from the political heights.

So on July 4, 2013, Shepelev's forty-third birthday, his party at a hotel in Budapest was stormed by police with an Interpol warrant for his arrest for two murders — of the banker in Donetsk and a policeman in Kyiv — as well as the $30-million Rodovid Bank fraud and the attempted murder of Dyadechko.

Shepelev's immediate response was to ask for refugee status in Hungary, claiming that the Ukraine oligarchs — the same ones that he offered to turn in to the police — were conspiring against him.

I was surprised to see mention of Kasyanov in the press reports of Shepelev's arrest. They reported for the first time that the newly formed KSG Bank was in fact the successor to Shepelev's money-laundering operation at the European Bank for Rational Finance, and Shepelev was still believed to be a part owner. The news that Kasyanov was being openly tied to a criminal like Shepelev gave me at least a faint hope that things were moving in Ukraine. If they arrested Shepelev, maybe Kasyanov was next?

◇◆◇

During this period I was still regularly travelling back to Canada, spending at least half my time there and working on some large-scale commercial real estate developments. When I was in Kyiv I was often putting in eighteen-hour days at my home office, working from 8 a.m. to the late afternoon on Ukraine business and then, as the day was ending there and the office in Canada was just opening, I was in contact throughout the evening on Skype with my CEO Cathy Hellyer in Westbank to keep abreast of daily developments. These Kyiv/Westbank work marathons would generally last until ten or eleven at night Kyiv time, and it felt more like I was living in the office than working from home.

My business in Ukraine was no longer just real estate and fighting to get my Unirem assets back — although that did take a depressingly large chunk of my time. I was also in the process of building a new company, but this time I was careful not to go into business with any Ukrainian nationals as partners.

The new initiative began when I was having dinner in one of the private rooms at Da Vinci's with Richard Spinks and Joseph Valoroso, a friend of mine from Kelowna who had visited me a couple of times in Kyiv and became interested in the business opportunities there. Joseph had a colourful history of his own. A Sicilian kid who had travelled first to Germany in the 1950s and then came to Canada with only a couple of dollars in his pocket, Joseph had managed to launch a logging company in northern B.C. and then finally retire in Kelowna with the money he made when he sold it twenty years later. But when he found it impossible to buy decent Italian sausages and cheeses and pastas in Kelowna, he launched a specialty market called Valoroso Foods, which is where I met him. My mother was a superb chef and she loved to shop at Joseph's market. He was a friendly and good-humoured presence in the store, and we became friends. And in Ukraine, we became business partners in a company that had no Ukrainian partners.

After Landkom, Richard Spinks was also looking for a new business opportunity. His London connections turned up a wood-chip company, Active Energy, that had some investment capital but very little action within it. A Ukrainian operation would be possible because Ukraine forestry licences were up for bidding and there were very few bidders. While we ate and lingered over Da Vinci's excellent coffees, we knocked around a few ideas. The most promising seemed to be to find a company like Active Energy that was already set up and listed on the stock exchange, and buy it up.

We spent a couple of weeks researching the company and the people involved, and everything about it seemed legit. It was listed on the London Stock Exchange and its owners had clean records, but its only problem was that they appeared to be asleep at the switch. We decided that we would put in $500,000 each for a total of $1.5 million, which would give us majority ownership, and try to build a profitable operation in the Ukrainian wood-chip business. It may seem harsh to people who have never done business in Ukraine, but by this time I understood the always-cheater mentality there and a large part of the appeal of this operation was that it did not have Ukrainian partners involved. We would also keep the headquarters of the company safely rooted in London.

After we bought the stock, Richard was the point man and took our proposals to the company shareholders meeting. With our majority interest we voted Richard in as the new CEO, and he went to work securing the forestry licences and material we would need and exploring markets for the material. We found them in Turkey, where there was interest in wood chips for both particle board and biomass, and we expanded our production by 300 percent in the first year. Soon we were looking for equipment upgrades and our own port facility in Yuzhne, a town on the Black Sea fifty kilometres east of Odessa.

The fact that we were able to successfully launch Active Energy in Ukraine helped reassure me that all was not lost in this country. You could do well, although with the sad proviso that you avoided partnering with Ukrainians!

Contributing to my admittedly low opinion of Ukrainian business people at the time were my dealings with the owner of the building where I was living while in Ukraine, which by now was about half the year. The conflict began when I arrived at my apartment, on Darvina Street in Kyiv, and the elevator was not working. The elevator had become a big issue between me and Alexander, the owner of the building. My apartment, which I had purchased, was on two levels, the fifth and sixth floors, and I had invested hundreds of thousands of dollars in renovating it.

When I bought the place, Alexander, who also had an apartment on the fifth floor, agreed to put in an elevator that we could both use, and I agreed to pay a certain amount for its upkeep. But suddenly Alexander added US$14,000 to the amount I was supposed to pay for the use of the elevator. He said I had to pay him then or he would shut off the elevator. I checked with a lawyer and he told me that the elevator had been written into the terms of my purchase and all I needed to pay was the $300 monthly upkeep fee, which I agreed to.

So it became a mini re-enactment of the grain elevator battle — but this time with an apartment elevator.

When I refused to give in to his demand, Alexander sent his own lawyer to strong-arm me into paying. Tempers were raised as the lawyer threatened to shut down the elevator, and I then threatened to literally throw him down the stairs if he didn't get the hell out of my apartment. The lawyer disappeared down the stairs in a flash, two steps at a time.

So Alexander went ahead with the next move in his US$14,000 extortion attempt: shutting down my access to the elevator.

That evening, I walked up the 101 steps — I counted them — to my apartment, cursing Alexander and cursing Ukraine. After that, every morning I walked down the 101 stairs and every evening I walked up the 101 stairs, a feat for a 70-year-old man. It wasn't long before I decided that I had to move to another apartment, but no matter what happened, I was determined not to give in to another Ukrainian extortionist. So I used the apartment only sparingly over the next several years, for employees and visitors, while it sat idle for most of the time. I would not give in.

That was how things were going in late 2013 when Ukraine, as it fairly regularly does, exploded.

CHAPTER 16

A NEW UKRAINE STRUGGLING TO BE BORN

Burning tires in the square, a fleeing president and the beginning of a war.

The rumblings of greater or lesser political turmoil were part of the background noise throughout my years in Ukraine, with people on and off the streets, beginning with the "Ukraine without Kuchma!" demonstrations twenty years ago, and then the mass protests of the Orange Revolution in 2005, which finally went nowhere when the oligarchs and gangsters returned to take back control of the country.

But tensions remained because the popular will for something better carried on. In the fall of 2013 and into early 2014, the underground rumblings finally erupted into a political volcano that shook the country to its very core and filled the night sky in Kyiv with fire. For a time it seemed Ukraine was about to change for good.

The actual flames were coming from burning tires and bonfires on Maidan Nezalezhnosti, the central square in the city, a fifteen-minute walk along Khreshchatyk Avenue from where I was living.

The spark had been a deal with the European Union that President Yanukovych refused to sign at the last minute — apparently thinking he could get better terms with the Russians. Ukrainians feared that Yanukovych was about to lock them into a common market with Russia that would tie them in perpetuity to a new version of the Russian empire, which Ukrainian nationalists had struggled to escape for hundreds of years.

On November 25, 2013, more than 100,000 people gathered in the Maidan. They carried Ukrainian and EU flags and chanted "Ukraine is Europe." The government reacted by firing hundreds of canisters of tear gas to disperse the crowd. I remember even as far away as Bessarabska Square my eyes were stinging when I went out to the late-night market to buy groceries.

When the protesters returned the following week, the government upped the ante. The police mercilessly beat hundreds of protesters and arrested hundreds more. From that point on, the battle for most people in Kyiv became as much a fight against a corrupt, brutal government as it was about a trade deal. At the same time, hundreds and even thousands of nationalists from Lviv — people who were determined to push the pro-Russian government from Donetsk out of power for good — began to flock to Kyiv. Lviv had long been the centre of the armed nationalist struggle against the Soviets — in fact many of their heroes fought in the Nazi Galician SS Division during the Second World War — and their presence in Kyiv gave the movement a measure of organization and leadership.

I was returning to Canada for Christmas on December 8, 2013, and Volodya, himself an ardent nationalist, was quite happy with all of these developments. He took me through a long detour to avoid the massive, 500,000-person anti-government demonstration that was pouring into the downtown area. When I was in the airport waiting room, I noticed the headlines in the *Kyiv Post* about an assault on the square the previous evening. The right-wing Svoboda Party had torn down the statue of Lenin and smashed it to bits with sledgehammers to shouts of "Revolution!" When my plane took off toward the West, I wasn't sure what I would find in Ukraine on my return.

By December 2013, it seemed that everyone was involved. The Americans, as well as the Europeans and of course the Russians, were all in a tug-of-war for the heart and soul of Ukraine.

When I arrived back in Kyiv at the beginning of February, the centre of Kyiv was a hellscape. The Maidan was filled with thousands of protesters camped out, and the air was thick with smoke from tire fires. The city seemed to be on the brink of revolution. Two protesters had been killed, and demonstrators were no longer holding protest signs but throwing Molotov cocktails and, in some cases, shooting back at the police. A number of the Lviv leaders, identified as the Parasiuk Group led by Zinoviy Parasiuk and his son Volodymyr, were quietly bringing higher-grade weapons into the square to use as self-defence if the government launched a deadly offensive against them.

There is still a dispute about who started shooting — for seven years, successive governments in Ukraine have been unable to hold an inquiry into the events — but in the end, as many as a hundred protesters were dead, along with about a dozen police officers. The brutality of the government response shocked the country and the world. There was a hurried backroom deal brokered by the EU to form a national unity government in Ukraine that shared power with the opposition parties, to be followed by early presidential elections. The deal apparently had the blessing of the Russians and it seemed that, at long last, the Ukraine crisis was over, and the hated president was being eased out of power.

But things would not be so simple. That night the deal was denounced by key people in the Maidan, and the leader of an armed group of Maidan fighters, Volodymyr Parasiuk, who I would later meet and who would briefly work for me, warned that if Yanukovych was not out of the country by dawn, Parasiuk and his armed nationalist group would launch an assault on the presidential palace. No one, especially Yanukovych, doubted his sincerity and the president disappeared into the night, eventually turning up in a Russian provincial capital near the Ukrainian boarder.

But even with this development, the turmoil was far from over. In fact, it was only beginning.

◇◆◇

In Donetsk, the reaction to the revolution couldn't have been more different than in Kyiv. Donetsk was largely ethnically Russian and the hometown of the deposed president, Viktor Yanukovych, who had been democratically elected less than four years earlier. The worst fears of the people of eastern Ukraine were confirmed on the day after Yanukovych fled the country: on February 23, 2014, the first legislative act of the new government was the abolition of the Kivalov-Kolesnichenko law of 2012, which made Russian, the language of the overwhelming majority in the east of the country, an official language alongside Ukrainian.

The language issue was part of the long-standing split in Ukraine that went back for centuries of being ruled by different empires. The division had clearly shown up twenty years previously, during the country's first post-independence parliamentary elections in 1994, when the people of Donetsk not only voted for the Communists, they voted 90 percent in favour of a formal association with Russia in a referendum. They also voted for protection of the Russian language in the newly independent Ukraine, while the people of western Ukraine elected a slate of ardent Ukrainian nationalists devoted to a complete break with Russia and all things Russian.

After the fall of Yanukovych in Kyiv, it was pro-Russian protesters in the eastern part of the country who were taking over government buildings and police stations, in open defiance of the Ukrainian nationalist-led revolution in the rest of the country.

In Crimea, the Russians wasted no time in profiting from the turmoil. Ethnic Russians were a majority there as well and had voted to secede from Ukraine and join Russia in the first parliamentary election in 1994. In fact Crimea was part of Russia from 1783 until 1954, when the territory became part of the Ukrainian Soviet Socialist Republic, so the seeds of secession were well developed there.

On February 23, 2014, pro-Russian demonstrations were held in the Crimean city of Sevastopol, where the Russian navy still had its Black Sea fleet, and the next day balaclava-wearing Russian servicemen occupied the city. On March 16, the Russians held a hurried referendum, declared Crimea's independence from Ukraine and then reincorporated it into the Russian Federation.

In Donetsk, Richard Spinks found himself, unwillingly, with a front-row seat of the turmoil. His first intuition that something was up came a couple of weeks before the final explosion of violence on the Maidan that swept away the old regime. He was getting a ride to the airport in a high-end Mercedes with a Ukrainian friend, one of the most successful businessmen in Donetsk. When they were stopped in front of the departures door, his friend helped him with his luggage. When he handed Richard his bag, he said he thought there was going to be a big blowout between Ukraine and Russia in Donbas (eastern Ukraine). Then he asked Richard what he thought. Should he go with Ukraine or go with Russia?

Richard was surprised by the question. At the time, the events in Kyiv seemed far away and he was not expecting any sort of Russia-Ukraine battle. But when the question was put to him he said, of course his friend should side with Ukraine. It was his country. You had to stand by your country.

"But Russia is richer and more powerful," his friend said.

Richard had no answer to that, other than to say that when your country is in trouble, you should stand by it. But the whole thing sounded very hypothetical at that point and he was in a hurry to catch his plane.

Very soon after that, Richard saw how decisively the tide in Donetsk had turned against the new regime when he heard there was a massive fight in the centre of the city. Back from his trip, he went down to Lenin Square with some friends and saw a running battle between a few hundred pro-Maidan Ukrainian nationalists and thousands of locals, who had the nationalists surrounded and were beating them and ripping the Ukrainian flags from their hands. The police, who were tasked with protecting the pro-Maidan group, were doing nothing. If a policeman did try to defend the Ukrainian nationalists, he, too, was beaten and his fellow officers abandoned him to the crowd. For ethnic Russians in Donetsk, what was called the Revolution of Dignity in Kyiv was seen more as a right-wing nationalist coup than a revolution, and this was the message that the Russian government would repeat to justify their own military incursion into the country.

After the street battles were over, the anti-Maidan forces were in control and Richard learned that he, like all Western businessmen, was on an enemy-of-the-people list. He, Tanya and their children fled to a country property they still owned in Lviv Oblast in the west of Ukraine, leaving their US$6-million Donetsk home and even their cars in the garage. When the war started, he said, Russian officers moved into his house. Tanya was from Donetsk and had enough connections to get the cars back, but the rest he lost.

In Kyiv, these skirmishes in Donetsk seemed remote at first. In the capital it was once again a time of wild hope that Ukraine would rid itself of the corrupt rulers of the past and set itself on a shining path to Europe.

But when the dust cleared, the guy who took the presidency in a rushed election, with large-scale support from the United States, Canada and Europe, was not one of the young idealists on the Maidan. It was billionaire Petro Poroshenko of the Roshen chocolate empire, who, like all of the corrupt oligarchs in the past, had a habit of following power. He had originally been part of the founding group of Yanukovych's Party of Regions, and had quit as Yanukovych's trade and economy minister only a few months before the uprising began. This gave him just enough distance from the previous regime to win the support of EU, American and Canadian backers of the revolution, and they had a definitive voice in a country that now was desperate for Western aid.

As we have seen, for Canada, Ukraine had been a high priority since its declaration of independence in 1991. In the years following independence, virtually every Canadian foreign affairs minister made the trip to Kyiv for a photo op and to dispense advice and cash. In 1999, Prime Minister Jean Chrétien visited the country promising important Canadian investment, but adding that it would only come to pass if Ukraine cleaned up its corruption rackets. This was a wise proviso on Chrétien's part — to put anti-corruption conditions on future economic deals with Ukraine — but it would unfortunately be ignored by all future Canadian governments, and as a result Canada, along with the rest of the Western world, would become prime enablers of the Ukrainian mafia.

This was immediately apparent under Prime Minister Stephen Harper. With his political base in Western Canada, where Ukrainian-Canadian voters were numerous, Harper lavished attention on Ukraine, and all of his foreign affairs ministers visited the country. After the pro-Western Revolution of Dignity, Ukraine was elevated to a full-fledged Canadian government obsession. In 2014 alone, Stephen Harper made three trips to Ukraine and proclaimed Canada the most Ukrainian country in the world after Ukraine. He then invited newly elected President Petro Poroshenko to Ottawa to address Canada's parliament, and Poroshenko proclaimed Ukraine the most Canadian country in the world after Canada. In fact, both proclamations were true in ways that didn't flatter either country, but the floodgates of Canadian financial, political and military aid were opened.

While Canada was warmly embracing the new Ukraine, the Ukrainian oligarchs and gangsters were also lining up with the new government — as they had done after the Orange Revolution ten years earlier. After fence-sitting through the early stages of the Revolution of Dignity, the Dnipropetrovsk mafia led by Igor Kolomoisky announced its support for the new government. Kolomoisky even made a deal with Poroshenko to have himself named as head of the Dnipropetrovsk Regional Administration, a job he took on with gusto, putting together gangs of street fighters to knock the heads of the separatists in the region. Kolomoisky even funded the first volunteer battalions under the command of a local criminal, Yuri Bereza, that set off to fight the Russian-backed separatists in Donetsk and Luhansk. Bereza, whose bio would include accusations of rape, torture and murder, as well as general gangsterism, would also soon be working with Sergey Kasyanov on violent raider schemes. With a bio like that he was a natural for Ukraine's parliament and was elected to the Rada as a People's Deputy in the fall of 2014.

The only oligarch who was momentarily out of step was the Donetsk-based Rinat Akhmetov. He had been the main bankroller of Yanukovych's Party of Regions and initially made a calculation to go with the anti-Maidan groups in Donetsk. As the resistance to the new government in Kyiv stiffened, Akhmetov was paying the salaries of the separatist fighters — until they began to seize and "nationalize" his own holdings. Then he retreated to Kyiv and proclaimed himself ready to do everything possible to protect the Ukraine homeland against the Russian-backed separatist threat. So in the end, all of the oligarchs were backing Poroshenko and they were reintegrated into the political and economic map of Ukraine, just as they had been with Yanukovych, Yushchenko and Kuchma.

◇◆◇

As I watched these historic events unfold, I was 100 percent behind the revolution. I believed that Ukraine needed to free itself from Russian dominance and had high hopes that this would at last allow Ukraine to address the corruption that had infested the country for so long. With the new regime, I even had renewed hope that finally I, too, might get justice.

I had my first concern about the seriousness of the revolution when in the parliamentary elections that fall, the man who engineered the theft of my properties with Viktor Fesun, Oleg Kryshin, was once again elected to the Rada as part of the new regime.

People's Deputy Kryshin, like all of the national and local oligarchs in Ukraine, including the guy who had my properties, former People's Deputy and Dnipropetrovsk governor Sergey Kasyanov, moved with the times. And at the ground level, the election was not much different from previous Ukrainian elections.

As in the past, voters were showered not only with promises but also with various degrees of vote-buying. Gifts from candidates to voters that traditionally included sacks of buckwheat had evolved into bottles of champagne, frozen chicken and giant cakes. As in the past, many candidates put together small food parcels with things like sunflower oil, condensed milk, a kilo of pasta and tea with sweets to buy the votes of impoverished pensioners. One enterprising candidate even gave his older constituents portable blood-pressure monitors.

Daryna Rogachuk, a Ukrainian journalist who put together a "Political Trash" exhibition of vote-buying in Kyiv, says this "buckwheat sowing" has deformed Ukrainian society, and it continued after the revolution. "People still refused to learn about political programs and analyze them. Politicians sell voters goods or entertainment, not their ideas or solutions," she said.

In one of her favourite examples, a candidate installed playground equipment for kids in his district during the election campaign. But when he lost the election, the playground equipment disappeared the next day.

While Ukraine was sorting itself out after the Maidan revolution, my struggle to get my property back was temporarily on hold because of the general turmoil and the escalating civil war with the now openly Russian-backed separatists in the border regions. So while I waited for the dust to settle, I devoted my business time to my new venture with Richard Spinks.

Active Energy was surviving the political chaos — the company actually expanded its wood-chip business with new markets in Turkey. A law forbidding the export of unprocessed lumber from Ukraine put some of our competitors out of business but allowed us to continue with our processed exports. In fact, our main challenge during this time was simply scaling up production to meet the demand. If we had had the capacity, we could have easily sold 400,000 tons a year. As it stood, we increased our revenues from a few million in 2013 to US$17.4 million in 2014. And working with Richard and Joseph, I didn't have to worry about thievery and deception.

But in Ukraine, my highest priority remained getting my property back, which I hoped would come with the country embarking on a path to reform. The political upheaval had temporarily paralyzed the courts, along with everything else, but this was a time when many people I spoke with in Ukraine sincerely believed that a new era was dawning, and that Ukraine would soon have a basic justice system for the modern era. I wasn't so sure about this, but I was not immune to hope. And I very much wanted it to be true.

CHAPTER 17

PLUS ÇA CHANGE

*Fesun behind bars. The Ukrainian court
and the press declare victory in my case.
The gangsters regather their forces.*

One area where the changes after the Maidan revolution were clear in Ukraine was name changes — the packaging, in a sense — as the new government moved to change the language of place names from Russian to Ukrainian, and to replace names left over from Soviet times with new Ukrainian ones.

In the first recognition of the country's change in orientation, English-language newspapers changed their spelling of the capital from the Russian-language "Kiev" to the Ukrainian "Kyiv."

Within Kyiv, streets and squares began to slowly change their names from those of obscure figures from Russian imperial or Soviet times into what were, for the most part, obscure figures from Ukrainian history or mythology. These changes often came with controversy — for example, the country's Jewish committee reacted with alarm as figures from Ukraine's past who were allied with the Nazis, some of whom even served in the Ukrainian SS division or other nationalist groups accused of participating in the Holocaust, suddenly had streets named after them or plaques installed in their honour.

This name-changing game was very much in play in the Dnipropetrovsk region, where there was a long tradition of changing city names to fit in with the new power in Moscow or Kyiv. For example, the city of Dnipropetrovsk. In czarist times, the city was known as Ekaterinoslav, after Catherine the Great, who ruled over the Russian empire from 1762 until 1796. In 1926, the name was changed to Dnipropetrovsk, after G. Petrovsky, the head of the Ukrainian Communist Party, who grew up in the city. In 2016, the new regime in Kyiv chopped the "petrovsk" from the name to leave a dangling Dnipro as the official name.[1]

Dniprodzerzhynsk followed a similar trajectory. The original Russian-language name, Kamenskoye, had been changed during Soviet times to Dniprodzerzhynsk, after Felix Dzerzhynsky, the founder of the Bolshevik secret police. Felix Dzerzhynsky was one of the leading forces of "decossackization," which led to the civil war in Ukraine in the early twentieth century. But in the Soviet Union, Dzerzhynsky was considered a patriot and one of the stalwarts of the revolution, so the city was named after him in 1936. With the new regime in Kyiv after the Maidan revolution, Dniprodzerzhynsk became Kamianske, which is the Ukrainian-language version of the original Russian name Kamenskoye.

Even Shchorsk, where my grain facilities were located, was changed back to its original name of Bozhedarivka. Meaning "God's gift" in Ukrainian, the name was chosen in 1861 when a train pulled into the station with the news that serfs in the entire Russian empire were now free men and women.[2] It was renamed Shchorsk by the Soviets only in 1956, after Nikolai Shchors, a Red Army commander during the revolutionary war who died in battle in 1919 near Volyn and had nothing to do with the town or the region.

For most of 2014 and well into 2015, few other significant changes were made. The country was consumed by the war with the Russian-backed

---

1   This only holds for the city name, however. The oblast is still called Dnipropetrovsk because it is so named in the constitution and would require a constitutional amendment to change.

2   The catch with the freeing of the serfs was that the now-former serfs had to purchase tiny plots of the least productive lands to live off at what turned out to be almost 35 percent more than the market price. So the land was definitely not a gift. But now a tiny piece of it was theirs.

separatists in Donbas. After a few initial successes, Ukraine's poorly equipped and trained military suffered a number of major defeats at the hands of the Russian tank infantry. Finally in early 2015, the Poroshenko government had to accept the freezing of the conflict with the Franco-German brokered Minsk Agreement, which called for the pullback of all weapons from the front and European-monitored elections in Donetsk and Luhansk, the two breakaway republics, which would be given a kind of provincial status within the country.

◊◆◊

For me, the confirmation that it was business as usual in post-Maidan Ukraine, as far as corruption was concerned, came in November 2014, when press reports described a brutal raider scheme in Chumaki, a farming village south of Dnipro. A group of armed men from Yuri Bereza's volunteer battalion, which was supposed to be fighting Russians at the front, was hired by Sergey Kasyanov for an armed assault on a local farm in a brazen takeover.[3]

The press openly compared Kasyanov's raid on Chumaki to what he had done to my Shchorsk operation.

"In 2011," a popular Ukrainian investigative journalist wrote, "the KSG Agro holding swallowed the Unirem-Agro subsidiary of the Canadian business man Ronald Michael Derrickson. As in the case of Chumaki, the Unirem-Agro company unexpectedly changed the director and the founder [from] the lawful owners. Further, the criminals, blocking the work of the enterprise, 'transferred' the entire land of the company to another legal entity with a similar name (Chomaki Agricultural was changed to Chomaki Agricultural Production Company), which was subsequently transferred to KSG Agro. As we can see, this [strategy] is Kasyanov's 'corporate signature.'"

As one press report put it, "The raider seizure of Chumaki in the Dnipropetrovsk region took place according to a typical 'branded Ukrainian' scheme: at first, scammers, with the help of purchased officials, replaced documents about the meeting of shareholders and appointed their director, then

---

3   "Chumaki agricultural company was represented by Kasyanov, Ation and Koshlyak" (Агрофирму Чумаки сообразили на троих Касьянов, Астион и Кошляк). Skelet Info. June 22, 2015, https://skelet .info/agrofirmu-chumaki-soobrazili-na-troix-kasyanov-astion-i-koshlyak/.

carried out a forceful seizure of the office and production facilities of the agricultural company.

"According to a new tradition, the capture was carried out by forces of an unknown paramilitary formation without decals. The faces of the invaders were covered with balaclavas, and in the hands [they had] machine guns."

What was different this time, and even more pernicious, was that the raid was not done to put the operation under new management, it was to sink a competitor and put the 5,500 hectares in the KSG Agro land bank. The report said that when the raiders arrived, they first "engaged in looting — they removed valuable property and unique equipment from the shops of the enterprise. On the same day, residents of nearby villages heard explosions — bandits with grenades destroyed what could not be removed."

For local farmers and agricultural workers, it was a disaster. They were thrown off their land and left with nothing. Eventually, Kasyanov would find another use for the land as part of a new bank loan scheme that would net him another US$40 million.

What was more ominous now was that Kasyanov was working with People's Deputy Bereza, who was using his Kolomoisky-funded brigade as a mercenary force at the service of the Dnipropetrovsk mafia.

Reports that Bereza's nationalist army was now working as a criminal gang for the oligarchs were confirmed a few months later when Bereza led his battalion in a takeover of the government-owned Ukrnafta oil company, in which Kolomoisky was a minority shareholder. In retaliation, Poroshenko removed Kolomoisky as governor of Dnipropetrovsk, but the pattern was set. Bereza was the preferred hired gun for Dnipropetrovsk gangsters.

So the new Ukraine was, unfortunately, a lot like the old one. Perhaps the most telling statistic on the continuing and even accelerating pace of corruption after the Revolution of Dignity came from the area I was most familiar with and that Kasyanov was most involved in: corporate raiding. The number of these corporate thefts did not fall after the revolution, it dramatically increased — from 279 in 2014, when the revolution took place, to 724 in 2017. Ukrainian businesses found these attacks almost impossible to guard against, with the fraudsters protected by the country's political and legal institutions.

By 2018 the Ukrainian Agrarian Council, a farmers' advocacy group, did a study of five hundred mid-sized agricultural firms around the country and asked them about raiding. More than 70 percent said they were worried about gangsters moving in, re-registering their business to another entity and seizing their farmlands with the help of crooked bureaucrats, courts and law enforcement officials.

"What's more," said Viktoria Kipriyanova, a lawyer for the UAC, "today the raiders act brazenly and openly, since they're confident in their impunity."

According to the UAC, this type of raiding was a direct descendant of the shoot-'em-up gangsterism of the 1990s, and often still contained those elements. But the modern tools also included bribery, blackmail and fraud to establish control over an enterprise and force it into bankruptcy as a way of transferring assets.[4]

All of this was made "legal" by the thoroughly corrupt legal system. Something that I was living through every day with a front-row seat at the Commercial Court on Bogdan Khmelnitsky Street in Kyiv. The building was of the common Kyiv style — yellow stucco decorated with white-painted imitation dorics and arches over the windows. Inside, I felt as though I was in a primary school from the 1920s: polished cement floors, narrow hallways and a series of small, cramped rooms that served as courtrooms. In the hallways, wooden benches were filled with litigants and their lawyers, and the halls were jammed with the overflow, making it hard to pass through and difficult to talk because of the din.

I hate to think of how many hours I spent there with my lawyer and with someone from my office to translate. What I found was a system that seemed to be run without rules by judges who interrupted and often mocked lawyers and plaintiffs, cutting them off or refusing to hear from witnesses. Then the judge would allow the lawyer for the favoured side to read the case file and endlessly drone on while the court secretaries played with their phones or, occasionally, even chatted with family or friends in a low voice while the proceedings were going on.

---

4   For a more detailed profile of current raiding in Ukraine, see Appendix III.

Receiving the Golden Key to Dnipropetrovsk from Governor Yekhanurov at the grand opening of Unirem-Agro, September 7, 2007.

Unirem-Agro was the best equipped and the most advanced grain operation in Ukraine.

Shaking hands with the three scorpions — Viktor and Anna Fesun and Yuriy Yekhanurov, Dnipropetrovsk governor and former prime minister of Ukraine.

Lyuba Chernysh, the crooked bookkeeper (standing) with my honest bookkeeper Yulia and people from my Canadian office (sitting).

My Ukrainian office manager, lawyer and friend, Vika Balenko.

My friend and business partner Richard Spinks and his lovely wife, Tanya.

Early days in Ukraine with my interpreter, Lena Konolova.

Lunch stop with Yulia and Volodya at the Two Sisters Café on the road to Bozhedarivka during my final visit to Unirem-Agro.

My apartment in Kyiv across from Lvivs'ka Square.

Taras Dumych, Ukrainian lawyer and corruption fighter.

Anton Makashov, the honest cop in Dnipro.

Because I didn't know the language I would focus on the judge. There were as many women judges as men, and neither tried to hide their feelings. They would react through facial expressions — rolling their eyes, smirking or grimacing — always making it perfectly clear how they were going to decide the case.

The cases were as dull as commercial cases almost always are. The lawyers took turns making speeches that featured versions of the circular arguments lawyers use everywhere, but without any conviction. In the end, the judges generally just adopted the argument of the side that was paying them and then repeated their arguments, word for word, to the court as their judgment.

I wasn't seeing any changes in the Ukrainian justice system after the Maidan revolution, but I told myself I had to give it time. And I did. But month after month passed and the hoped-for changes did not come. And I kept returning to court. In the end, my case would amass over one thousand court appearances and 350 delays as I followed the process to the end.

The legal cha-cha-cha continued. I would move two steps forward and one step back. Then one step forward and two steps back while I listened to the thieves perfecting their story.

In written testimony, Aleksei Gershun would inform the court that after the March 2009 meeting, where Viktor Fesun and Lyuba Chernysh had run out before Richard Spinks arrived, he returned to Dnipropetrovsk to meet with them. They then decided that since Mr. Derrickson was so upset and wanted out of the company, they would take it upon themselves to find a new owner for my share. Gershun said he searched for a buyer and the only company he found that was interested was Interlineprom, a company that subsequent documents showed was actually set up by Fesun and taken over by Oleg Kryshin.

Gershun said that since there were no more buyers for the elevator — conveniently omitting the fact that he was in the room when Richard Spinks arrived with his US$28 million offer — they decided to sell the property to LLC Interlineprom, which made an offer of UAH 18 million, or about US$2.4 million. He claimed that amount was the book value of the elevator, rather than the actual $28 million that Spinks had submitted in his written offer, which Gershun had been given a copy of. Nevertheless, the sale to LLC

Interlineprom was then carried out at a notary office on Chelyuskina Street in Dnipropetrovsk. During the sale agreement, Kryshin's lawyers would assert triumphantly, the notary verified Fesun's authority to sell the property.

In the true spirit of chutzpah, Kryshin's lawyers would then accuse me of an attempted raid, of using the law to try to take property from the Unirem-Service company, which was legally acquired, its acquisition registered by the Bozhedarivka (formerly Shchorsk) Council and confirmed by several previous court decisions.

The judges, who nodded their approval to Kryshin's lawyers as they went through this ridiculous deception, would invariably find that there was no evidence that Fesun had done anything to abuse his office or commit any other unlawful act.

So that was it — the shit had been wrapped, the notary put ribbons and bows on it, and the Ukrainian courts certified it as chocolate.

So we would go back again and again to challenge the obvious problems with the thieves' version of events, pointing out that according to Ukrainian law, more than 50 percent of the company's assets could not be sold without a vote by the board, that the sale had been done with forged documents and in the end I had lost all of my money.

In fact, in the case of the equipment on the site, it was already illegal to sell it because of the import tax exemption that prohibited its resale for at least five years. So we would work to get the file opened again and new criminal charges would be brought against Fesun. As soon as this file was opened, one of our opponents' hand-picked judges would review it and drop the charges. When another investigator opened it again — often after our intervention in another court — another investigator would close it.[5] After every cycle was complete, we found ourselves back where we started.

---

5   April 1, 2013: Criminal proceedings against Fesun were re-initiated for his role in the theft. September 23, 2014: The pretrial investigation confirmed that "Fesun V.V. Acting Director of Unirem-Agro LLC and Unirem-Oil LLC, abusing his official position, seized the property of these companies." December 29, 2014: Then out of nowhere, the Dnipropetrovsk arbitration manager, L.G. Talan, who had actually worked on the bankrupting of my companies and was known locally for his close ties to both Igor Kolomoisky and the local judiciary, recommended the closing of the criminal proceedings. December 30, 2014: the prosecutor of the Department of Procedural Management of Pretrial Investigation issued a decision to close the criminal proceedings. February 12, 2015: The investigating judge of the Babushkinsky district court of Dnipropetrovsk cancelled the decision on the closure of criminal proceedings.

I had some insight into what was going on behind the scenes with the police from the investigator in Dnipropetrovsk, Anton Makashov, who came to Kyiv to speak to me. He was young, in his late twenties, but had one of those youthful faces that could have passed for ten years younger. He was also well educated, with degrees in law and economics, so he was assigned to the commercial cases in Dnipropetrovsk. Apparently he came from a line of policemen; his father had been a cop in Soviet times.

When Makashov was working at the Department of Combatting Economic Crime in the Dnipropetrovsk region, he received the file from my lawyer charging Fesun and others with stealing my property. He saw that the case had already been opened and closed a few times, most recently by the investigator in Krinichansky district, where Bozhedarivka (Shchorsk) was located. In Ukraine this usually meant that a powerful person wanted to keep things hidden, so they bribed or threatened the local officials to bury the case. As he sifted through the paperwork, Makashov confirmed that a crime had obviously been committed and someone was trying to cover it up. He put together a report to that effect for the head prosecutor in Dnipropetrovsk, and his boss said okay, take it on and see where it leads.

Then things got murky, as the case disappeared into the swamp of Ukrainian police corruption.

It began with Makashov as the prosecution analyst working with Viktoria, a police investigator, and her assistant Elena. Viktoria and Elena (these were the only names I knew them by) quickly confirmed Makashov's evidence that the theft's trail led directly from Fesun to Kryshin, then discovered that every one of the managers of the phony pop-up companies that participated in the fraud had worked for Kryshin in the recent past, or were still working for him.

Makashov told me that while the evidence strongly identified Kryshin at the centre of the theft, he would focus on Fesun to bring him in and put maximum pressure on him so he would offer up Kryshin as the brains behind the fraud.

But just as things were moving forward, the two women investigators who had responsibility for the case were transferred to Kyiv, and the lead investigator, Viktoria, was given a promotion. I was at first encouraged when I heard about this, thinking that perhaps my case was getting a higher profile in the Ukrainian justice department. But I was not taking into account the deformities of the system. The promotion and transfer of Viktoria might mean they were going to fast-track my case in the anti-corruption drive — or, more likely, it meant that Viktoria had been bought off with a promotion by the powers-that-be in Kyiv, and her job was to slowly strangle the case against People's Deputy Kryshin and bury it so deep in the Kyiv bureaucracy that it would never again see the light of day.

The whole thing became even more confusing when Viktoria and Elena visited my lawyers. They said they had been working hard on the investigation but were being foiled at every turn by an operative in the Dnipropetrovsk office named Anton Makashov, who they believed was on the take from the Dnipro mafia. But they reassured my lawyers that they were onto him and were in the process of isolating him and having him thrown out of the department.

Viktoria and Elena then came to interview me personally. They seemed competent enough. They were forthright and asked the right questions, and told me they were tired of the corruption in Dnipro and were determined to see that I received justice. Then they walked off with many of the remaining documents I had on the case.

Everything went silent for a few months. Then I heard from Anton. He said Viktoria was suspected of corruption, and when confronted by these suspicions had quietly left the force. I heard later from my lawyers that she had long since stopped investigating my case and had, in fact, transferred all my files to a police department that was in the midst of being dismantled.

It was then that Anton returned to interview me in Kyiv. When he described the situation in Dnipro, he did not sugar-coat it. He said I had been dealing with people with a different mentality. A lot of rich people built the bulk of their business on the criminality of the region, he said, but he was determined to change that.

"The honest people and the honest businessmen in Ukraine will not accept this forever," he said, "because it is destroying the country. If Ukrainians keep allowing investors to be robbed like this, there will soon not be any investors at all."

Then he made a promise: "I will not stop until I get your money back," he told me. "And I will make sure Fesun answers for his crime."

Anton told me he was working on a plan to arrest Fesun on the evidence he had for criminal conspiracy.

That was the last I heard from Anton for a couple of months. Then he called and said he would like to meet me again in Kyiv to fill me in on the latest developments. When he arrived, he was his usual amiable self. He had tracked down Gershun at his home in Connecticut, where he was living with his wife, Lori, and two children. The house was not far from the Prestone lab in Danbury, where he was still working as a senior technical fellow. Makashov said he could not convince him to come to Dnipropetrovsk for an interview, but Gershun agreed to speak to him on Skype.

Gershun, especially at such a safe distance, was not easy to pin down. He still held that the whole issue was an unfortunate falling-out among partners, he had great sympathy for Ron Derrickson and thought Viktor Fesun had acted immorally, but as he understood it, everything was done on a completely legal basis. Regarding Oleg Kryshin, he said he knew nothing. His understanding was that Kryshin had acquired the companies through some kind of bankruptcy proceeding, and Gershun imagined that it had all been decided through the court.

Makashov saw that Gershun had learned the official set of stories that the theft had been carried out under, and he understood he would not be able to move him off this ridiculous story — which was contradicted by all of the facts of the investigation — on a Skype call from Connecticut. Gershun felt too safe there. But Makashov knew that Gershun returned to Dnipropetrovsk on a regular basis to visit his parents, and he made a note to try bringing him in for a more pointed, and less polite, discussion of the case when Gershun was back in the city.

Makashov then had the police bring in Fesun for questioning. He knew all about Fesun by this time, including that he had an engineering degree and, like all young Soviet men, had done his military service, and he had seen file photos of Fesun's round, beefy face. But he was surprised at how much of a simple crook — someone of limited intelligence who was always on the lookout for easy money — Fesun seemed, compared to the cosmopolitan Gershun.

He said he did not give Fesun an easy ride. As the son of a Soviet police colonel, the usually amiable Anton knew how to bring the storm clouds down on a reluctant witness. With Fesun sitting nervously only a metre across from him, he began to lay out the case against him in a harsh prosecutorial tone: the forgeries, the embezzlements and the final teaming up with Kryshin to steal the companies from the Canadian businessman and sell them off to Kasyanov.

According to Makashov, Fesun was literally squirming in his seat while the evidence against him was listed. When Makashov began to pepper him with questions, Fesun sputtered and froze before trying to deny the undeniable, or claimed he couldn't remember. It was a very bad performance by a guilty man desperately trying to bluff his way out of an interview.

Makashov said he didn't arrest Fesun at that moment, because he wanted to make sure the case against him was so ironclad that even a crooked judge would have trouble freeing him. But in the meantime he was keeping tabs on Fesun. He always knew where to find him.

◇◆◇

This more or less positive news on the criminal case was matched by positive developments in the commercial court. My young lawyer Sergey Tarasov had an important victory when the economic court decided, in its own words, to "completely satisfy" my claim.

In essence, Judge Spichak of the Commercial Court of Kyiv found that Fesun's actions since December 7, 2006, had been invalid, since they were backed by fraudulent and forged documents. The judge also pointed to the forgery of my signature that was found in the phony meeting minutes of March 18, 2008, where I was supposed to have approved awarding Fesun almost unlimited powers to sign deals for the company. As a result, the court put a freeze on the elevator complex to forbid the current owners from selling it while the final ownership was being assessed in the economic court.

Then, in a surprising move, the court issued an arrest warrant for Fesun and the police were sent out to his modest house at 68B Sanatorna Street, a muddy lane in Kamianske's Zavods'kyi district, to bring him to jail in Dnipro. Anton Makashov was moving in.

It seemed that at last everything was falling into place. Fesun was behind bars, and my lawyer Sergey Tarasov assured me we were within one step of getting all of my property back after seven years of fighting. Finally, I told myself, we were seeing the results of the new Ukraine.

These sudden advances in my case were even noted in the Ukrainian press as a source of hope that things were improving. The *Kyiv Post* showed its confidence in this article:

> Ronald Derrickson, a Canadian citizen and honorary Indian grand
> chief, is on the verge of restoring his ownership rights in a farming
> enterprise in Dnipropetrovsk Oblast in which he invested some
> $20 million.
>
> The business includes rights to over 8,000 hectares, a $13-million
> grain elevator made with Canadian technology and $7 million
> worth of New Holland machinery. Derrickson alleges that his
> erstwhile partner Viktor Fesun and Dnipropetrovsk Oblast regional
> lawmaker Oleg Kryshin swindled him by orchestrating fraudulent
> bankruptcies and conducting an illegal shareholders meeting that
> took over Derrickson's stake.
>
> The Canadian's land eventually ended up part of Warsaw-listed
> KSG Agro, which belongs to former member of parliament and
> ex-Dnipropetrovsk governor Serhiy Kasyanov. Kryshin and Kasyanov
> both rigorously denied involvement in the takeover in April 2013
> telephone interviews with the *Kyiv Post*. Kasyanov furthermore
> denied Derrickson's farming assets are a part of KSG-Agro and
> maintained that whatever assets he bought from Kryshin were done
> legally after conducting proper due diligence. Kryshin also had
> threatened to sue the Canadian for slander, which he hasn't.

Two Higher Commercial Court rulings, in November 2013 and January, reversed the bankruptcies of Derrickson's former companies, thus paving the way for him to restore his ownership rights to the assets.

Derrickson said that if the guilty aren't prosecuted, including Kryshin and Kasyanov, he will sue the Ukrainian government in Strasbourg's European Court of Human Rights for violating a 1994 bilateral treaty between Canada and Ukraine that guarantees each side's investments.

The *Kyiv Post* article had most of the facts right — except for the idea that my case was a success story in the making. The newspaper was engaging in the same wish fulfillment that I was. Nothing had changed in the gangster state.

Within days of his arrest, Fesun was set free after the quick intervention of Kryshin's lawyers. Within two months, the People's Deputy Kryshin and former People's Deputy and governor of Dnipropetrovsk Kasyanov had the freezing of their assets lifted, and we were quickly back where we started.

I heard that Fesun then fled the country and I asked Makashov if he knew where he was. He said he had information that Fesun was in hiding in Azerbaijan. But he told me not to worry. When the time came, he would pick him up again. He told me not to lose faith.

I told him it was already too late for that.

CHAPTER 18

END OF THE LEGAL CHARADE

Attempted murder, bank fraud and more corporate raiding by force of arms. Kasyanov is in and out of the revolving door of Ukrainian courts with a smile and a wave.

Officially during this period, Canada, America and Europe were insisting that Ukraine was making impressive progress in fighting corruption while they poured billions of dollars in loans into the country.

But by 2016, inside Ukraine there was already a feeling that the air was leaving the balloon. No one expected that corruption would be immediately defeated with the Maidan revolution and the election of the new pro-Western Poroshenko government, but there was hope that the situation would at least improve.

Petro Poroshenko had won the presidency in 2014, and in later parliamentary elections his political party and party of the future prime minister Arseniy Yatsenyuk — who was a leading figure in Yulia Tymoshenko's corrupt Fatherland Party — won a majority of seats. But the elections also brought a wave of young anti-corruption campaigners into the Rada, and they set about to write new anti-corruption laws. The International Monetary Fund (IMF) then oversaw the setting up of the National Anti-Corruption Bureau of Ukraine, and the investigators were trained by the FBI and set loose on the country. They were, however, only one of several competing police forces in the corruption battle — with the police often on different sides of the fight.

The anti-corruption bureau had some early success in uncovering the corruption in the political class by publicizing their family and personal incomes. It was not unusual to discover that many of the relatively poorly paid public servants had incredibly rich wives who earned millions, and owned impressive amounts of real estate. In a typical instance, the *Kyiv Post* reported that while military prosecutor Anatoliy Matios earned US$17,000 in 2014, his wife's income was over $2.2 million from mysterious sources in the same year. But most of the corrupt officials were too smart to get caught and took advantage of the many financial instruments the wealthy used to hide their money.[1] This was confirmed in 2020 when the National Agency on Corruption Prevention reported that 99 percent of audited asset declarations filed by Ukrainian officials in 2017–2019 contained false information.[2]

In the political arena, there only seemed to be a rearranging of the staff, with a lot of lateral moves. The first prime minister after Maidan, Arseniy Yatsenyuk, was chosen by the Americans in a famous bugged phone conversation between a U.S. State Department official and U.S. Ambassador Geoff Pyatt.[3] Yatsenyuk was from Tymoshenko's party, so he was a colleague of Oleg Kryshin and Alexander Shepelev. Yatsenyuk was removed from office after it became too obvious that he was part of the corrupt system he was supposed to be bringing down. But then he was replaced by a Poroshenko appointee who was even less diligent in addressing the corruption issue. Gradually, the

---

1   The most talented money-hider in the country was probably President Poroshenko himself. International corruption investigators at the Organized Crime and Corruption Reporting Project have shown that throughout his presidency, Poroshenko secretly controlled at least six offshore shell companies handling tens of millions of dollars in transactions, including luxury furniture for his home and expensive art. Drawing on banking records, correspondence, invoices and other documents, an OCCRP investigation found that Poroshenko used a friend with accounts at the Austrian bank Raiffeisen to mask his control of the offshore companies used to fund business activities and personal dealings.

2   "99% of Audited Ukrainian Officials Asset Declarations Contain False Information," *Kyiv Post*, July 26, 2021, https://www.kyivpost.com/ukraine-politics/99-of-audited-ukrainian-officials-asset-declarations -contain-false-information.html.

3   In the call between Assistant Secretary of State Victoria Nuland and the U.S. ambassador in February 2014 that was leaked to the press, Nuland is heard personally selecting the members of the next Ukraine government. When concerns are expressed about EU acceptance of the American plan, Nuland is heard saying "Fuck the EU," which caused an international scandal.

voices of young reformers, who had made so much noise when they were first elected, fell silent. By the time the dust cleared two years after the revolution, it was clear that it wasn't reformers but the oligarchs — Igor Kolomoisky, Viktor Pinchuk, Rinat Akhmetov and local mini-garchs like Sergey Kasyanov — who were running the country.

There had already been ample reason to question Poroshenko's commitment to anti-corruption measures when he made Arsen Avakov, Ukraine's chief law-and-order man, head of the Interior Ministry. Avakov was central to the continuing corruption in Ukraine and his appointment by Poroshenko and reappointment by Poroshenko's successor, Volodymyr Zelensky, tells you all you have to know about the power centre in Ukraine.

Arsen Avakov, who has the neat, buttoned-down look of a corporate CEO, was the chief law officer of the country. He began his political career in 2000 as a local leader in Kharkiv, where he amassed a US$100-million fortune from illegal land grabs — the same type of gangsterism that Kasyanov was engaged in against me. In 2012, Avakov was finally charged with "illegally transferring land" and fled the country. He was placed on Interpol's international wanted list and was arrested in Frosinone, Italy, with the Italian court placing him under immediate house arrest and beginning proceedings on extradition back to Ukraine for trial.

But while under house arrest in October 2012, Avakov did a deal with Tymoshenko's Fatherland Party to run in the parliamentary elections that were taking place in Ukraine — presumably with a large payment into Tymoshenko's coffers. While in jail in Italy awaiting deportation, Avakov was elected in absentia to the Ukraine parliament. This led to a Ukrainian court ruling on December 10, 2012, that cancelled the Interpol arrest warrant for someone who was now a People's Deputy, and Avakov returned to Ukraine the following day to take his seat in parliament. Within eighteen months he was the chief legal officer in post-Maidan Ukraine — a post that he held right up to 2021.[4]

At the Interior Ministry, Avakov solidified his position by making an alliance with the Azov Battalion, a military group with far-right, some say

---

4   "Avakov's dubious legacy to remain intact under his proposed successor," *Kyiv Post*, July 15, 2021. The article states that the man appointed to replace Avakov, Denis Monastyrsky, "will promote Avakov's interests. Avakov is going into the shadows but one of his people will replace him."

neo-Nazi ties[5] that fought against the Russian invasion and at the same time set itself up as a well-armed power within Ukrainian society. In November 2014, Avakov made one of the Azov leaders, Vadim Troyan, the Kyiv police chief and was condemned for this by Ukraine's chief rabbi, Yaakov Bleich. Bleich said that "if the interior minister continues to appoint people of questionable repute and ideologies tainted with fascism and right-wing extremism, the interior minister should be replaced." After Avakov was in power, calls for badly needed police reform in Ukraine fell on deaf ears.[6]

With Azov support and control of the national police, Avakov became an untouchable in Ukraine. Despite the obviously corrupt interior minister, the United States, EU and IMF continued to send billions into Ukraine. By 2016, the economy was clearly on life support and was being fed intravenously by a steady drip of IMF and other international loans, which were supposed to be tied to the anti-corruption fight. But that continued to be a fight in word and not deed, because the international money flowing into the country actually fed corruption rather than reducing it.

My favourite example of Ukrainian corruption during this period, and an apt symbol of it, resulted from a US$221-million European loan to Kyiv to repair a crumbling dam on the Dnieper River. The repairs were not made and the money almost instantly disappeared from the Ukrainian government account. One year later, a dozen luxury houses were under construction on prime riverfront property. They were built with the stolen European money, downriver from the crumbling dam the money was supposed to repair. So in a literal sense, corruption in this part of Ukraine will continue living the high life until the dam bursts. Which may come sooner than we think.

◇•◇

5   "In 2018, the U.S. House of Representatives also passed a provision blocking any training of Azov members by American forces, citing its neo-Nazi connections. The House had previously passed amendments banning support of Azov between 2014 and 2017, but due to pressure from the Pentagon, the amendments were quietly lifted. This was protested by the Simon Wiesenthal Center, which stated that lifting the ban highlighted the danger of Holocaust distortion in Ukraine." *Greek City Times*, April 7, 2022, https://greekcitytimes.com/2022/04/07/greek-parliament-azov-battalion/.

6   "Kyiv Regional Police Head Accused of Neo-Nazi Ties," *Jerusalem Post*, November 12, 2014, https://www.jpost.com/diaspora/Kyiv-regional-police-head-accused-of-neo-nazi-ties-381559.

It was during this period that a dam did burst for Sergey Kasyanov and his Ukrainian-Canadian partner Alexander Shepelev.

In a stunning development on August 1, 2016, Kasyanov was arrested in Dnipro on charges of money laundering, bank fraud and attempted murder. For once I saw in the newspaper photos that his usual self-satisfied smile was wiped from his face and replaced by a look of genuine alarm as he stood in the docket and listened to the prosecutors read the charges against him.

This was a bombshell. The fact that Kasyanov was arrested at all surprised me, and I was even more surprised by the seriousness of the accusations against him. There was nothing about the theft of my property; instead the charges involved his participation in the massive Rodovid Bank fraud and his role in a second attempt to murder the Rodovid Bank vice-president Sergei Dyadechko.

According to the accusation, this occurred in 2013 when Shepelev was still in custody in Hungary. The prosecutor's report said that Shepelev got in touch with Kasyanov with instructions on who Kasyanov should contact to arrange a hit on Dyadechko. Shepelev then wired Kasyanov US$1.3 million from a Swiss bank account to Kasyanov's KSG Bank, which had formerly been under Shepelev's control, to pay for the hit. The murder money was then transferred to Kasyanov's business account.

The plot failed only because Dyadechko fled the country, but according to the prosecutors, Kasyanov and Shepelev were still in touch with one another even though Shepelev was now in hiding in Moscow. He had arrived there in typical Shepelev fashion. After being extradited from Budapest back to Kyiv in 2013, he had spent a year in prison in Kyiv before he managed to land in the prison hospital, where he paid a guard a million dollars to help him escape. Then Shepelev's father-in-law, Mikhail Friedental, the same one who bought the house in Westmount for him, paid the Russian mafia US$10 million to whisk him away to Russia. He was there when Kasyanov was arrested and during Kasyanov's house arrest, and a Moscow court refused a Ukrainian request to extradite him.

But the main military prosecutors' office in Dnipro had been tapping Kasyanov's phone calls with Shepelev, and they had the bank records, so they knew everything about his role in the second murder attempt on Dyadechko, who was now publicly accusing Kasyanov of trying to murder him.[7]

Kasyanov had his first hearing in the Dnipro court on August 1, 2016, and prosecutors applied to keep him in jail at the pretrial detention centre for at least sixty days while they built the case against him.

As the prosecutor put it, "The circumstances that give grounds to suspect Sergei Kasyanov of committing these offences are confirmed by the statement of the commission of criminal offences, the testimony of the victim Sergei Dyadechko, the testimony of witnesses, audio recordings, conclusions of the relevant expert studies, and other evidence in the proceedings." Releasing Kasyanov, they said, "would risk having him engage in witness tampering and intimidation."

The Dnipro judge was more trusting of the former Dnipropetrovsk governor. He listened while Kasyanov's lawyers suggested that bail be set at UAH 30 million. While the terms were being discussed, People's Deputy Yuri Bereza, head of the militia funded by Igor Kolomoisky and himself a man who had at various times been accused of torture, murder and rape, arrived at the court and said he could vouch for Kasyanov's integrity. Bereza also said he would personally put up the UAH 30 million in bail money. The judge was surprisingly unsurprised by this sudden development and said that with Bereza's bail bond, Kasyanov could be released to six weeks of house arrest while charges against him were prepared.

So Kasyanov's chauffeur picked him up at the courthouse and drove him home to his wife and kids. Journalists covering the trial said it was "the pressure of Kolomoisky's man Yuri Bereza that was the key factor in the freeing of Kasyanov to unmonitored house arrest."

In the end, the charges against Kasyanov were not so much dropped as allowed to evaporate. The only real consequence for him for his years of fraud and attempted murder was that the National Bank of Ukraine seized

---

7   For his part, Dyadechko was said to be one of the leaders of the first fraudulent bankruptcy of the Rodovid Bank and as the chief money launderer for Yanukovych and the Donetsk gang. After the attempt on his life by Shepelev and Kasyanov, he fled to Monaco, where he bought the local professional basketball team and is said to be "close to Prince Albert II of Monaco and maintains business relations with him."

the assets of KSG Bank, then owned by Kasyanov and his wife, Ksenia, and Alexander Shepelev and his son.

When the National Bank of Ukraine regulators audited KSG Bank, they found that it was involved in money laundering and had a pattern of transferring millions of hryvnia in "loans" to the accounts of selected clients, who then took the money and never repaid. Along with these frauds, the National Bank investigators discovered all sorts of small-time hood activities, including accounts opened with stolen passports by an account holder who had dozens of credit cards in their name and ran up exorbitant balances before disappearing. But mysteriously, even after the National Bank publicly chronicled KSG's criminal practices, no charges were laid against Kasyanov. Instead, the bank was quietly liquidated at the same time that the attempted murder charge against Kasyanov disappeared into thin air.

That is how things worked in Ukraine. Gangsters launched banks and stole billions of dollars from their clients and depositors. The state then liquidated the banks and paid off the creditors. Since 2014, the official fund for reimbursing funds for failed banks had raised and paid out only US$1.4 billion. But the taxpayers paid out another US$20 billion in compensation to replace the funds stolen by the gangsters, who simply pocketed the money and walked away.[8]

A new bank governor, Poroshenko associate Valeria Gontareva, was appointed to clean up just this sort of fraud and was frank in her initial assessment of Ukraine banking, telling the press, "Unfortunately, Ukraine is a country of complete lawlessness."

As if to prove her point, Gontareva was also forced to resign because of accusations of corruption, and she fled to London, where she said she was getting threats from Kolomoisky for seizing his Privatbank assets. She was soon after hit by a car in London and her Kyiv house was burned to the ground, both of which she said were done by Kolomoisky's people.

But Kolomoisky shrugged off the accusation. He said a lot of people were mad at Gontareva, and he had a point. In 2019, Gontareva herself, with Investment Capital Ukraine (ICU) top manager Konstantin Stetsenko,

---

8   The *Kyiv Post*, April 2, 2021.

was charged with "the illegal seizure of another's property — monetary funds of PJSC Agrarian Fund worth UAH 2.069 billion" through "fake contracts of sale and purchase of government domestic loan bonds with the Agrarian Fund under direct repurchase agreements with the National Bank of Ukraine."

Once again it was clear that the lawmakers in Ukraine proved to be the most lawless of all. To illustrate this, we only have to check back in with Sergey Kasyanov.

In November 2016, less than two months after his house arrest was lifted, Kasyanov was involved in another armed standoff, this time at his Agro Soyuz property. The financial institution that had loaned his company UAH 70 million, which Kasyanov refused to pay back, won a court order to repossess the property. When the court officers arrived on the site to enforce the court order, they were met by heavily armed guards, likely from Yuri Bereza's security company, who drove them off at gunpoint. The officers never returned.

The following year, when creditors of Kasyanov's massive Rantier pig farm won a court decision to seize the property after another US$20-million loan went unpaid, Kasyanov arrived with several busloads of Bereza's men, who terrorized the farm workers and people in a nearby village. They stole all of the 55,000 pigs that the court had awarded to the creditors. Local villagers were shocked by the actions and by the fact that the local police had not only failed to protect them, but were obviously working with Kasyanov and his armed security force. In a confrontation with the local people trying to protect their property, Bereza's men were accused of murdering one of the farm workers.

Bereza was also later accused of kidnapping one of the farmers who had tried to offer resistance to the pig farm raid. The farmer was taken to Bereza's home where, it was reported in the media, he was tortured for more than four hours until he died with four broken vertebrae, several broken ribs and numerous intracranial hematoma.

To this day, none of the criminals in this murderous operation has been charged with the deaths.

By 2017, I no longer had any hope of getting my property back through Ukraine's sham justice system. Even when we had another favourable court judgment and managed to restart the criminal case against Fesun, I knew this was another pointless exercise. It was only when I heard that Fesun was subpoenaed to appear at the courthouse in Kamianske (Dniprodzerzhynsk) that I told my lawyer, Sergey Tarasov, to go there with my assistant to find out what they could about Fesun's current status. I wanted to know how Fesun, who was now long out of jail, was weathering the storms he had flung us both into.

I can't say I was surprised when my assistant sent me a detailed note about her day in court. She said the Kamianske courthouse was even more rundown than it had been when she visited it a year earlier. Garbage was piled outside, and inside the building the walls were dirty and the plaster was cracked, and there was a bitter smell of disinfectant.

As always, the hallway was crowded with people, and she and Sergey pushed through them to take their seat inside the empty hearing room. There was a type of cage in the middle of the court, and my assistant wondered if Fesun would be brought in and placed there. While they were waiting, two men — one older and one younger, likely the lawyers hired by Kryshin or Kasyanov — stopped by but left soon after.

Five minutes before the hearing was supposed to start, a court secretary came to tell them that the judge had gone to lunch, and after lunch there would be a consultation with other judges that would take a long time. She suggested that the hearing would likely be postponed and they should go home. My assistant said they had driven all the way from Kyiv, a good six hours away, so they would stay and wait.

Two and a half hours later the judge, a woman in her fifties, returned. She was obviously surprised, and not at all pleased, to see them still there. The judge said that usually people leave, and she seemed put off having to deal with them. She added that rather than travelling from Kyiv to Kamianske for the court hearing, they could have simply asked to listen to it through video conference.

Sergey said he was there to question Fesun and he wanted to do it face to face, and pointed out that Fesun was under a court order to appear.

The judge then pulled out a letter and read it out loud. It was from Fesun's lawyers and said their client had not been given proper notice to appear, and for that reason he was not able to prepare his defence so obviously could not be expected to appear in court.

When Sergey tried to protest, pointing out that both sides had been given a great deal of time to prepare for the hearing, the judge cut him off. Speaking hurriedly and aggressively, she said the hearing was adjourned because of a lack of proper notice to the defendant.

The judge disappeared into her chambers, the court secretary got up and wandered off, and Sergey and my assistant were left sitting alone in the empty courtroom.

When I read this account, I thought, fine. This was my last stand in the courts. That is the end of justice in Ukraine. The legal route to getting my property back seemed to be at its end. But I was not ready to give up.

What we needed, ultimately, were people who could play the political game. People who could put pressure on the Ukrainian government to step in and use the president's security service, if necessary, to send the maskis[9] in and seize my assets back from the thieves. That was my only hope. There was no justice in Ukraine, but there was politics, and political power generally followed the law of quid pro quo. That, finally, was the only hope I had in solving this.

---

9   *Maskis* is the common term in Ukraine for the shadowy masked security agents who suddenly move in to seize people or property.

CHAPTER 19

THE CANADIAN CARD

*In his first appearance, Zelensky bursts
onto the scene and slowly fizzles out.
My lawyer puts on a bow tie to confront
Avakov in Toronto. Canada continues to
write blank cheques to the gangster state.*

There are not many countries in the world where you can play the Canadian card. But Ukraine is definitely one of them.

As we have seen, the largest Ukrainian population outside of Ukraine and Russia was in Canada. In the Soviet years, Ukraine's president-in-exile lived in Canada, and Canada was the first country in the world to recognize an independent Ukraine in 1991. Ukraine remained a high priority for Canada through 2014, the year of the Maidan revolution and the civil war with the Russian-backed separatists in Donbas. That year, as previously described, Prime Minister Stephen Harper took the relationship to an almost obsessive level with three visits to Ukraine and the proclamation that Canada was the most Ukrainian of countries.

At that point, it seemed that Canada's influence in Ukraine could not possibly go beyond this mountaintop.

Then it did.

In 2015, the Liberal Party replaced the Conservatives in office and Chrystia Freeland was appointed first as Canada's international trade minister, then global affairs minister and finally deputy prime minister.[10]

Freeland has deep family roots in Ukraine. Her grandfather, Michael Chomiak (in Ukrainian: Михайло Хом'як), was from Lviv and during the 1930s worked as a journalist for a popular nationalist newspaper there. In 1939, when the Soviet troops were moving in from the east, he fled to Krakow, where the Nazis had set up their administrative base in occupied Poland. Chomiak then worked as the editor of a Nazi-funded, Ukrainian-language newspaper, *Krakivski Visti* (*Krakow News*), for the rest of the war. The newspaper published Nazi war propaganda laced with anti-Semitic diatribes — something that today would be considered a war crime for contributing to the climate of hate that set the stage for the Holocaust in Ukraine.

Chomiak met his wife, Freeland's grandmother, in Krakow, where he also took his PhD in law at a local university. His eldest daughter was born there, before they had to flee the approaching Red Army for German-controlled Austria in 1944. He continued to publish the Nazi-backed paper in Vienna right up until April 1945, when Austria was also overrun by the Red Army. Before the Soviets arrived, Chomiak and his wife and daughter fled to a transit camp in the American sector in Germany, the Blonhofen Displaced Persons Camp, where Freeland's mother was born. The family immigrated to Western Canada in 1948, and Chomiak worked for a short time as a labourer in Edmonton before finding a job with the Sherritt Gordon Mines just north of the city.

In Canada, Chomiak was active in the Ukrainian community as a member of several Ukrainian nationalist organizations, and he was for a time a teacher at the Ivan Franko School of Ukrainian Studies in Edmonton. He also continued his journalistic work in Canada, editing an important Ukrainian-language newspaper that was backed by the Ukrainian Catholic Church.

So Chrystia Freeland was raised in a family steeped in Ukrainian culture. After getting a journalistic start working on her grandfather's community

10   Freeland was minister of international trade from 2015 to 2017, minister of global affairs from 2017 to 2019, and as of 2022 was deputy prime minister.

newspaper, Freeland went on to earn a bachelor of arts degree in Russian history and literature from Harvard University, and a master of studies degree in Slavonic studies from St Antony's College, Oxford as a Rhodes Scholar. In 1993, she served for a time as the *Financial Times* correspondent in Russia while she worked with nationalists in Ukraine, and kept in touch with her uncle Bohdan Chomiak — who, as we have seen, was working as a consultant in the Ukraine grain industry.

By the time Freeland was appointed to Justin Trudeau's first cabinet in 2015, her uncle was well situated within the Ukrainian power structure. Chomiak worked in a consulting firm with Gilles Farley, a director with ICU, the company founded by Poroshenko's personal asset manager and National Bank president appointee Valeria Gontareva. Other ICU appointees included a number of key government managers in Poroshenko's team.[11] After Poroshenko was turfed from office, Chomiak turned up as a director with G.N. Terminals, a Odessa grain-handling outfit registered in Cyprus that had been charged with gangsterism for illegally moving more than UAH 4 billion through the port.[12]

When Freeland was elected to parliament in 2015 and appointed minister of international trade and then foreign minister in the Trudeau government, Ukraine and Ukrainian issues reached new heights in Ottawa. There was a bump in the road when news reports about Freeland's grandfather covered his Nazi past, including a series of what historian John-Paul Himka described as "vehemently anti-Semitic" articles Michael Chomiak published in *Krakivski Visti*. This was embarrassing for Freeland, because she had always said that her grandfather was an inspiration to her, but her reaction hinted at Canada's future Ukrainian policy. Instead of admitting the truth, that

11   Poroshenko appointed the founder of ICU, Valeria Gontareva, as National Bank of Ukraine governor and three other ICU employees were given top jobs in the administration as heads of the National Energy Regulatory Commission, the Energy Ministry and the National Communications and Information Regulatory Commission. Together they involved the government in a massive coal price-fixing scandal with the oligarch Rinat Akhmetov.

12   G.N. Terminals is a subsidiary of GNT Olimpex Holding Ltd., which is controlled by Vlodymyr Naumenko and Sergiy Groza, who have been part of numerous police investigations, including criminal proceedings No. 42017000000001712 launched by the Prosecutor General's Office under 9 articles of the Criminal Code of Ukraine (including article 364 — abuse of power or official position; article 255 — creation of a criminal organization; and article 212 — tax evasion).

her grandfather was indeed a Nazi collaborator during the war, she tried to dodge the controversy by suggesting it was all Russian disinformation.[13]

Of course Freeland is no way responsible for the sins of her grandfather. But dismissing accusations about him as Russian disinformation is a rather typical example of Canada's serial dishonesty when it comes to Ukraine. Freeland was well aware of her grandfather's activities in Krakow, and the nature of the newspaper he edited, because the information came from the family archives at the University of Alberta. All of the facts had been publicized in 1996 in a peer-reviewed academic paper by Himka, who, as well as being a widely respected historian, is Freeland's uncle by marriage. Freeland herself was listed as someone who was directly consulted in the drafting of the 1996 paper that exposed her grandfather's role in editing the virulently anti-Semitic paper in Krakow.

The controversy reached the point that Canadian journalist Sheldon Kirshner wrote a column for *Canadian Jewish News* and the *Times of Israel* urging Freeland to "come clean" and acknowledge the fact that her grandfather was editor of "a mouthpiece of the Nazi propaganda juggernaut, that solicited Ukrainian support for the Nazi cause and published anti-Semitic articles during a period when Polish Jews were being slaughtered by the thousands." Kirshner added that by "presenting the 'Jewish Question' within the framework of Nazi conspiracy theories," Michael Chomiak "contributed to the Holocaust."[14]

Freeland refused to bend in the face of the facts. She still clung to the story that her grandfather was himself a victim and blamed "the Russians" for leaking the information. The charade continued to the point where Canada actually expelled two Russian diplomats for tweeting about the information that Freeland's own uncle had been exposed in an academic journal twenty years earlier.

As an elected official, Freeland pursued the Ukrainian nationalist cause in the Canadian government in a very high-profile way. On May 19, 2015,

---

13   She said "there were efforts on the Russian side to destabilize democracies in the West" and that it "shouldn't come as a surprise if these same efforts are used against Canada."

14   Sheldon Kirshner, "Canadian Foreign Minister Should Acknowledge the Truth," *Times of Israel*, March 9, 2017.

Ukrainian's Vyshyvankas day, which celebrates the country's colourful embroidered shirts, Freeland convinced Prime Minister Trudeau and most of the cabinet to pose in the House of Commons atrium wearing a Ukrainian folk costume and, according to her uncle Bohdan Chomiak's social media post, they sang a Ukrainian song.

At this point Canada quickly became deeply involved in every facet of Ukrainian life, including its border conflict with Russian-backed separatists in Donetsk. Hundreds of Canadian soldiers were sent to train the Ukrainian army in Operation UNIFIER, a Canadian Armed Forces military training mission in Ukraine, and more than 2,500 military personnel from Canada supported the NATO-Ukraine Joint Working Group on Defence Reform, offering staff officer and peacekeeping training for Ukrainian military and civilian personnel. This military aid generated controversy when it was disclosed that the Canadians were training the Azov Battalion fighters, a group that the U.S. Congress had described as neo-Nazi.

Along with offering generous government-to-government support to Ukraine, Freeland completed negotiations on the Ukraine-Canada Free Trade Agreement, which led to a slight increase in Ukrainian exports to Canada but was somehow accompanied by an actual drop in Canadian exports to Ukraine. Freeland also led the push for Canadian non-governmental organizations to join the government in providing aid and assistance. The Canadian International Development Agency funded the establishment of the Centre for Small Business and Economic Development in Ivano-Frankivsk. An additional CDN$3.8 million was committed to a regional network project to support small-business growth and economic development in five additional communities in the same oblast of western Ukraine.

The Canada-Ukraine Chamber of Commerce played an important role in promoting trade and business ties between the two countries. In 2016, Global Affairs Canada established the Canada-Ukraine Trade and Investment Support Project, which was budgeted for five years and designed "to lower poverty in Ukraine through increasing exports from Ukraine to Canada and investment from Canada to Ukraine."

There was even a major grain industry project that had been started under Harper. With Freeland's uncle Chomiak assisting, Canada launched a project that involved buying five hectares of land to build co-op silos near the railways that cross the village of Vasilkivka, which is just the other side of Dnipro from my stolen grain elevators at Bozhedarivka.

The official name of the CDN$13-million project was the Ukrainian Grain Storage and Marketing Project, and their point man met with Freeland's uncle as well as with Volodymyr Klymenko, the president of the Ukraine Grain Association — an association that Bohdan Chomiak had set up when he was working with USAID.

But it turned out that Ukrainian farmers were interested in Canadian cash and not local co-ops. The first meeting of the Canadian co-op group attracted around twenty-five local farmers who had come expecting to find a barrel of Canadian cash they could dip into. When it was clear that the funding was for a co-op and not the individual farmers, the room began to clear. By the end of the evening, only three farmers remained in the room.

◊•◊

The irony of the Canadian government wanting to build grain elevators in the same neighbourhood where mine had been stolen was not lost on me. And by 2017, I was ready to press the point with them.

Surely, I thought, in return for Canada lavishing all sorts of aid on the country, Ukraine could be expected to repay the favour by offering simple justice to a Canadian businessman who had invested in the country and built a much-needed resource. Especially when the injustice was caused by People's Deputies in the Ukrainian government.

I had been listening carefully to the Canadian and other Western rhetoric in Ukraine, which declared that Ukraine had to fight a two-front war: in the east against the Russian-backed separatists, and against corruption throughout the country. I was about to test the waters to see if Canada and the West were really serious about the second front: fighting corruption in Ukraine that over the previous decades had been far more damaging to the country than the Russian-backed separatists.

What I needed in order to move down this new avenue was someone who had contacts in the Ukrainian government and with Canada, and I found a law firm in Ukraine that had a track record in this kind of international relations. The firm was Wolf Theiss, which had branches throughout Eastern Europe and specialized in serving the interests of foreign investors. What they sold were direct government connections in the countries they did business in — they were known to work so closely to those in power that they were said to have a role in rewriting business laws in these countries.

The man to speak to, I was told, was Taras Dumych, the managing partner at the Ukraine branch of the firm, who specialized in mergers and acquisitions and in agriculture markets and had taught law at the University of Lviv. Like Oles Kopets, he had studied in North America and spoke excellent English. At our first meeting, I asked Dumych to take a look at my case from a political perspective, to try to find a way we could get around the corruption of the courts to find justice in the backrooms. He was also, I noticed from his Facebook page, personal friends with Chrystia Freeland's uncle Bohdan Chomiak.

Dumych began by reviewing the case up to that date, and when he was finished he told me he saw a gap between the current legal team's strategy and the final step to getting my assets back. He thought Sergey Tarasov should continue the court case while we worked with the Canadian embassy staff and in the backrooms of the government in Kyiv.

So that is what we decided. We would try a two-pronged approach: Sergey continuing to go through the motions in the courts while Taras Dumych worked with the embassy to get them to put pressure on the government in Kyiv.

Taras sent an initial wake-up call to the Canadian embassy in the form of a letter signed by me and addressed to the Canadian ambassador, Roman Waschuk. The letter said I had made state-guaranteed investments in the economy of Ukraine with a total sum of approximately UAH 100 million, bringing hundreds of jobs and other benefits to the people of the Dnipropetrovsk region of Ukraine.[15]

The letter then detailed my case, from the theft of my properties by Fesun and Kryshin to the fencing of them to Kasyanov. I reminded the Canadians

---

15   The full letter to the Canadian embassy is provided in Appendix I.

that the Maidan revolution was supposed to "change the balance of power in the corrupt and ineffective governmental institutions of Ukraine, but so far, I am still denied access to fair and reasonable justice and yet, still unable to reinstate my rights as the owner of my property. That is why I now ask for help from the Canadian Embassy to influence the situation by all means necessary."

With the first volley sent to the embassy, our plan hit a roadblock when I informed Sergey Tarasov, our courtroom lawyer, that a lawyer from a prestigious international law firm would be working on the case to press the Canadian government to act — and I asked him to brief him on the details. Sergey agreed to do it, but I noticed he had a sullen look on his face. When Taras Dumych contacted him, Sergey refused to meet. Eventually they had a couple of meetings, and I even sent Vika in to try to mediate between the two, but Sergey made it clear he was not going to work with another lawyer. So finally, I had to let Sergey go.

In his final review of the files, Taras said Sergey had not been a bad lawyer, he was good at launching cases and winning some important judgments along the way, but he didn't seem to have an end strategy to get the case off the ten-year merry-go-round in the Ukrainian courts. "What you see in all of these documents," Taras said, "is a lot of puck-passing, sometimes even fancy puck-passing, but never actually shooting on the goal."

◊•◊

Taras Dumych's hockey reference was an apt one because he was already using hockey as a way to curry favour with the Canadian embassy in Kyiv.

In the spring of 2017, he invited the Canadian ambassador and Adam Barbolet, the senior trade commissioner at the embassy, to the World Hockey Championship qualifying tournament that was being held at the old Soviet-era Palace of Sports near Bessarabska Square. He had tickets for the game between Ukraine and Austria, where Ukraine's place in the A Division was on the line. The home team ultimately lost by a score of 1–0, but it was a great game and it gave Taras a chance to get together with the Canadians in a friendly way.

His hockey diplomacy went so well that the following June he called up the embassy and said that Ukrainians really appreciated all that Canada was doing for the country and he would like to do something for Canada Day in Kyiv on July 1. He suggested organizing a friendly street hockey game in the Maidan square, within a block of the Canadian embassy, that pitted Canadians against a group from the Ukrainian foreign office, followed by a Canada Day picnic. The Canadian embassy liked the idea and Taras Dumych became a welcome figure at the embassy, later being invited by Adam Barbolet to give his input to the organizing committee of the Ukraine Reform Conference scheduled for Toronto in June 2019.

The conference was a big deal for Canada, allowing the country to show off its importance to Ukraine. The main themes were to be international support for Ukraine in its military conflict with Russia and Ukraine's own fight against corruption. The two elements were to be linked — new aid to Ukraine in its external battles depended on Ukraine making headway on the anti-corruption front.

Tackling corruption in Ukraine was something Western governments had been claiming to be a priority for the previous five years, but up until then they had proven they were not at all serious about it. Billions were flowing into the country and disappearing, and no one was holding anyone to account. The Ukraine Reform Conference was supposed to be a new watershed, and personally I hoped that Canada was finally getting serious about holding Ukraine's feet to the fire and demanding an end to corruption in exchange for continued support.

I was happy to hear that Taras was getting the royal treatment from the Canadian embassy. But I was still wondering why, after receiving the detailed rundown on my case, they weren't offering to put pressure on the Ukrainian government on my behalf. After all, up to that point, post-Maidan Ukraine had received CDN$785 million in Canadian taxpayer money, as well as massive military and NGO support. Wouldn't it be natural for Canada to ask that Ukraine return the property of a Canadian businessman that had been stolen by a group of People's Deputies?

I was skeptical, but Taras had high hopes that we would get the ball rolling in Toronto.

The conference was taking place at what seemed like yet another decisive moment in Ukrainian politics. In the presidential election a few weeks earlier, which was expected to be a battle between two corrupt old rivals, Petro Poroshenko and Yulia Tymoshenko, the political newcomer Volodymyr Zelensky jumped into the race and won in a landslide.

Zelensky was far from an unknown, however. He was one of the most familiar faces on Ukrainian television, as the popular comedian who wrote and starred in a television series about a schoolteacher who was accidentally elected president with a promise to end the corruption in the country. That, along with the promise of an honourable end to the conflict with Russian-backed separatists in the east, was what Zelensky ran on and he took almost 75 percent of the vote, winning in every region of the country except for the nationalist stronghold of the Lviv Oblast.

Zelensky arrived in Toronto for the conference like a conquering hero. The CN Tower shone with the blue and yellow colours of the Ukrainian flag, and his speech to the packed hotel ballroom was the hottest ticket in town. The evening was hosted by then–Foreign Affairs Minister Chrystia Freeland, and the hall was full of wealthy Ukrainians, representatives from the IMF and World Bank, and investors from around the world.

Zelensky had a special message for Canadian-Ukrainian business relations. He spoke in glowing terms of the CDN$65-million investment by a Canadian energy company, TIU Canada, in massive new solar-power fields in Ukraine. The deal was the first investment under the new Canadian-Ukrainian Free Trade Agreement, and Canada and Zelensky promised it was a turning point in building a new Ukrainian economy. He spoke about reforming his country to rid it of systemic corruption, thus opening the way for Ukraine to join the European Union and cut a peace deal with Russia on favourable terms.

The speech was greeted with wild enthusiasm. But no one raised the difficult question of how, exactly, he was going to accomplish these things in a country that was essentially controlled economically by gangsters and the corrupt politicians who worked for them.

I, for one, already had my doubts. One of the reasons for my skepticism came immediately after Zelensky's election, when he decided, or some say was forced, to keep Arsen Avakov as his interior minister. The Kharkiv land thief, who was originally elected People's Deputy while in an Italian prison cell, was still the most powerful man in Ukraine, being in charge of the justice system. He was, to put it mildly, unlikely to bring about any meaningful reform while he was in office.

Taras Dumych also believed that Avakov, and not the president, was the real power in Ukraine at the time, so he targeted him as the person in government who could actually return my property to me. Avakov would be at the Toronto summit and Taras was determined to meet with him there to force his hand, in the Canadian setting with — he hoped — Canadian backing.

Taras put on a bow tie, because he said everyone always remembers the guy with the bow tie, and went to the Toronto conference panel Avakov was speaking at. When it was over, he cornered Avakov and told him he was working on a case that was important to the Canadian embassy and wanted to speak to him for a few minutes. Avakov was trapped and agreed to speak to Taras in a corner of the hotel lobby, with Avakov's assistant taking notes.

Taras outlined my case and again underlined its importance to Canadians. Avakov's interior ministry was receiving a lot of aid money and police training from Canada, and the Canadian government was at the time secretly giving military training to the Azov Battalion, which the U.S. Congress had identified as a neo-Nazi organization. Avakov appeared to be very interested in the case of a Canadian businessmen who'd had a $28-million agricultural business stolen from him by the Dnipropetrovsk mafia.

Avakov indicated that he would definitely look into the matter and told Taras to give his card to his assistant and get back in touch with them in Kyiv. They would see what they could do to help the Canadian find justice in Ukraine.

Taras was quite enthusiastic about this. As soon as he was back in Kyiv he provided Avakov's assistant with a more detailed outline of the case — how the theft had been stage-managed by People's Deputies Kryshin and Kasyanov, and how the resulting legal case was stymied by corrupt police and judges.

Taras asked for a meeting to discuss possible courses of action. Then he waited for a reply. And waited. And waited. But there was nothing. Silence.

What was clear was that Avakov was receiving absolutely no pressure from the Canadian government to open my file. Taras said he checked with the Canadian embassy to make sure they would not be upset if he contacted Avakov directly in Toronto, and they shrugged it off. They had no intention of moving to pressure Ukraine about the theft of my grain operation. When I later pushed Taras on what, exactly, the Canadian embassy had done to support my case, he said they had "shown an interest in it" to the prosecutor's office. But nothing beyond that.

That was it. They had "shown an interest" at a low level but asked for nothing and had not moved the issue up the political ladder.

A short time later we received a notice from the prosecutor's office of Dnipropetrovsk region. It said that according to the results of the pretrial investigation on April 26, 2019, "the investigator of the Shevchenkiv Police Department of the Dnipropetrovsk Police Department of the Main Department of the National Police in Dnipropetrovsk region made a decision to close the criminal proceedings based on Clause 2 of Part 1 of Article 284 of the Criminal and Procedural Code of Ukraine in view of the lack of criminal violation."

I had had $28 million stolen from me and according to the justice system of Ukraine, there was no "criminal violation." When Taras got in touch with the Canadian embassy to ask them to intervene, once again there was silence.

◊•◊

The communiqué that Chrystia Freeland released after the Toronto conference was full of praise for Ukraine's "reform agenda." It then went on to offer a wishy-washy caveat regarding "key reform areas that we believed could be vulnerable or where there was risk of backsliding."

"It is critical that Ukraine continue to work with its partners — the IMF, EU and bilateral donors," Freeland said, "to meet and complete reforms agreed as part of these programs. We will work with Ukraine to ensure continued progress in these areas to further assist Ukraine in implementing reforms, including by allocating funds."

That was it — reforms if necessary but not necessarily reform. Either way, Canada would keep shovelling money into the bottomless pit. There would be no consequences for Ukraine when, once again, it failed to implement the drastic reforms needed to break the stranglehold of the oligarchs and gangsters like Kasyanov on Ukrainian society. No matter what they did, the billions would keep enriching the ruling class in Ukraine while the mass of Ukrainians slipped even further into poverty and despair as the poorest country in Europe, living at a level far below their Polish neighbours and even the Russians.

Even inside Ukraine, voices of protest against Western sponsorship of the de facto gangster state had been rising. A series of editorials in the *Kyiv Post*, a very pro-Western newspaper, condemned the West — in this case the European Union — for approving another 600 million euros in unconditional assistance to Ukraine. The *Post* wrote:

> By attaching no conditions, the EU guarantees that Ukrainian officials will get the wrong message: that they need to do nothing on reform or corruption. They gave Ukrainian authorities the opportunity to dodge, weave and pretend to act. Everyone says 'we are for reforms' while oligarchs continue to control lawmakers, ensuring the absence of any changes.
>
> The International Monetary Fund is barreling down the same path. The IMF has long been Ukraine's financial drug of choice and enabler when it comes to cheap loans in exchange for half-hearted reforms — or flat-out hypocritical lies — that don't change anything for the better.
>
> The IMF is the same institution that lent money to Ukraine without requiring the nation to have any effective police, prosecutors or courts — or basic banking regulations — such as who owns what bank. This negligence allowed a $20-billion theft from Ukrainian taxpayers, engineered by banking insiders, forcing Ukraine's government to borrow more billions to cover the billions stolen, saddling future generations with needless debt.

Canadian-Ukrainian consultant Yuri Polakiwsky summed up the status of Ukraine as "a country of failed promises led by nonsense-speaking pretenders, who make promises only to then break them." Polakiwsky, who is based in Kyiv and specializes in foreign policy and transatlantic relations, pointed out that, sadly, "the Maidan was a wished-for revolution that actually wasn't." According to Polakiwsky, Ukraine would change only if it was forced to by donors, and it was the habit of donors to continually look the other way that allowed corruption to continue to be part of the accepted way of life in Ukraine.

The reform czar in Ukraine at the time, Mikheil Saakashvili, was even more blunt. He said that corruption costs the country US$37 billion a year and he is frank about why Ukraine can't move forward.

"Ukraine has so few foreign investors because the country is seen abroad as a place where they will get scammed. [Official] foreign investment in Ukrainian GDP is less than two percent [actually less than 0.2 percent].

"Why? Because no one likes scams. Ukraine, Ukrainian officials and the state all have a clear reputation for scamming. They screw everybody," he said.

This is not a Russian propagandist saying this, it's the guy who was head of the reform committee in Ukraine.

In fact, we were arriving at the point where even many of the country's European supporters were now admitting that Ukraine had entered the territory of a failed state, where you could not be sure if the billions of dollars of Western cash was intravenous fluid keeping it alive, or embalming fluid being pumped into an already-dead country to make it look like it was still alive.

CHAPTER 20

THE FINAL HAIL MARY

*The revolution that wasn't. Their gangsters
become our gangsters and the plunder
continues with funds from the West
and cheerleading from Canada.*

I was preparing to walk away from my stolen property in Ukraine for the last time when my friend Richard Spinks suggested I try one final Hail Mary pass. He said I should hire Volodymyr Parasiuk, the young hero of the Maidan revolution who had gone to fight against the separatists in the east and been elected to parliament while he was away at the front. So again I was dealing with a People's Deputy, although this one was supposedly from the *new* Ukraine.

Parasiuk was from a nationalist family in Lviv and had received some military training from the radical right-wing Congress of Ukrainian Nationalists. During the Maidan battle in the winter of 2014 he arrived in Kyiv with his father and was a commander of his own unit, known as the Parasiuk Group. In court filings he and his father were said to have brought a substantial number of weapons to the square to battle with police and paramilitaries in the closing days of the uprising.

Parasiuk rose dramatically to national prominence on February 21 when, dressed in his army fatigues, he stood up and seized the microphone from opposition politicians in the Maidan who were announcing the power-sharing deal they had just signed with President Yanukovych. Parasiuk denounced the deal and announced that if Yanukovych was not gone by 10 a.m. the next morning, he and his comrades would attack Yanukovych's compound and remove him by force of arms. That speech, spoken with a revolutionary's passion, reignited the crowd and instantly killed the power-sharing deal. Yanukovych understood that the end had come, and in the dead of night he fled his heavily fortified presidential compound. A few days later, after meeting in secret with mafia bosses in Kharkiv and Donetsk, he turned up as a political refugee in Russia.

Volodymyr Parasiuk and his father continued the battle by enlisting in a hastily assembled militia called the Dnipro-1 Battalion, set up by the Dnipro gangsters Igor Kolomoisky and Yuri Bereza, and went to fight the Russian-backed separatists in Donbas. Parasiuk was taken prisoner in the disastrous battle of Ilovaisk, but was quickly released three days later in a prisoner exchange between Kyiv and the separatists.

In the October 2014 elections, Parasiuk was elected as a People's Deputy along with Yuri Bereza, the commander of the Kolomoisky-funded Dnipro battalion. As a member of parliament Parasiuk joined a cross-party reform caucus. But he didn't confine his politics to the Rada. In 2017 he was part of an armed group that blocked the railway in Luhansk to prevent coal imports to Ukraine from the territory held by separatists. The role of Volodymyr Parasiuk, a sitting member of parliament wearing battle fatigues, was given front-page news throughout Ukraine and led to a war of words between Parasiuk and President Poroshenko, who had been quietly permitting this illegal trade with the enemy. Parasiuk finally won, forcing the president to send in the Ukrainian army to seal off railway transport between the separatist regions and the rest of Ukraine.

These sorts of actions, as well as a number of actual fist fights in the Rada, including one with his former commander Bereza, made Parasiuk something of a legend in Ukraine. Even though he was a bit of a hothead, he was known as one of the few uncorrupted men in government, and among the young,

Parasiuk had what almost amounted to a cult following. He was the action hero of the revolution — seen as an incorruptible force who represented the fierce demand for change in the country. His importance was confirmed in the Ukrainian way in 2016, when someone threw a grenade under his SUV.

Parasiuk hadn't run for re-election in the 2019 legislative election because of a glitch in his filing papers. But there were rumours in the press that he might be appointed by Zelensky as governor of Lviv Oblast. In the end, it was either only a rumour or the offer was made and refused, but the fact that people saw him as the next governor of the oblast told me that Volodymyr Parasiuk, poster boy of the revolution, was still a force to be reckoned with in Ukraine.

Richard Spinks was a friend of Parasiuk and his family in Lviv. They were close enough that after the grenade incident, as a joke, Richard bought Volodymyr a selfie stick with a mirror on the end for checking under his car for bombs.

Inside the Rada, Parasiuk had distinguished himself by co-sponsoring an important anti-corruption bill. By the time that Richard suggested hiring him to get my property back, I had already met him a few times and was impressed. In person, he was polite and good-natured and obviously smart. And his national reputation for doing the right thing — even if it meant taking up arms — made him an appealing force to be aligned with.

When Richard and I spoke to him about a contract to get my assets back, he seemed happy with the idea and positive that he could make a difference.

Parasiuk brought in his lawyer and they spent some time going through my court document until they had a clear enough picture of the case. Then Parasiuk headed down to Dnipropetrovsk to supposedly take the bull by the horns. He did have important contacts there, including with the ruling mafia don Igor Kolomoisky, who had funded his Dnipro-1 Battalion. At one point during the war, Parasiuk reportedly called Kolomoisky for assistance and Kolomoisky sent him a Privatbank armoured car to use as a troop carrier. Kolomoisky was also reported to have funded Parasiuk's coal blockade in Luhansk because Kolomoisky was fighting his own private war with rival Donetsk oligarchs. But Parasiuk had also shown his independence with his fist fight in parliament with Kolomoisky's and Kasyanov's enforcer, Yuri Bereza. I expected that Parasiuk, who was still said to have a good relationship with Kolomoisky and also had the backing of many in Ukraine's powerful right-wing militia movement, could bring pressure to bear on Kasyanov that others could not.

But when Parasiuk returned from Dnipro, he was vague about what he had done and who he had met. He said it might take a little longer than he thought to get my property back and that he would have to travel to Europe and possibly Israel to meet some people. But I would have to give him expense money. I was disappointed with the news, but I transferred CDN$16,000 to his bank account to fund his trips.

Then I heard nothing. He disappeared. I asked Richard to find out what was going on. Richard did not find out much, but did confirm that Parasiuk had never travelled to Europe or Israel and wasn't really doing anything to advance my case. And he kept my money.

That was it. The hero of the Revolution of Dignity was as crooked as the rest. I had made my last-second Hail Mary pass, and Parasiuk hadn't so much dropped the ball as run off with it through the stands and disappeared down the street. Another crooked former People's Deputy to add to the list.

And now the clock had definitely run out.

◊•◊

It was time to wrap it up. I made a quick trip to Ukraine in late 2019 to let Volodya, Vika and Yulia know that I would be winding things down and selling off my remaining property there. To help the staff make the transition, I paid them all a CDN$10,000 bonus and let Volodya and Vika go, keeping only Yulia on while I sold off my remaining properties. I returned to Canada with a plan to make my final wrap-up trip to Ukraine in the spring, when I would oversee the sale of my remaining properties in Kyiv and my dacha (country home) forty kilometres north of the city.

As it turned out, the COVID-19 pandemic would delay my return to Ukraine by eighteen months. During that time, I started a new renewable energy business venture in North America called RMD Environmental, with Richard Spinks and Oles Kopets as partners. I listened with interest to the news coming out of Ukraine in the summer and fall of 2021, and unfortunately, all of it was bad.

Old-time repression was returning to the country alongside the old-time corruption. In the spring of 2021 Zelensky found himself briefly trailing behind the pro-Russian party in the polls, so he ordered the closure of three opposition television channels that were officially owned by a member of the pro-Russian Opposition Platform Party. The financial backer of the stations was Viktor Medvedchuk, a prominent oligarch who was said in the press to be a close friend of Vladimir Putin. Based on that friendship and the more serious crime of Medvedchuk's party gaining in popularity over Zelensky's Servant of the People Party, Zelensky accused Medvedchuk of treason and put him under house arrest, along with another member of his party. Zelensky would go on to close several other media outlets, including the only English-language paper in Ukraine, for the crime of being critical of him.

In the summer, Zelensky's own adviser, Mikheil Saakashvili, head of the executive committee of the National Council of Reforms, warned that the country was becoming a haven not only for Ukrainian gangsters but for gangsters from across Eastern Europe.

"Ukraine is a gateway, there are criminals from all over the post-Soviet space," Saakashvili said. He spoke about prosecutors and cops for hire and said the system was sick. "In the migration service you will stand in line for a long time, but for [enough] money [Osama] bin Laden will be given a certificate that will testify that his great-grandfather lived in Ukraine. Anyone will drop in, any will leave, any will shoot, any will blow up. And all this is happening in front of everyone."

The most serious blow was against Zelensky himself. When the Pandora Papers, a load of information on tax havens around the world, was published in the summer of 2021, not only did Ukraine have more politicians on the list than any country in the world — including twice as many as Russia — but Zelensky's name was prominent among them. The "reform president" had a slew of secret investments in partnership with his cronies from his native Kryvyi Rih region. Subsequent reporting showed that when he was elected, he "sold" some of his hidden shares to a friend and partner, but the friend continued to pay him the dividends from the shares. This was the same type of under-the-table dealing that he had denounced in the Poroshenko government, so add hypocrisy to the corruption charges. Up until then, Zelensky had been accused of being a power-hungry incompetent. Now he was also seen as corrupt and his approval ratings dropped ten points in a week.

It seemed that no one was untouched by the corruption in Ukraine. That was the dismal situation when I headed there in the fall of 2021 for my final visit.

CHAPTER 21

BEFORE THE DELUGE

The last goodbye to Bozhedarivka.

I arrived in Kyiv once more, in my twentieth year of involvement with the country, on October 14, 2021 — just four months before the Russian invasion. October 14 also happened to be Defenders of Ukraine Day, a national holiday that had been proclaimed by Poroshenko to mark the official formation of the Ukrainian People's Army (UPA) to fight the approaching Red Army in 1942.

Yulia had booked me for a VIP arrival in Kyiv, and a young airport official was waiting for me when I stepped off the plane onto the passenger boarding bridge. He asked for my luggage tag and then opened a door that led to stairs down to the tarmac, where a Jaguar was waiting. The young man opened the car door for me and then disappeared inside the airport to pick up my suitcase at the baggage carousel. The driver took me to the next small terminal for the VIP arrivals. Inside, a strikingly beautiful Ukrainian woman in military uniform stamped my passport and welcomed me to Ukraine, then pointed to the plush leather chairs where I would wait for the young man to bring me my suitcase. I was the only one in the waiting area, and after a long flight I noticed with pleasure that there were ashtrays set out so I could smoke, something that was of course forbidden in the rest of the airport.

TV monitors showed the live broadcast of the Defenders Day events in Kyiv. In past years, there had been tens of thousands in the streets supporting their troops. But more recently the battle with the Russians in Donetsk had faded into a frozen conflict and I saw only a few military vehicles assembling in the square, and a few hundred people gathered there. From the banners they were displaying, it seemed the crowd was largely made up of nationalists celebrating the UPA, and not veterans of what was still the low-grade conflict in Donetsk.

The celebration of the UPA and related nationalist groups was always a bit dicey because along with fighting the Red Army, the UPA were at times allied with the Nazis and were accused of murdering tens of thousands of Poles and Jews. The related nationalist militias were also accused of assisting the Germans in carrying out the Holocaust, which killed millions of Jews, so these Ukrainian nationalist fighters were frowned upon by the Europeans and Ukraine's other Western allies, to put it mildly. This iffy status was illustrated that day when the TV camera panned across a massive White Lives Matter banner in the middle of the square. This was not supposed to be the message of the Ukrainian revolution.

This off-balance Defenders Day set the tone for my trip. Everywhere I went, the mood was bad. In fact, in my twenty years in Ukraine I had never seen the local people so cynical and devoid of hope.

My long-time driver and friend, Volodya, was waiting for me outside the door after I passed the customs desk, and we were happy to see each other. But as we drove we spoke about the latest news, and I found that even Volodya, who was one of the fiercest supporters of the nationalist revolution and a person who had always been full of hope, had become despondent about the situation in Ukraine.

He said that personally, things were very difficult since our contract had ended. Work was hard to come by. The economy had been sinking over the past few years and COVID was making everything worse.

"I read a lot of bad news about Ukraine in the papers," I said.

Volodya said, "Yes, very bad. This government is bad. And now, internationally Ukraine is losing support. Nothing is good." That was the message I would hear again and again.

I was planning to meet with Taras about the final legal status of my case and with Oles about other business. Oles had offered to take care of selling my flat and the dacha, my final two pieces of property in Ukraine. Then I would travel with Volodya and Yulia down to Dnipropetrovsk to meet with the prosecutor, Anton Makashov, for a final police report before I had to abandon my $28-million investment stolen by the thieving politicians of Ukraine. I did not expect much in the way of concrete results from this visit; I was visiting out of a need to close things off. To say goodbye and to put a period at the end of the sentence of my years in Ukraine.

But despite this, I was still content to arrive back in my flat across from Lviviski Park, on the height of land above the ancient St. Sophia Cathedral and the Maidan square. Ukraine had been an important part of my life for the past twenty years and even though it was not ending well, it would not be easy to say goodbye for good.

In the evening, battling jet lag, I watched the CNN European news channel before collapsing on the couch. There was another piece about Ukraine, this time about COVID. The news clip said the country had skyrocketing rates of COVID and the lowest rate of vaccination in Europe.

The vaccine was readily available, but the people didn't trust it, and officially only 15 percent of the population was vaccinated. The actual number was much lower than that, the reporter said, because fifteen hospitals in Kyiv sold under-the-table vaccination certificates for around US$80, without actually vaccinating you, and these certificate purchasers were then included in the already low official numbers. The fake vaccination certificates, the newscaster said, were needed by wealthy Ukrainians because they didn't trust the vaccines, but they needed a certificate when they were travelling abroad. As a result of the low level of actual vaccinations, COVID was continuing to cut a murderous swath through the population.

The idea of hospitals selling these certificates did not surprise me. A couple of years earlier, the government embarked on a mass "Ukrainization" program

BEFORE THE DELUGE ◊ 177

that required all civil servants to pass a proficiency test in the Ukrainian language, even though only 65 percent of the population spoke it fluently; the rest were mainly Russian speakers. On the face of it, the program was an instant success as civil servants from around the country quickly acquired the necessary language proficiency certificates — which, of course, could be purchased under-the-table without a test from the government department responsible for issuing them.

Neither the vaccination nor language certificates were backroom forgeries by the criminal class. These were government officials selling the certificates, which were duly recorded in the national statistics. In Ukraine, even the bureaucrats were corrupt.

◇•◇

My first meeting in Kyiv was with my lawyer Taras Dumych. I met him in the morning in his office in Podil, the old city district. In the end, it was more a courtesy call, or maybe more precisely a curiosity call, than a lawyer-client meeting. I was not asking him to do anything more for me than make sense of things.

We spoke of Saakashvili's comments describing Ukraine as "a sump" for Eastern European criminals and the prime minister of Estonia telling people not to invest in Ukraine because of the rampant corruption. That was when Taras told me, frankly, that I would never get justice in Ukraine and it was, for all intents and purposes, a failed state.

Taras admitted that he'd still held a glimmer of hope in 2019 when he was in Toronto for the conference on Ukraine reform. He said he now realized there was no hope, and for him this was symbolized by the fate of a Canadian solar energy company in Ukraine. He said that while he was in Toronto, Zelensky made a big deal of the investment by a Calgary-based energy company, TIU Canada, in a massive CDN$65-million solar power operation in Ukraine. The company did everything right. TIU Canada went on to become a major sponsor of both Ukraine House Davos and the Mariupol Conference on Ukraine, where Zelensky again cited TIU Canada as a model for the future. So it looked like Ukraine just might take a new direction with the new president.

Unfortunately, Ukraine's future would look glaringly like its past. Shortly after Zelensky held up the Canadian company as an example of what was possible in Ukraine, TIU had its assets stolen. In this case, the raiders were associates of Igor Kolomoisky in Nikopol, the city in Dnipropetrovsk Oblast where Yulia was from. The Canadian company was strangled to death by Kolomoisky, who used his control of the surrounding land to cut off the Canadians' access to their own site. The courts stood aside and let the obvious extortion happen until TIU was forced to sell Kolomoisky its solar power plant at a cut-rate price and, like me, close down all of its operations in Ukraine.

While the elites fought about ethnic and linguistic rivalries and East versus West and the names of cities, towns and streets, the people were abandoned to poverty and desperation. And the misery was increasing. A UN study a few months earlier had revealed that Ukraine had more people classed as "severely food insecure" than any other European nation, with almost nine million hungry people. The UN Development Programme found that 60 percent of Ukrainians were living below the poverty line, and Credit Suisse ranked Ukraine 123rd of 140 countries in the median wealth of its citizens.

It was during this meeting that Taras told me about his client who had invested in the post only to have his property and his entire US$20 million investment stolen by the municipal government. It became his Ukrainian scorpion moment when the government went to court to say, basically, that his client had no right to complain because he knew Ukraine was corrupt when he came here.

I asked Taras why Canada and the rest of the West kept pouring billions of dollars and other forms of aid into this cesspool. Two years ago I had asked Taras a version of that question and he deflected it, saying that reform was underway. But now he hesitated only a moment.

"I don't know," he said. "When the Estonian prime minister told her business people not to invest in Ukraine, everyone was upset that a friend had said this. They complained about her and denounced her, but I was saying, listen, listen to this woman. You know she is right. Let's admit that she has good reason to say that and look at ourselves and seriously address the problems. But no one listened. Not in Ukraine and not donor governments like Canada. Everyone prefers to pretend. But this is killing Ukraine."

So instead of reform, Ukraine has another presidential administration centralizing power and lashing out at its enemies. Taras had hope with the gang of reformers elected in 2014 right after the Maidan, but they were long gone. Poroshenko worked to centralize powers in the executive and crush the Rada, Taras said, and Zelensky was doing the same. As Taras saw it,

> The problem with Ukraine is that we think we should be in the big
> leagues, in the NHL, when really we should be playing in maybe
> the Manitoba junior league. We pretend we are on the same level as
> not only Canada but the same level as Russia and the United States,
> when really we should be in the league with more modest countries
> like Poland, Austria and even Romania and Bulgaria. These
> countries have done better than us because they set more realistic
> goals and worked to follow them. Ukraine pretends to be playing
> in the league with Russia and America and we will be used when it
> suits them, but discarded after. That is what is happening now.

◊◆◊

I was glad to escape Ukrainian politics for the rest of the day. I had set up a lunch with Vika to say goodbye.

She had taken a course in computer design after I closed out the real estate company in 2019, but she found it dull and had finally taken a job with a firm that produced software for online gaming. We met at a small café near her office.

It was a pleasure to sit with her and reminisce about an almost twenty-year friendship that began when she was a kid just finishing law school and working as a waitress at the Arizona. She was now a woman of forty with a child who was thirteen years old and, from the photos she showed me, a good-looking young man.

I asked about her work, and she said that COVID had actually been a boon to their business because people were stuck at home and looking for something to amuse themselves with. So she had landed on her feet work-wise.

While we spoke the initial pleasure was tainted by the sad realization that this was probably the last time I would see her. So I told her that I appreciated working with her and thanked her for being one of the bright memories of Ukraine for me. Vika was someone who always looked people directly in the eyes and did not shy away from saying what she thought. But she combined that forthrightness with a profound kindness that made her a wonderful friend.

She returned the compliment in a touching way. She said she had learned a lot from me and appreciated that from the beginning I had given her responsibilities and trusted her. "You have been like family to me and you will always be like family to me," she said. Then she added, "And family is the most important thing."

We said goodbye on the sidewalk. She turned up the street to return to work and I caught a taxi back home.

◊•◊

Oles dropped by my apartment the next morning. He was his usual good-natured self. On his way through the door, he was already telling me about the potential buyer he had taken through my apartment the week before who had made a US$390,000 offer. I was looking for more, but it was the best opening offer we'd had, so I said I would think it over.

We spent a few minutes discussing RMD Environmental, the new business project we were working on with Richard Spinks in Canada. Oles told me he was very glad the company was founded in Canada and operated under Canadian law. He said he had decided a year ago to no longer bring foreign investors into Ukraine. "And I am even cutting back on all of my own business activities in Ukraine. It just isn't worth it."

To control the managers of the small wood-chip company he was a partner in, Oles told me, they had to set the maximum transaction the general manager could authorize without board approval at a ridiculously low $5,000. But that's the way it had to be in Ukraine. You could not trust anyone in business and without that, you couldn't really move forward. The always-cheat environment killed not only foreign investment, it killed initiatives in the domestic economy as well.

As with virtually all of my discussions with people on this trip, the conversation veered into the disastrous shape of Ukrainian politics. Like Volodya and Taras, Oles said that things were getting worse, not better. "Our comedian president is becoming a bad joke. Zelensky is a performer and like all performers he wants to be loved by his audience, the people of Ukraine. But he also tasted the sweet fruit of power and he fell in love with it. Now he has forgotten about the people. He uses the power to suit his personal needs — to help his friends and harm his enemies."

Zelensky seemed, in fact, to be using Vladimir Putin as his model. When Putin first got into power, he, too, had posed as a reformer and went after a few designated oligarchs with some spectacular takedowns. What people didn't notice at first was that Putin had surrounded himself with a select group of oligarchs, and at the end, it was Putin and his own criminal gang that was left standing with a considerable portion of the country's wealth and almost all of the political power under their control. Zelensky seemed to be heading down the same road. A hint of this had come a couple of months earlier when Zelensky held a kind of anti-oligarch summit that was sponsored by — you guessed it — one of his preferred oligarchs, Victor Pinchuk.

Oles had never believed in Zelensky, and in the last election he hadn't even bothered to vote. "Zelensky had no solutions to offer and Poroshenko had, at a time of war, used power as leverage for his business interests. Our only hope is the fact that Russian opposition is even less adept than we are.

"In the end, I think it is stupidity that makes the world go round," he said. "I used to see complex plots everywhere, but gradually I have come to see that no one really knows what they are doing."

Oles left a short time later, after we finished discussing the sale of my apartment and the dacha.

"You will be happy to say goodbye to Ukraine," he said.

"I will not be happy to say goodbye to my money," I replied. "And my friends here. But Ukraine, sure, it is time to say goodbye."

◊•◊

That afternoon, Volodya picked me up for a kind of farewell trip to Volodimirsky Market, the main market in Kyiv, which was something of a wonderland for me. The market was founded in the nineteenth century, but in Soviet times it was rebuilt into a massive glass-and-steel structure with an architectural flair — it had a winged roof and its walls were made of small glass squares embedded in concrete squares, like honeycombs in a beehive.

There were hundreds of stalls with the finest fruits and vegetables, cheeses, fresh fish and meats in what was the city's largest market. There were even several restaurants inside and a juice stand where a young woman served a fresh pomegranate juice that left a wonderfully pure taste memory.

I enjoyed just sauntering through the aisles and absorbing the incredibly diverse sights and smells. I stopped at the stall where for almost twenty years I had come to buy my fruits and vegetables. When the woman behind the counter saw me, she smiled and came out into the aisle to greet me. When I first saw her so many years ago, she had looked to be about forty years old. Two decades later, she still looked forty. She stood in front of me smiling, with her hands in her apron pockets.

With Volodya translating, I said, "You look as young as when I first saw you here."

The woman nodded and said, "It is because I have never been touched." Then she laughed and slapped me on my shoulder. "What do you want from me?"

I bought two big bags full of fruits and vegetables that I knew I didn't need — I would give them to Volodya. On the way out, I stopped for a glass of the best fresh pomegranate juice in the world. There were many things in Ukraine I would miss. But in the morning I would head to Dnipropetrovsk to meet with the prosecutor Makashov and say a final goodbye to my stolen assets in Ukraine.

Volodya picked me up at 9 a.m. and we stopped to pick up Yulia on our way out of the city. She had heard that Dnipro would be declared a COVID Red Zone on Monday, and because she was not vaccinated, she wanted to get a test so she wouldn't be barred from hotels or restaurants. I had my vaccination certificate so I was in the clear. Volodya didn't seem worried.

The testing system in Ukraine, it seemed, was very efficient. Yulia had her test in the morning and would be sent her results on her phone by the end of the day. Although in Ukraine, you wonder if lab work was actually being done or if the company simply took the $20 they charged for the test, waited a few hours, then cranked out an automatic negative result without bothering to go through the actual lab test. But then, in Ukraine, the important thing was to have the right form with an official stamp, and she would have that.

As we crossed the bridge over the Dnieper River, I recalled that I had also been travelling with Volodya and Yulia on that day in September 2007 when my grain elevator operation was officially opened. I remembered the prime minister of Ukraine, the Cossacks on horseback, and the giant key that I originally thought opened nothing — but in fact it opened the scorpions' nest of gangster politicians, crooked judges, thieving lawyers and legions of small-time crooks and fraud artists.

During the drive, I sat alone in the back because I was reading the draft business plan for RMD Environmental that the office had pulled together. At the halfway mark, Volodya said, "Ron? Hungry?"

"Sure," I said. "Let's stop."

"Two Sisters?"

It was the same restaurant we had stopped at fourteen years ago and, in fact, on every trip to Dnipropetrovsk. The restaurant was as pleasant as always, with the folksy charm and excellent cabbage rolls and varenykys with sides of black bread, pork fat and horseradish — reminding me again of the pleasures of Ukraine.

Three hours later, we were crossing the Dnieper again to enter Dnipro. We had some difficulty finding the hotel. Yulia had tried to book us into the Grand Hotel downtown where I usually stayed, but for some reason all the downtown hotels were full. The only decent one left was a new one, the Bartolemeo. This was out of the ordinary, as well as out of the city. The Bartolemeo had been built as a kind of Caribbean-style resort on an artificial beach on the polluted Dnieper, and the grounds were planted with palm trees and littered with fake pre-Columbian statues. The restaurant in the middle was a full-size replica of a Spanish galleon — and I mean full-size, with upper decks at least thirty feet above the ground. Inside there were two separate restaurants, one that specialized in fish and the other in red meat. After 10 p.m. it also served as Dnipro's largest disco, and the whole project looked like the brainchild of some spoiled 21-year-old child of a local mafia leader or an elaborate money-laundering scheme. Or perhaps both.

While we ate the so-so tasting, overpriced meal, giant screens at both ends of the dining room flashed scenes from the fake beach in summer: the sands and adjacent pool packed with reclining lawn chairs under white parasols, and beautiful young women swimming, paragliding or zipping past the beach on Sea-Doos. It then switched to night scenes, with those same women dancing or swaying in front of a pop singer performing on the large outdoor stage. The film was on an endless loop and was accompanied by hard-pounding disco music blasting out from speakers located around the room. I ate quickly and left, telling Yulia to charge the meal to my room.

I took a stroll along the deserted beach, which even in late October was still covered in the white parasols. There was a boarded-up beach bar and food shack like you would find in an all-inclusive Caribbean resort. All this on the edge of a sooty Ukrainian industrial town and on the shores of a river that was known for its toxic waste problem. The place was demented. A product of a country that had lost its way.

Back at the hotel, my thoughts turned to my lunch meeting with Anton Makashov. I had a few questions that I wanted answered, though I wasn't expecting much. Time had run out.

Yulia, Volodya and I were supposed to meet Makashov at the Вікінг (Viking), an upscale restaurant not far from the downtown area, but when we arrived there was only one car in the lot and the restaurant was shuttered. Volodya knocked on the door and the restaurant owner came out.

He said he was closed that day because of the COVID Red Zone order in Dnipropetrovsk. He said that all the city's restaurants were closed by law.

While we were debating what to do, Anton Makashov arrived in his Kia station wagon. He nodded when he heard the restaurant was closed and said, "Follow me."

We drove behind his Kia for two blocks and pulled in behind him in front of a small café that seemed to specialize in Turkish fast food. He led us into the large restaurant, which had Arborite tables and a few cushioned booths. "Is this all right?" he asked. "It is not very fancy."

"It's fine," I told him. And we settled around a large round table in the back.

Despite the COVID order, no one was wearing masks. We were served by a middle-aged Turkish woman who seemed to be the owner. Makashov said they had a very good businessman's lunch here and we all ordered that, which included borscht and a meat and cabbage dish.

The food was good. The conversation was, at times, a bit difficult because I was not going to sugar-coat anything.

"Last time we spoke," I said to Anton, "you told me that this story would have a happy ending. That I would get my money back. But now it is clear I won't. So why, finally, couldn't you give me justice?"

Anton tried to duck the question.

"A big question," he said. "I am not sure that I am the right person to answer it."

So I rephrased it. I asked him what, at his level, had prevented him from delivering justice in my case.

I knew I was putting him on the spot, but I wanted him to be open about it all. But instead, Anton struggled very hard to find a way not to answer the question. He spoke about individuals here and forces over there — a battle between abstractions that no one was responsible for. But he did admit at the end of the bobbing and weaving that it was true: there was now very little hope that I would get justice in Ukraine.

The only thing I pressed him on was Sergey Kasyanov.

"Why hadn't Kasyanov ever been charged with the theft? Or at least brought in for questioning?"

Anton looked uncomfortable at this. "Kasyanov had all the paperwork ..." His voice faded at the end of the sentence.

"Of course he had paperwork," I said. "This is Ukraine. Everyone has paperwork for everything."

I had brought with me a copy of an article, in Ukrainian and English, that described Kasyanov's violent takeover of the Chumaki property in 2017 and compared that raid to the one on my property. I pushed the article across the table to Anton. He read it carefully.

The English version stated:

> In 2011, the KSG Agro holding swallowed the Unirem-Agro subsidiary of the Canadian businessman Ronald Michael Derrickson. As in the case of the Chumaki, the Unirem-Agro company unexpectedly changed the director and the founder [from] the lawful owners. The criminals blocking the work of the enterprise then "transferred" the entire land of the company to another legal entity with a similar name (Chomaki Agricultural was changed to Chomaki Agricultural Production Company), which was subsequently transferred to KSG Agro. As we can see, this [strategy] is Kasyanov's corporate signature that he had already used on the Canadian.

Anton leaned back. "I don't know what can and what cannot be proven against Kasyanov," he said. "But, yes, you are right. It is certain that Kasyanov at least knew that your property was stolen."

"So you also agree that there is a good chance that Kasyanov was in on the theft from the beginning."

Anton nodded. "Yes," he said. "Very possible. He certainly knew that it was stolen property. I didn't question him but the case was transferred to Kyiv ... maybe someone from there questioned him. We should have pressed the issue."

That was a small concession at least. But I could see Anton was not happy that I sprung this on him. I did not know if he had been prevented from confronting Kasyanov or steered clear for his own reasons. But he would not give me more. I backed off. I knew you could not really blame people in Anton Makashov's position for the mess of Ukraine. The treason went much higher up and it was, after all, supported by governments like Canada, who propped up the corruption because Ukraine was a useful tool in elections at home and in the competition with Russia abroad.

So I offered Anton an out.

"I was wondering if you had ever been contacted by the Canadian embassy about my case," I asked.

Anton understood and took the offered escape route.

"No," he said. "The Canadian government should have helped you. This is really a political case and it needs a political solution."

A few minutes later we had moved on and were talking about the highway from Kyiv. Anton asked if I noticed that it was in much better shape.

I said I did. The highway had been greatly improved since my last trip.

"It is because it is also the highway to Kryvyi Rih," Anton said.

Everyone laughed. Kryvyi Rih, as everyone around the table was aware, was the hometown of President Zelensky and his friends and partners in illicit offshore investments.

I mentioned that I had also heard that the IMF was investigating the highway improvements to the president's hometown because the construction funds were alleged to have been illegally taken from the IMF's UAH 13.3 million allocation to Ukraine's COVID support fund. Everyone laughed again, as Ukrainians often do when they speak of government corruption. This was safer territory in Ukraine. Blaming the system in general terms, or the sitting president, but not the people caught in the middle of it.

◊◆◊

The final stop on my journey was Shchorsk, now known as Bozhedarivka: God's Gift.

Driving through the countryside to the village, I saw that the land looked much as it had on my first visit eighteen years earlier. The villages still had the same shabbiness, and the giant Soviet war memorial outside the town of Krynychky, with the giant medallions of Lenin and CCCP insignia, had somehow escaped the various waves of "decommunization" and still dominated the landscape.

Shchorsk seemed frozen in time, too, with abandoned buildings and a pronounced state of rubble everywhere. We stopped for a coffee at the village café, which was in the same building as the agriculture feed store. But both were closed. So we walked down the main street toward the same small grocery store where I had met the young woman with rotting teeth fifteen years before and saw the need to bring a dentist to the village. That woman was not there, but the store seemed the same — maybe with a few more items to sell but still smelling of stale milk and wet cement.

The shopkeeper, an old woman, watched us wander aimlessly around, then asked what we were looking for.

Yulia told him I was the Canadian who used to own the grain elevators. She was instantly friendly. She said she thought we were from the government and gathering evidence of the village's disobeying the COVID restrictions. The village was supposed to be in the Red Zone today, she said. Although I had noticed that not one person in the village was wearing a mask.

We bought Cokes and left.

◇•◇

It was Sunday and the grain operation was closed, but I could see even from a distance that the steel bins were rusted and the place had a rundown look.

Volodya pulled up in front of the office. The sliding metal entrance gate was half open. I could not resist walking inside for one last look at the complex I had built with such pride.

When I last checked online, the owner of Unirem-Service was officially Lubov Alexsandrivna Khimanich, and her husband, Sergey Sergeivitch, Khimanich was listed as the director. The founding date of the company was given as April 9, 2009, when Kryshin and Fesun's theft occurred, but Sergey and his wife had only been listed as owners for the past two years. When I later had a researcher look into the other recent owners, the search quickly turned up literally a hundred pages of interconnected companies that were impossible to follow.

One important fact that emerged from the search was that Sergey Khimanich was listed as a member of Zelensky's Servant of the People Party and had been an unsuccessful candidate in the 2019 election. His consolation prize, apparently, was the ownership of the grain operation, or more likely the role as front man and director.

While I was looking around, a big, unshaved security guard came out, eyeing me suspiciously. Just to see his reaction, I told him, with Yulia interpreting, that I was Ron Derrickson. "I am the owner of the property," I said.

He replied with a kind of smirk and said, "No, you aren't. Сергій Сергійович Хіманіч (Sergey Sergeyovich Khimanich) is the owner."

A smaller man dressed in worker's coveralls wandered over. He didn't say anything, but he was listening with obvious interest.

"I built the operation," I said. "I bought all of those grain elevators in Canada. And the machinery in Canada and in Italy."

The burly fellow shook his head. "No. It was built by local people."

"No," I said. "It was built by me with my money."

I noticed that the worker, who was standing just off to the side, seemed to nod in agreement.

"No," the security guard said. "It was local people."

"Nyet, nyet, nyet, I built it!" I said, and Volodya laughed.

We turned back to the car. When I looked back, I saw that the worker in coveralls had caught up to Yulia. He was speaking to her and pointing at me.

Yulia said he told her, "We know that this place was built by Ron and they took it from him." And he told her to tell me they remember that I built the company.

I looked in his direction. He was watching near the gate for my reaction. I waved to him. He smiled and waved back.

So that was it. Some of the people, at least, still knew the truth.

We drove off and I did not look back.

◇•◇

The next day, Volodya drove me to the airport for the last time, across the bridge spanning the Dnieper River and past the rundown apartments from the Soviet era, which had ended in Ukraine thirty years ago. But the shoddy old Soviet apartments were still crowded with people — you could tell by the laundry hanging from the balconies. These people were still waiting, after thirty years, for the new era to begin.

In my small way I tried to help. But like so many others, I had to make a strategic retreat from the failed state.

After I was back in Canada, I called Richard Spinks and asked if he could help me accelerate the purchase of two houses I had been looking at in Poland. I would close everything in Ukraine and handle the rest of my Eastern European business from the safety of Poland, within the EU and free from the corruption and instability that had defined Ukraine for the past thirty years. He called me in January 2022 and said the deals were done, the houses had been purchased and registered in Poland. I was finally done with Ukraine.

◇•◇

Then Ukraine blew up. On February 24, the first of hundreds of Russian missiles slammed into Kyiv, Kharkiv and Dnipro, and Russian tanks crossed the border in a massive invasion that had been threatened for weeks. That is when my Skype lit up with calls from friends throughout Ukraine. Over the next six weeks I worked around the clock with Richard, who had moved his family to one of my houses in Poland, to try to get our friends and colleagues to safety. For the first week it was utter confusion. I was first in touch with Yulia, whose mother had had a heart attack and passed away shortly after the first Russian missiles reached her city, Nikopol, in the east. Yulia's husband, like all men in Ukraine between the ages of sixteen and sixty, was called into military service, leaving Yulia and her son under siege in Kyiv. Richard began working frantically to find drivers, often for a high fee that I would pay, who would go into Kyiv and get people out to the relative safety of Lviv, where they could be hustled across the border to Poland. Yulia was one of the first people we got out.

But many were shell-shocked or understandably furious at the Russians, like Vika, who at first refused to leave Kyiv. The next person I succeeded in getting out was Susana, my former girlfriend. Richard found a driver to take her to Poland and usher her though the growing throngs — from thousands, to hundreds of thousands, to millions of people that were desperate to get out of the country. Susana moved into one of my houses in Poland and expressed her great gratitude. But after two weeks, she said she was returning to the border area. People there were mad with fear and grief, she said, and as a psychologist she could help them cope, so she left the house and went to the border area to help her people.

Eventually, Vika relented and she was ready to make a break for it. Richard and I got her and her son, along with her sister and her sister's children, out to Poland and they then went on to Prague, where Vika had friends. Lena followed a similar trajectory. First she said, "No, I am staying," and then later decided to take up the offer to leave. Richard got her out and eventually she made her way to Canada, specifically Quebec City, where she had a friend, and planned to stay there for good.

Volodya, I knew, was a determined nationalist. Initially he told me that he would stay and fight. He already had military training, ironically in the Red Army in the 1980s, so there would be a front-line position waiting for him. But he had just had a child with his new wife and was sixty years old, so he was eligible to leave the country. And he did. He left Kyiv for Poland with millions of other Ukrainians.

Volodymyr Parasiuk, the "hero of the Maidan," did go and fight as part of the defence force around Kyiv. But I noticed on his Telegram channel that he seemed to spend most of his time and energy making pleas for money for the war effort. At some point, he disappeared from the front entirely and returned home with some kind of injury to his leg; now in civilian clothes, he continued to collect money for the war. When he healed, he returned to battle.

I checked on Anton Makashov in Dnipro, which was a transport point for weapons being sent to the Donbas front, so it was under regular Russian missile attack. Makashov was still there but had sent his wife and kids to England where they would be safe. He was not sure if he would stay or join them.

Not all of our rescues worked. The most tragic one was when we were trying to get a 17-year-old girl out of Kharkiv with another family, who had a small baby and were making a run for it. The car was hit by an artillery round on the highway out of the city, and tragically the only survivors were the 17-year-old and the baby. The girl took the baby with her and managed to cross the country to the Polish border, where we picked them up and brought them to one of our houses.

Richard did the math. He calculated that in all we had saved forty people from the Russian assault, and he counted more than $50,000 that I paid for their transport. Of course the money was nothing and I was glad to help my Ukrainian friends get to safety. I refused no one help if they asked for it. Along with the rest of the world I was appalled by the invasion and the stories of Russian brutality. And by the fact that while the West was generous with weapons, the Ukrainians were left to fight the Russian marauders alone.

POLAND 2022

*Old habits die hard. Russian
aggression and internal corruption
continue to devastate Ukraine.*

In June 2022, I travelled to Eastern Europe again, to Poland, to meet with my Ukrainian friends and with Richard Spinks.

The final leg of my flight was from Toronto to Warsaw, and while I sat in the airport lounge in Toronto I watched CBC News on the overhead television. The topic was of course Ukraine, and the news was not good as the Russians continued their slow-motion conquest of the east of the country, village by village, city by city.

But what caught my interest was an item on the theft of grain from terminals in the Black Sea port of Kherson, where the grain from my Shchorsk/Bożhedarivka operation used to be shipped. They were showing a long line of trucks with the Russian military's Z symbol emblazoned on the side being loaded with grain, and then cut to the same trucks on the highway heading south to Crimea. Fifty thousand tons of stolen grain were being shipped to the port in Sevastopol, where it was loaded on ships for export. The chances were good that several tons of the grain stolen by the

Russians were from my operation in Shchorsk, which would mean that assets from my property stolen by the Ukrainians were now being stolen from them by the Russians — a harsh illustration of the saying, "What goes around comes around."

When I landed in Warsaw, Richard Spinks was waiting for me and drove me out to one of the three houses I had purchased around the capital. This house was in Magdalenka, a village south of Warsaw, and while we drove Richard spoke about the continuing clusterfuck of corruption that he was seeing in Ukraine. He told me that no one was reporting it, but the wartime corruption and theft had reached obscene levels. With tens of billions of dollars of cash and equipment flooding the country, oligarchs and mini-garchs were in a feeding frenzy, loading up their massive hauls and trucking them off as fast as possible so they could hurry back for more. If this was known, he said, there would be hell to pay, but Western governments were doing everything they could to keep the thefts out of sight. The facts occasionally slipped out, as in a CBS report that quoted the director of a Lithuania-based organization responsible for shipping military supplies across the border to Ukraine. The director said, "All of this stuff goes across the border, and then something happens — kind of like 30 percent of it reaches its final destination." The other 70 percent disappears into the web of "power lords, oligarchs [and] political players."[1]

The amounts were staggering. The United States had pledged $100 billion to Ukraine, and at the rate of theft quoted in the CBS report, Ukrainian crooks would be pocketing some $70 billion from the Americans alone, and billions more were flooding in from Canada and Europe.

We have already had glimpses of the type of thing that has been going on in Ukraine during the war. Within months of the invasion, it was learned that city authorities in Zaporizhia were stealing humanitarian aid on an industrial scale. An official at the National Anti-Corruption Bureau (NABU) said top

---

1   This was known since the beginning. A U.S. intelligence source told CNN in April 2022 that Washington has "almost zero" idea what happens to these arms, describing the shipments as dropping "into a big black hole" once they enter Ukraine. Canadian sources said they have "no idea" where their weapons deliveries actually end up. Andy Milburn, a retired U.S. Marine colonel, told CBS, "If the ability to which you're willing to be involved in that stops at the Ukrainian border, the surprise isn't 'oh, all this stuff isn't getting to where it needs to go' — the surprise is that people actually expected it to."

officials had stolen a whole freight train's worth of goods, which included 389 rail cars with 22 shipping containers and 220 trucks. This is just one operation by one group of local gangsters. There are countless more operations throughout the country that have not yet been recorded. But more ominous are the revelations that both the interior ministry and defence ministries were guilty of billions of dollars of theft.

These stories are just beginning to come out, and those in the know in Ukraine tell me that, indeed, tens of billions of dollars' worth of goods have already been siphoned off.

The rest of my days in Poland were full of meetings with Richard and Oles Kopets discussing our business development, but with enough time for a lunch with Volodya and Yulia, who were now working with us in Poland and living in a large and very comfortable house I had purchased just a ten-minute walk from my house there. Volodya was living there with his wife and infant child and with Yulia and her sister and child, so we had reconstituted a bit of Ukraine in Poland. I had purchased three other houses that I was using for Ukrainian refugees who were still coming across the border.

Poland was safely within the EU and NATO and with a government that ran by the rule of law. There were gangsters there, as there are everywhere, but they weren't running the government and courts as they were in Ukraine. There was a sense of justice in Poland, however imperfect, that Ukraine has never achieved, even in the best of times.

It is far from certain that, even at the end of hostilities, Ukraine will be allowed into the European club. The celebration of Ukraine having its application to the EU accepted during the war was muted when it became clear that "acceptance" was only an agreement to set up "a formal framework for negotiations." While Ukraine was urging a speedier process, the EU let it be known that it would be a long process, lasting ten to twenty years before Ukraine could hope for admittance into the EU Without a serious and successful battle against corruption, one that frees the economic, political and legal spheres of the country from the control by oligarchs and gangsters, EU membership for Ukraine will be put alongside Turkey on the membership path to nowhere.

Canada and the other supporters of Ukraine have always only given lip service to the fight against corruption and, today, brush it aside because of the need to fight the Russians. They would be wise to listen to my Ukrainian lawyer, Taras Dumych, a Ukrainian patriot and corruption fighter all of his life, who has concluded that, in fact, "corruption in Ukraine has been the best ally of Russia."

This has also been the conclusion of Richard Spinks, a true friend of Ukraine who probably understands the country better than any other foreigner, who warns that even today powerful forces in Ukraine are plotting on how to steal, misappropriate and divert every piece of equipment and every dollar to the portfolios of the criminal oligarchs and local minigarchs, and unless the corruption issue is seriously addressed, any victory paid in blood by the Ukrainian people will be squandered and lost in peacetime. That is, after all, the nature of the story of the frog and the scorpion. Ukraine will never make it across the river with the gangsters and oligarchs on its back.

APPENDIX I

MEMORANDUM TO THE CANADIAN EMBASSY

Re: Fraudulent Actions Committed Against Mr. Ronald Derrickson in Ukraine in Connection with his Investment into Agricultural Assets and an Elevator in Dnipropetrovsk Oblast

This Memorandum provides an overview of facts and history of the developments with respect to the fraudulent actions that were committed against Mr. Ronald Derrickson in Ukraine, and which led to Mr. Derrickson losing his investments into agricultural assets and an elevator in Ukraine.

Unirem-Agro. LLC "Unirem-Agro" was established in July 2005. The company cultivated wheat, soybean, canola, had a land bank of more than 9,000 ha and used the latest technologies in its operations.

Mr. Derrickson became a majority founder and shareholder of Unirem-Agro holding a 51 percent share. He did not participate in day-to-day management of the company and was relying on his Ukrainian partners in this respect. Mr. Derrickson fully paid his contribution to the charter capital of

Unirem-Agro by 10 October 2005, including agricultural machinery imported from Canada, which was used to set up the agricultural machinery storage and servicing facility in the village of Adamovka (the "Adamovka Facility").

Other Ukrainian co-founders of Unirem-Agro (Mr. Victor Fesun and five other individuals) failed to make their contributions to the charter capital of the company. Therefore, the business was completely run with Mr. Derrickson's money.

Ukrainian shareholders (with Mr. Fesun being a mastermind) forged certain pages of the charter of the company during incorporation of Unirem-Agro as well as at later stages — as a result, inter alia, the charter contained no limitations for the director of Unirem-Agro regarding transactions with the company's assets. Financial accounts of the company were also forged over the years of operation of Unirem-Agro to falsely represent to Mr. Derrickson that the company was in a good financial condition.

Incorporation of Unirem-Oil. LLC "Unirem-Oil" (shareholding held: 49 percent by Unirem-Agro, 51 percent by Mr. Derrickson) was incorporated in December 2006 at suggestion of Mr. Fesun to operate the Elevator.

Mr. Fesun convinced Mr. Derrickson that Unirem-Agro should contribute the Elevator to the charter capital of Unirem-Oil, which was done in March 2008.

The Elevator. The grain storage and processing facility in the village of Bozhedarivka (before 2016 — called Shchorsk) in Krynychansky Rayon of Dnipropetrovsk Oblast with the capacity of 20,000 tons per year (the "Elevator") was constructed and commenced operations in September 2007. The construction was financed by Unirem-Agro with funds and equipment received from Mr. Derrickson. The Elevator was constructed on the property that was owned and leased by Unirem-Agro.

In 2007–2008 the charter capital of Unirem-Oil was gradually increased to UAH 36,072,150. Additional contribution of Unirem-Agro to the increased charter capital was made with the Elevator.

Unlawful action of Mr. Fesun. In the beginning of 2009 Mr. Derrickson received information that Mr. Fesun (as director of Unirem-Agro) misappropriated funds of Unirem-Agro. Moreover, the acreage of land cultivated by Unirem-Agro had decreased for some unknown reason. The company also stopped being profitable. Therefore in March 2009, Mr. Derrickson, as a majority shareholder, ordered (unfortunately only orally) Mr. Fesun to stop any transactions with assets of Unirem-Agro and Unirem-Oil.

Apparently, at around this time Mr. Fesun started fully implementing the scheme aimed to deprive Mr. Derrickson of his investments. As it appears, Mr. Fesun was cooperating closely with Mr. Oleg Kryshin (currently an MP, formerly — a deputy of the Dnipropetrovsk Oblast Council) and his people in implementing this fraud.

Illegal sale of assets of Unirem-Oil and Unirem-Agro. In April 2009, Mr. Fesun, without informing Mr. Derrickson and without receiving approval from him, executed a number of contracts on the sale of various assets of Unirem-Agro and Unirem-Oil.

The illegal disposal of the Elevator. In 2009 the Elevator, that was then the property of Unirem-Oil, was sold for UAH 20,651,903 to LLC "Interlineprom." In fact, according to the charter of Unirem-Oil, property of the company constituting more than 51 percent of its assets could have been sold only subject to approval of the general meeting of shareholders. Mr. Fesun found a way to avoid this requirement — the balance sheet of Unirem-Oil was prepared where it was fictitiously stated that the Elevator represented only 40 percent of the assets of the company. However, apart from the Elevator, Unirem-Oil hardly had any meaningful assets. Therefore, no approval of the general meeting of shareholders of Unirem-Oil was received for the sale of the Elevator.

The purchase price of the Elevator (UAH 20,651,903) had been transferred to Unirem-Oil by the purchaser of the Elevator but subsequently disappeared from the bank account of Unirem-Oil. The same happened to funds received by Unirem-Agro as a result of sale of its assets — the funds have disappeared.

After April 2009 the Elevator changed owners three times within just six months. This was apparently done in an effort to make it as hard as possible for Mr. Derrickson to trace the transfer of title and claim the property back. After Unirem-Oil had sold the Elevator to LLC "Interlineprom," LLC "Interlineprom" in its turn contributed it to the charter capital of LLC "Avtoinvestcentr." The present owner of the Elevator — LLC

"Unirem-Service" — obtained the Elevator in the course of court proceedings on enforcement of mortgage against LLC "Avtoinvestcentr." It is sufficient to just read the court decision according to which the title to the Elevator passed to Unirem-Service to see that the litigation was orchestrated specifically to transfer the property to Unirem-Service:

- the cause for enforcement of the mortgage was failure by Avtoinvestcentr to perform its obligations under a commission agreement. As had already been the case with Unirem-Agro and Unirem-Oil, funds had been transferred to Avtoinvestcentr by Unirem-Service based on the commission agreement but have disappeared without a trace leaving Avtoinvestcentr unable to perform its obligations under the agreement;
- in the court proceedings Avtoinvestcentr did not at all dispute or object to its loss of title to the Elevator and agreed to all the claims of Unirem-Oil;
- the decision has never been appealed;
- the decision apparently was expeditiously enforced.

The trick with the court decision was aimed to make it harder for Mr. Derrickson or his companies to return the property, as under Ukrainian law the standard of protection of disputed property obtained under a court decision is much higher than that obtained under an agreement.

Importantly, all three companies in the chain of transfers of the title to the Elevator (LLC "Interlineprom," LLC "Avtoinvestcentr," LLC "Unirem-Service") were either controlled by or related to Mr. Oleg Kryshin. All the three companies were liquidated shortly after the title to the Elevator had passed to Unirem-Service.

The illegal alienation of assets of Unirem-Agro. All meaningful assets of Unirem-Agro, including the Adamovka Facility, were also transferred to LLC "Unirem-Service," LLC "Unirem-Agro Plus" and LLC "Unirem-Service Plus" — the companies directly or indirectly controlled by Mr. Oleg Kryshin. The assets were transferred under a number of bogus contracts. The fact that the contracts were fictitious was confirmed by the court-economical expert examination No. 1108/1109-13 dated 31 July 2013 conducted by Dnipropetrovsk Scientific Institute of Court Expertise in the criminal investigation (which is described below).

It may be the case that some corrupted local authorities were also aware and supportive of the illegal actions committed against Unirem-Agro and Unirem-Oil. As an example, according to the law, the agricultural machinery that was contributed to the charter capital of Unirem-Agro by Mr. Derrickson in 2006 had been imported without paying import duties and could not have been sold by that company until 2011. However, the local tax inspection that was supposed to control compliance with the law in this field apparently did not react at all to the improper disposal of the machinery.

Insolvency of Unirem-Agor and Unirem-Oil. In the end of 2009 insolvency proceedings with respect to Unirem-Agro and Unirem-Oil commenced at request of fake creditors having insignificant claims against the companies. Insolvency of Unirem-Oil was initiated by a creditor with a claim of UAH 300,000 — ten times smaller than the company's charter capital.

It turned out that despite the sale of virtually all meaningful assets early in 2009, by December 2009 neither Unirem-Oil nor Unirem-Agro had any funds to satisfy insignificant claims of their creditors. Mr. Derrickson has no information on how and where the funds from the bank accounts of both companies have disappeared.

Furthermore, the creditors (the companies) of Unirem-Oil and Unirem-Agro that initiated and participated in the liquidation proceedings were related to or founded by persons either close to Mr. Fesun or who worked at Unirem-Oil and Unirem-Agro. Some of the creditors were related to LLC "Vilnohirske Sklo" — a large glass producer in Dnipropetrovsk Oblast controlled by Mr. Oleg Kryshin (currently a Member of the Parliament).

Insolvency of Unirem-Agro and Unirem-Oil was important for Mr. Derrickson's adversaries so as to ensure that there would not exist anymore an entity that could claim the Elevator and other property from their current owners.

It should also be noted that in the process of liquidation of Unirem-Agro and Unirem-Oil the majority of the corporate and business documentation of these companies was lost.

Liquidation of Unirem-Agor and Unirem-Oil. In May-July 2010 both Unirem-Oil and Unirem-Agro were liquidated according to a simplified procedure. Mr. Fesun, as the director of both companies (or anyone else from both companies), did not appeal the decisions on liquidation.

Mr. Derrickson tried to prevent the liquidation. Through his attorneys and representatives Mr. Derrickson even appointed a new director (Mr. Oliynyk). But Mr. Oliynyk also turned out to be close to Mr. Fesun and acted in collusion with him in the process of liquidation of both companies.

Actions of Mr. Derrickson to return the investments. Starting from mid-2012 Mr. Derrickson has been taking active actions to return the Elevator and other assets: lawyers were retained, meetings with law enforcement authorities were held, Unirem-Agro and Unirem-Oil were "revived" in 2015 and their liquidation was cancelled, a number of commercial litigations were successfully completed, etc.

Criminal investigation. The criminal investigation No. 12013040460000012 in connection with the above events was commenced. Mr. Fesun for some time was a primary suspect in that case. In the course of the criminal investigation a lot of pressure was exerted on the investigators in Dnipropetrovsk Oblast. The case was closed several times for unknown reasons, whereupon Mr. Derrickson's lawyers (with considerable effort) reopened it each time. In order to avoid pressure on the investigators that was exerted in Dnipropetrovsk Oblast, the criminal case was transferred from the city of Dnipro to Kyiv and received high attention of investigators and officials of the police due to the media coverage that the case received.

However, after a lot of investigative actions have been completed, solid evidence against Mr. Fesun collected and the end of the process was in sight, the investigators suddenly refused to proceed with the investigation and started acting in a strange way (this took place in 2016). It also turned out that some of the documents disappeared from the materials of the criminal case — there were just blank pages instead of important documents that had been there (e.g. charters of Unirem-Agro and Unirem-Oil) — which made a lot of allegations against Mr. Fesun unfounded (i.e. there was no basis to state that he lacked authority to perform certain actions on behalf of the companies if there were no documents evidencing his actual authority at that time).

Furthermore, the criminal case itself was transferred to a police department (railroad police) which was to be liquidated in the near future, whereupon it was assigned to various law enforcement authorities and was finally transferred to a police department in one of the districts in the city of Dnipropetrovsk. The chief investigator in the case refused to continue investigating the case and moved from Kyiv to Dnipro. Reportedly, the financial situation of her family improved significantly after the case was stalled.

All in all, throughout the criminal proceedings there was every indication that someone was improperly influencing the police, trying to stall any headway in the case and close the proceedings altogether.

Arrest of the Elevator. In November 2016 the arrest was imposed on the Elevator in the course of criminal proceedings. Unirem-Service could no longer freely dispose of the Elevator. However, in September 2017 the arrest was cancelled purportedly due to closure of the criminal proceedings. Presently there is no arrest or other charge imposed on the Elevator which means that Unirem-Service could dispose of the Elevator at any time in order to prevent Mr. Derrickson from returning it.

Litigations in commercial courts. One of the greatest difficulties for Mr. Derrickson and his legal counsels were that after the liquidation of Unirem-Oil and Unirem-Agro there were virtually no documents left evidencing the commissioning of the constructed Elevator, title to the Elevator, transfer of the title, business and corporate documents of Unirem-Agro and Unirem-Oil, etc. A number of commercial litigations were started (either by Mr. Derrickson himself or by his revived companies Unirem-Agro and Unirem-Oil) in order to collect the missing documents and information (e.g. documents evidencing transfer of title to the Elevator), recognize certain documents and actions as invalid. Among other things, the following results were achieved:

- the courts invalidated the appointment of Mr. Fesun as a director of Unirem-Oil, which should make it possible to invalidate documents executed by Mr. Fesun on behalf of Unirem-Oil, including documents on the sale of the Elevator;
- the courts also invalidated the minutes of the general meeting of shareholders of Unirem-Oil whereby the Elevator was contributed to the charter capital of Unirem-Oil.

A number of litigations are still pending in the court in Kyiv and in Dnipropetrovsk. The litigations are aimed, inter alia, to:

- invalidate the minutes of the general meeting of shareholders of Unirem-Agro where consent was granted to contribute the elevator to the charter capital of Unirem-Oil;
- invalidate the agreement on the sale of the Elevator by Unirem-Oil to LLC "Interlineprom";
- invalidation of the registration of title to the Elevator, etc.

The results achieved through these litigations should subsequently allow Mr. Derrickson (through one of his "revived" companies — Unirem-Agro or Unirem-Oil) to accumulate sufficient evidence to return his investments.

Should you have any questions or comments, please do not hesitate to let us know.

With best regards,
Taras Dumych
Wolf Theiss, Kyiv

LIST OF UKRAINIAN OLIGARCHS

The Ukrainian "core" rich, 2006–17

No.	Name	Average domestic business wealth (US$M)	Average share of national wealth (%)	Years on list
1	Rinat Akhmetov	9,989	2.08	12
2	Igor Kolomoisky	3,005	0.66	12
3	Victor Pinchuk	2,999	0.66	12
4	Gennadiy Boholyubov	2,898	0.63	12
5	Vadym Novynskyi	1,899	0.39	12
6	Kostyantyn Zhevago	1,558	0.33	12
7	Dmytro Firtash	1,461	0.30	12
8	Kostiantyn Hryhoryshyn	1,171	0.25	12
9	Vitaliy Haiduk	1,164	0.25	12

No.	Name	Average domestic business wealth (US$M)	Average share of national wealth (%)	Years on list
10	Yuriy Kosiuk	1,029	0.24	12
11	Serhiy Taruta	1,097	0.22	11
12	Oleksandr Yaroslavskyi	860	0.20	12
13	Petro Poroshenko	846	0.20	12
14	Andriy Verevskyi	821	0.20	12
15	Leonid Yurushev	812	0.19	12
16	Serhiy Tihipko	703	0.16	12
17	Leonid Chernovetskyi	640	0.15	12
18	Viktor Nusenkis	704	0.14	10
19	Valeryi Khoroshkovskyi	558	0.12	10
20	Vasyl Khmelnytsky	531	0.11	12
21	Oleksiy Martynov	510	0.11	11
22	Vyacheslav Boguslayev	429	0.10	12
23	Vitaliy Antonov	426	0.10	12
24	Hryhoriy & Ihor Surkis	411	0.09	12
25	Andriy Ivanov	420	0.09	12
26	Oleksandr & Serhiy Buriak	370	0.08	10
27	Mykola Yankovsky	335	0.08	12
28	Volodymyr Kostelman	331	0.08	12
	Total	38,015	8.21	

CORPORATE RAIDING IN UKRAINE

By the mid-2000s, "raiding" schemes were already developing into a science in Ukraine. Organized crime worked with corrupt officials at all levels — politically from local officials up to the highest reaches of parliament, judicially from the court registry to the Supreme Court, and with the police at all levels. The schemes are built on a foundation of forged documents and phony directors, meetings that delegitimize the real owners and then sell the stolen company to a "buyer" who will, on paper, "legally" purchase the stolen property.

The theft of Unirem-Agro and Unirem-Oil followed this familiar pattern. In my case, part of the fraud had already happened when my personal title was given as the company Президент (president) instead of Председатель (chairman). Chairman of the board and company director are recognized terms in Ukrainian law, but company "president" is not. So this strengthened Viktor Fesun's role as director. Then in the falsified charter for Unirem-Oil, Fesun included a clause that gave the director the power to sign any contracts for the company on his own. The next move was his setting up of the company Interlineprom on October 19, 2007, barely a month after our grand opening ceremony.

To this shell company Fesun was able to add the ownership of Adamivka, the large collective farm that we purchased in 2006.

If this had been the extent of the fraud, it would have been fairly easy to unravel. But what occurred after March 23, 2009, required the work of an advanced criminal enterprise, and that is where People's Deputy Oleg Kryshin came in.

Kryshin has a long list of fraud charges of his own. But in this scheme his role would be to arrange the alienation of my property and pass the operation through the courts to clear them for the later, symbolic "sale" to Sergey Kasyanov.

One of the first hurdles was that under Ukrainian law, management can sell company assets without the approval of a general meeting of the shareholders only if the assets are less than 50 percent of the value of the company. So under Kryshin's tutelage, Fesun began by falsely inflating the value of the agricultural side of the company until the grain elevator facility, which in reality represented 89 percent of the company assets, was listed as representing only 45 percent. At that point he could use the company's falsified charter to sell them off without the approval of the shareholders.

The first receptacle for my companies was Fesun's Interlineprom company. Kryshin made his first move by purchasing the controlling interest in Interlineprom from Fesun and on April 3, only two weeks after the March 23 meeting, Interlineprom purchased the grain processing facilities in Shchorsk for UAH 20,651,903, about US$3 million, which was about 10 percent of what they were worth. But even that payment was never made, instead sitting on the books as a receivable.

On April 8, the company's remaining assets were also sold to Interlineprom and they, too, were listed as a receivable in our books, thus completing the alienation of all of my property without a dollar changing hands. It was around this point that Kryshin, or perhaps Kasyanov, sent in a small armed security force to physically take control of the property.

They then had their friends in the Shchorsk Regional Council issue a new registration certificate showing the ownership of the elevator had been duly and legally transferred to Interlineprom. In Ukraine, villages have an executive authority in these matters, so this registration would be deemed binding under the constitution.

After April the elevator changed owners three times within just six months, to companies that the police later learned were headed by current or recent employees of Kryshin. This was apparently done in an effort to make it as hard as possible for me to trace the transfer of title and claim the property back. After Unirem-Oil sold the elevator to LLC "Interlineprom," Interlineprom founded LLC Avtoinvestcentr and transferred ownership there.

Then came the work of raider genius. Kryshin created a company called Unirem-Service, which initiated court proceedings against Avtoinvestcentr for a debt incurred on a relatively small deal between them. But to ensure payment, Unirem-Service put a lien on the grain elevators that Avtoinvestcentr then legally owned.

When the case of Unirem-Service v. Avtoinvestcentr (Case No. 10/236–09) for the unpaid debt went to court on October 8, 2009, Avtoinvestcentr did not dispute the debt or object to Unirem-Service's lien on the grain elevators. In fact, they agreed to their surrender as payment of the debt. When the court judgment transferred legal ownership of the elevators to Unirem-Service, the decision was never appealed and the court worked with startling swiftness.

This was an important move because now the pea-under-the-walnut game of moving my assets around had been given official status by a court of law awarding my assets from one Kryshin-controlled company to another one, making it infinitely harder for me to get them back. Legally, the standard of protection of disputed property obtained under a court decision is much higher than that obtained under an agreement.

Then on November 2, the first part of the charade ended with Kryshin holding a shareholders meeting for Unirem-Service Plus and Unirem-Agro Plus with Fesun, who was a 15 percent shareholder in the two companies. Fesun was secretary of the meeting and took the minutes, which showed the company formally integrating all of my assets into their structure.

But this was just the end of the beginning. There were several more moves on Kryshin's chessboard, including a kind of festival of liquidation. Kryshin began by liquidating all of the shell companies that had played a role in guiding my assets into Unirem-Service, to make it impossible to directly follow his financial footsteps. In a rapid series of court cases, beginning with Interlineprom and ending with Avtoinvestcentr, the shell companies were bankrupted and liquidated by the courts. In such a situation, it was almost impossible to say who owned the elevator after August 2010. There was neither an owner nor a founder of the company, just nothing.

The next-to-final stage of the fraud took place when Kryshin moved to bankrupt my two companies, like a pirate who scuttles captured ships after he empties them of treasure. The final case against Unirem-Agro was brought to the Commercial Court of Dnipropetrovsk by Orion-Centre Trade LLC, a company controlled by one of Kryshin's employees. Orion-Centre said they were owed a few thousand dollars by Unirem-Agro, but the court declared Unirem-Agro bankrupt and unable to pay and ordered its liquidation. A week later, on March 18, 2010, LLC Unirem-Oil was declared bankrupt by a resolution of the Commercial Court of Dnipropetrovsk because of a failure to pay another small debt to LLC Decorecvetranit, another Kryshin-controlled company. The companies were then delisted.

With my companies hollowed out and their assets transferred to Kryshin's companies, the fraud entered its final stage. The assets were sold to Sergey Kasyanov for what I imagine was a couple of million dollars, and Kasyanov absorbed my $28-million property into his KSG holding company, which he would soon list on the Polish stock market for a $40-million windfall.

As I was tracing this scam later, I was astounded by what seemed like the sheer audacity of it. I thought that in its own way, it was a work of creative genius. It was only later that I learned that these types of criminal raider schemes were so common in Ukraine that there were actually lawyers who specialized in them. You could even find annual statistics on them. And they were slowly killing the country, as foreign investment would sink to today's minuscule rate of 0.02 percent of the GNP. Now today, more than a decade later, there is a certain frankness about it, with the head of the reform committee of Ukraine, Mikheil Saakashvili, saying that people who invest in Ukraine will likely be "robbed of their money. Even if you take back some of what you put in, you're a very lucky man . . . They screw everybody."

This, however, was not what Ukraine backers were saying at the time and certainly not what Canadians were saying in their continuing promotion of Canada-Ukraine trade and investment.

For all of its seeming originality, the theft of my property fit the familiar pattern in Ukraine. The Ukrainian Agrarian Council study found that 100 percent of raids involved bribery of judges, 80 percent involved buying shares of the company, more than a third involved corruption of law enforcement agencies, more than half involved threats to business owners and a third involved forgery of documents.

It turns out that the Kryshin operation against me was a classic case, using all of the tools of the trade. In the breakdown of the raids, the study found that almost all raiders operate with someone inside the company and someone outside, like Fesun and Kryshin. With that, they create a parallel governing body by convening shareholders' meetings and re-electing them to the board of directors and the CEO role.

The agenda of such meetings is aimed at terminating the powers of the current board of directors and appointing a new one. In the third stage, one of the shareholders present at a legitimate meeting of the board files a lawsuit with a request to declare the meeting invalid. The court, in this case, examines the claim and finds the fees legitimate and competent, and the raider receives a final document. All of these standard procedures of raiders were part of Kryshin's method of operation.

And finally, the primary means of implementing a raid is by way of court decisions, without which the raiders' actions could be terminated fairly quickly by law enforcement agencies. Once the raiders have a legal decision bought and paid for, they can move on to the final stage of the raid against a company, which involves physically taking over the administrative buildings and territory of a foreign enterprise and establishing control over them — often by force of arms to prevent their victims from forcing their way back into the business.

The schemes are so common that now there is an official body called the Anti-Raiding Union of Entrepreneurs of Ukraine, which issued a report that found raiding has become the basis for further development of organized criminal activity by providing the gangster class with proceeds for their operations. As the report put it, "Raiding is no longer a rarity and an exception, but a marker that characterizes business in the agrarian sector of Ukraine. Moreover, raiding has become a profitable business. The same company-invaders regularly implement proven schemes for all new objects, gaining illicit profit and remaining impunity."

A noted Ukrainian lawyer, Maxim Lazarev, says that less than 1 percent of raiding cases are even sent to court because most often, criminal proceedings are not instituted when raids occur because corrupt law enforcement officers are covering the raiders.

This book is also available as a Global Certified Accessible™ (GCA) ebook. ECW Press's ebooks are screen reader friendly and are built to meet the needs of those who are unable to read standard print due to blindness, low vision, dyslexia, or a physical disability.

At ECW Press, we want you to enjoy our books in whatever format you like. If you've bought a print copy just send an email to ebook@ecwpress.com and include:

- the book title
- the name of the store where you purchased it
- a screenshot or picture of your order/receipt number and your name
- your preference of file type: PDF (for desktop reading), ePub (for a phone/tablet, Kobo, or Nook), mobi (for Kindle)

A real person will respond to your email with your ebook attached. Please note this offer is only for copies bought for personal use and does not apply to school or library copies.

Thank you for supporting an independently owned Canadian publisher with your purchase!